D0361143

INSIDERS' GUIDE

PHILADELPHIA &
PENNSYLVANIA DUTCH COUNTRY

HELP US KEEP THIS GUIDE UP TO DATE

We would love to hear from you concerning your experiences with this guide and how you feel it could be improved and kept up to date. Please send your comments and suggestions to:

editorial@GlobePequot.com

Thanks for your input, and happy travels!

INSIDERS' GUIDE® TO

PHILADELPHIA & PENNSYLVANIA DUTCH COUNTRY

FIRST EDITION

MARILYN ODESSER-TORPEY

INSIDERS' GUIDE

GUILFORD, CONNECTICUT
AN IMPRINT OF GLOBE PEQUOT PRESS

All the information in this guidebook is subject to change. We recommend that you call ahead to obtain current information before traveling.

To buy books in quantity for corporate use or incentives, call **(800) 962-0973** or e-mail **premiums@GlobePequot.com**.

INSIDERS' GUIDE ®

Editor: Amy Lyons
Project Editor: Lauren Brancato
Layout: Joanna Beyer
Text Design: Sheryl Kober
Maps revised by Alena Joy Pearce © Morris Book Publishing, LLC

ISBN 978-0-7627-5699-5

Printed in the United States of America
10 9 8 7 6 5 4 3 2 1

CONTENTS

Directory of Maps

ABOUT THE AUTHOR

Born and raised in Philadelphia and a current resident of Lancaster County, **Marilyn Odesser-Torpey** has been writing about the area for more than 15 years. She is the author of several books, including *Quick Escapes from Philadelphia* and *Insiders' Guide to Pennsylvania Dutch Country*, and is travel editor for *Main Line Today* magazine.

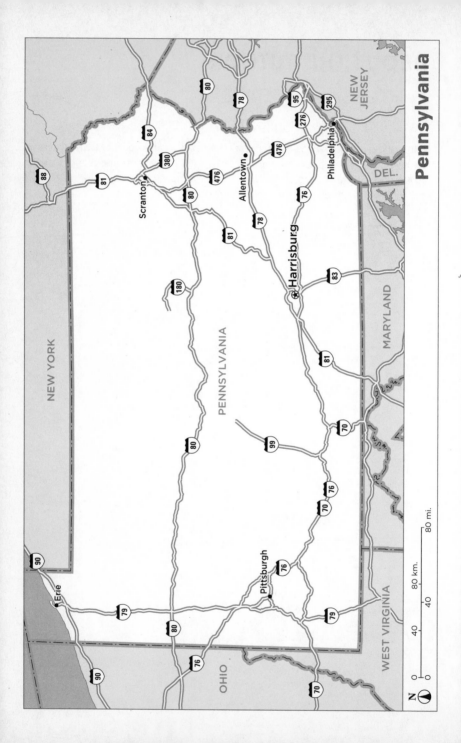

Pennsylvania

INTRODUCTION

Philadelphia is all about freedom of choice. It has been from the beginning when, in 1682, William Penn established his city as a refuge from religious persecution. Even the name he chose—a combination of the Greek words for love ("philos") and brother ("adelphos"), later to give the city its best-known nickname, "The City of Brotherly Love"—offered a warm welcome to all.

Almost a century later, our Founding Fathers gathered in Philadelphia to sign the Declaration of Independence, guaranteeing every individual's "unalienable rights" to "life, liberty, and the pursuit of happiness" and establishing the city as the "Birthplace of America." Philadelphia also earned the title "The Cradle of Liberty" (although Boston also claims bragging rights to that moniker) in 1787, when our illustrious forefathers put pens to parchment to secure our basic freedoms with the signing of the US Constitution.

Today, there's still no better place to exercise your freedom of choice in all things from culture to cuisine, outdoor to retail recreation, big city to small community living than this southeastern Pennsylvania city. Ask any of the more than 1.5 million residents (almost four million if you include the five-county Greater Philadelphia Area, as most people do) and millions of visitors (36 million domestic and at least 600,000 international in 2008 alone) and all will agree that the second largest city on the East Coast and the sixth largest in the nation is a great place to pursue—and find—your happiness, whatever it happens to be. Actually, you can just ask me.

Philly's my hometown. I was born, raised, and educated here from kindergarten through college. I got married and raised my family here. Even when I moved away a few years ago to satisfy my cravings for cornfields and country roads, I didn't go far. I live only a two-hour drive away in Lancaster County ("Pennsylvania Dutch Country"), on which I also share my "insider's" perspective with you in this book.

No matter where I travel, there will always be at least one person who will ask me, "Are you from Philadelphia?" It's not because I'm wearing a Philly tee-shirt or anything. It's my accent, a distinctive twang that is impossible to replicate on paper but is unmistakable once you've heard it.

Sly Stallone gave Philly-speak a good try when he starred in the *Rocky* movies, but, hey, he was born in New York! One thing he did get right was his use of the most versatile word in the native dialect, the simple, straightforward, yet super-expressive "Yo!" Depending on the facial expression that accompanies it, "Yo!" can be a friendly greeting (as in "Yo! How youse doin'?") or an expression of displeasure ("Yo! Get your hands off my car, girlfriend, cheesesteak . . . ").

If you want to have any prayer of passing as a native, you should also know the difference between the words "youse" and "yis." It's really quite simple; "youse" translates to the singular "you," and "yis" is more than one "youse." For example, a server in a restaurant might ask a table full of diners, "What can I get for yis today?"

But our little linguistic lilt isn't the only thing that sets Philadelphians apart from the rest of the world. With the accent comes a very distinctive attitude (pronounced a-dee-tood). It's a confident way of looking at and dealing with the world. Some people might mistake it for cockiness (after all, Philly is the home of the "Mummers' Strut,") but it's much more than that. It's a deeply felt pride in the place, the people, and the possibilities.

Over the years, I've seen Philadelphia evolve from stodgy to sophisticated, its retail personality develop from '60s department store to fashion-forward boutique, its downtown nightlife from roll-up-the-sidewalks to roll-out-the-red-carpet. And, of course, there's the sense of connection to American history that you won't feel anywhere else.

I could talk about Philly for days, but you can't know its heart until you experience it for yourself. So throw some clothes in your suitcase and hit the road. You'll know you've arrived when you hear someone say, "Yo! Welcome to Philadelphia!"

HOW TO USE THIS BOOK

Like any major city, Philadelphia can be overwhelming to the first-time visitor. To make it easier on yourself and avoid missing that attraction you've been dying to see, I suggest that you use this book to make up an itinerary of "must-dos" based on your particular interests, then to group these by geographical proximity. Of course, you'll want to keep your schedule flexible—don't even try to resist popping into that intriguing museum or taking a people-watching break in one of the city's beautiful urban parks. A good and extensive system of public transportation offers a variety of easy and economical ways to get around without getting bogged down in slow-moving Center City traffic and parking in expensive garages and lots. I also recommend that you start with a ride around the city on a tour bus that allows you to get off and back on as you wish to give you a city orientation and make it easy for you to explore areas and sites that are on your itinerary or simply catch your fancy.

If you're a new or veteran Philly resident, this book can be a handy reference for all kinds of useful information from the most basic city and community services to where to go for a quick casual or romantic dinner out to local events and festivals to less-than-one-tank week-end adults-only or family-oriented getaways in the 'burbs or beautiful, nearby "Pennsylvania Dutch Country" and Hershey, "Chocolate Town USA."

For your convenience, the chapters in this book are organized according to categories (e.g., Restaurants, Attractions, Shopping, Tours, Kidstuff, and more) and geographic location. Keep in mind that Philadelphia is generally an all-round kid-friendly town, so if you're looking for somewhere fun to go or something to do with the family, don't just limit yourself to the Kidstuff chapter. With its colorful colonial locales, costumed interpreters, and little-known tidbits of historic fact (and maybe a little lore—such as the longtime legend that tossing a penny onto Benjamin Franklin's grave at the southeast corner of 5th and Arch Streets will bring good luck)—even the historical stuff can appeal to all ages. To give you a few ideas on how to sneak some education into your recreation, take a look at the book's History chapter.

The Getting Here, Getting Around chapter will help you pick the most convenient (and economical) forms of transportation to get you to and around Center City, the neighborhoods, the 'burbs, and day-trip destinations. Of course, you'll have to eat, chill out, and sleep sometime. So we've put together Hotels and Bed-and-Breakfasts, Restaurants, and Nightlife chapters with options ranging from the budget conscious to the sky's the limit, the national names you know to the National Historic Registry–listed. And you'll always find something fun to do rain or shine if you use the Attractions, Arts, and other activity-oriented chapters.

Although prices seem to change every time you turn around—as do restaurants, to be honest—we've put together a general pricing guide for accommodations, dining, and attraction admissions. Each one is tagged with a symbol ranging from $ for the least expensive to $$$$ for big-budget. Keys to the guides are given in the introductions to those chapters.

We also have provided six maps to aid you in planning your stay and getting around. The maps show (1) Pennsylvania, (2) Philadelphia and its suburbs, (3) Center City and surrounding neighborhoods, (4) Old City (the Historic District), (5) Lancaster County, and (6) Hershey.

Throughout the book are **Insiders' Tips** (indicated by an **i**), which give you some tidbits gleaned from locals on things you might not otherwise have known about; sidebars, which condense practical information and basic facts into an easy-to-read list; and **Close-ups** that spotlight things worth spending more time on.

You'll also find listings accompanied by the ✳ symbol—these are our top picks for attractions, restaurants, accommodations, and everything in between that you shouldn't miss while you're in the area. You want the best this region has to offer? Go with our **Insiders' Choice.**

Those who are relocating to Philadelphia—welcome! Check out the blue-tabbed pages at the back of the book where you will find the **Living in Philadelphia** section. It offers information on relocation, education, child care, health care, and media and provides quick answers to common questions.

This book isn't a phone book. It must be said that businesses come and go as the city grows and changes, so information can change quickly. Even websites can be wrong if they aren't updated regularly. As such, the information provided here has been kept to generalities rather than specifics, and it is always a good idea to call beforehand to confirm things like hours of operation or entrance fees.

PHILADELPHIA

AREA OVERVIEW

If you've never visited Philadelphia, you might imagine a city frozen in the 18th century, with narrow streets lined with lovingly preserved colonial town homes and early American historical landmarks such as Independence Hall, the Liberty Bell, and the Betsy Ross House. And while "Old City," the centerpiece of "America's Most Historic Square Mile," is home to some of America's most iconic sites and treasures and colonial architecture, it is also a vibrant hub of soaring contemporary structures, commerce, and avant garde art galleries and boutique shopping (some of which are housed in converted foundries, factories, and warehouses from the city's industrial heyday). In an effort to brand the neighborhood, a group of Old City businesspeople define it as "Hipstoric."

Going west from Old City's Delaware River border are some of the nation's most prestigious art and science museums, including the Philadelphia Museum of Art, Rodin Museum, the Barnes Foundation, Franklin Institute, and University of Pennsylvania Museum of Archaeology and Anthropology. Other Center City area museums celebrate the ethnic diversity that gives Philadelphia its distinctive character. Don't miss the lighthearted tributes to the legendary Three Stooges and our own fine, feathered Mummers. Then there's the scientifically oriented but not-for-the-squeamish preserved body parts and anatomical anomalies at the College of Physicians of Philadelphia's Mütter Museum.

Along the Avenue of the Arts, you'll find the Kimmel Center, home of the Philadelphia Orchestra, Pennsylvania Ballet, Opera Company of Philadelphia, Peter Nero and the Philadelphia Pops, and all kinds of other grand and intimate performing arts venues. Jewelers Row is the diamond standard for outstanding adornments, Antique Row for timeless treasures, South Street for the fun and funky, and the Italian and Reading Terminal Markets for the food-focused.

Philly sports fans aren't shy about demonstrating their support for (or displeasure with) their home teams, so there are often just as much excitement and drama in the stands as there are on the field, the court, or the ice when the World Series–winning Phillies baseball, NBA Championship–winning 76ers (aka Sixers) basketball, Stanley Cup–winning Flyers hockey, and Super Bowl–playoff contender Eagles come home to play. On the college courts, you can get in on all of the hoopla of top teams the Villanova University Wildcats and Temple University Owls.

Throughout the city, there are also plenty of green and tranquil urban oases where you can grab a bench, kick back, and people-watch. True to William Penn's original physical design for his "green country towne" city, four open squares (the fifth is now the site of City Hall) have been preserved as public parks. If you can't get enough of the green, you can also head for sprawling Fairmount Park. Or walk on the wild side at America's first zoo.

No matter where you go, you'll never be far from nourishment (or just a yummy noshable to tide you over until your next meal). You'll want to try more than one cheesesteak so you can join in the long-standing heated debate as to which shop makes the best one. If it's street food you're craving, try one of the multitude of trucks that seem to be permanently parked in the areas around the city's major universities. Just so you know that Philadelphians do know how to eat with forks, you'll also find a wide range of dynamite dining spots from the highest of haute to little bitty BYOBs. Mix in some cocktail-centric clubs and you have some idea of the dining diversity you'll find here.

If you ask me to sum up Philly in less than 10 words, I would tell you this—you're never going to be bored . . . or hungry.

THE NEIGHBORHOODS

Philadelphia is often referred to as a "City of Neighborhoods." You know that's true because when you ask a native where he or she is from, the response won't be just Philly, but the more geographically pinpointed "Fairmount" or "Chestnut Hill." Some may go so far as to designate a particular neighborhood within a neighborhood—for example, Old City is part of Center City. It's really much less complicated than it sounds, but I thought it would be helpful to give you a geographic reference to some of the ones you're most likely to visit and how to make the most out of your experience when you do.

Art Museum Area/Fairmount

At the head of the Benjamin Franklin Parkway, the 1.5-mile-long Paris Champs Elysees–inspired thoroughfare located just northwest of Center City, stands one of the city's crown jewels, the Philadelphia Museum of Art. Also located along the parkway are many of the city's premier cultural and educational institutions.

Just west of the art museum is the beginning of Fairmount Park, a haven of recreational trails and fields, historic buildings, outdoor art, and gorgeous greenery. The surrounding Fairmount neighborhood is well-known for its lively restaurant and nightlife destinations. (Don't miss the nationally acclaimed Wine School.) It's also the site of one of the city's most famous bastions of the bizarre, Eastern State Penitentiary, a spooky, early-19th-century structure that was the first prison in the country focused on inmate reform rather than just punishment. Tours are available, and at various times of the year such as Bastille Day and Halloween, you can catch some truly offbeat special events.

Center City

When I was a kid, just about everybody did their serious shopping for everything from furniture to fashion "downtown," a designation that generally included the real estate between the Delaware and Schuylkill Rivers. The heart of the city was a magical place of multistoried, family-owned department stores with windows elaborately decked out

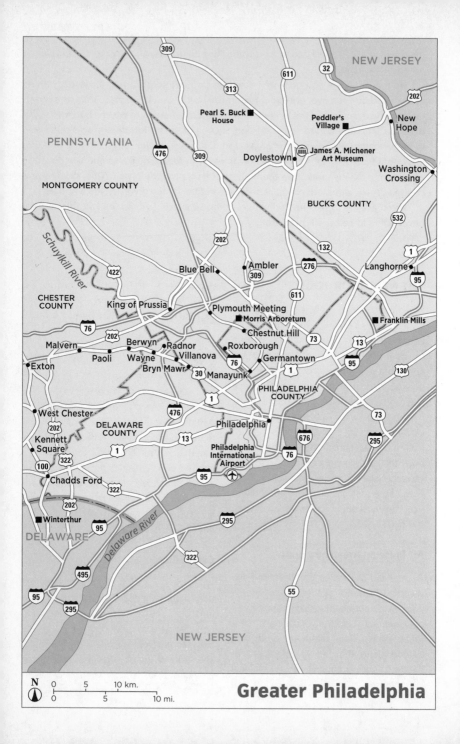

Greater Philadelphia

NEW JERSEY

PENNSYLVANIA

MONTGOMERY COUNTY

Schuylkill River

Pearl S. Buck House

Peddler's Village

New Hope

Doylestown

James A. Michener Art Museum

Washington Crossing

BUCKS COUNTY

CHESTER COUNTY

Blue Bell

Ambler

Langhorne

King of Prussia

Plymouth Meeting

Morris Arboretum

Franklin Mills

Malvern

Berwyn

Radnor

Chestnut Hill

Roxborough

Paoli

Wayne

Villanova

Germantown

Exton

Bryn Mawr

Manayunk

PHILADELPHIA COUNTY

West Chester

DELAWARE COUNTY

Philadelphia

Kennett Square

Philadelphia International Airport

Chadds Ford

Winterthur

DELAWARE

Delaware River

NEW JERSEY

N

0   5   10 km.

0   5   10 mi.

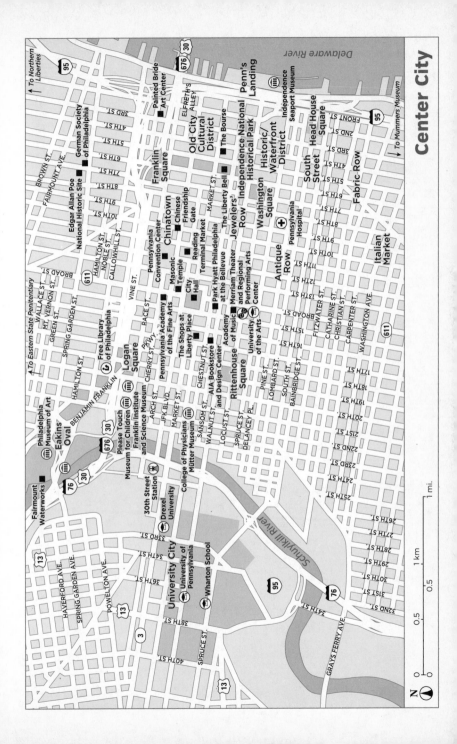

Center City

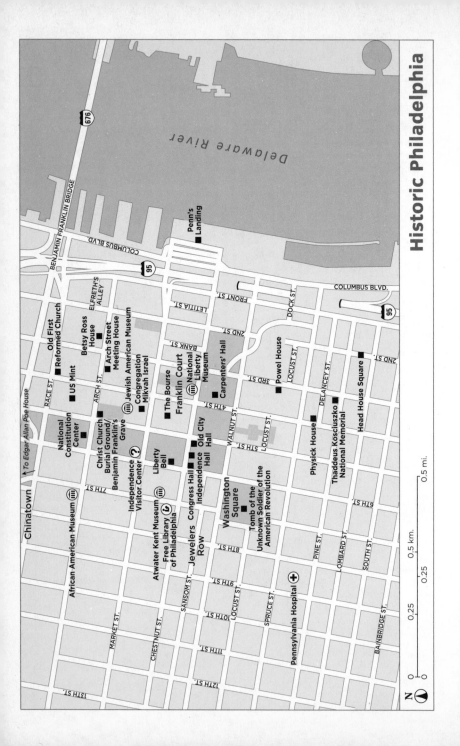

Historic Philadelphia

🔍 Close-up

Hoofing through History

Catch a warm, sunny day; put on some comfy shoes; and get ready to give your body, brain, and soul a good workout with a walk through Philly's Parkway Museums District. Within 2.4 miles along the Benjamin Franklin Parkway you'll find the Philadelphia Museum of Art, Parkway Central Library, Barnes Foundation, Rodin Museum, Franklin Institute, and Academy of Natural Sciences.

Along the way, you'll see close to 30 works of outdoor art ranging from Rocky Balboa to Rodin's *The Thinker*. Some of my favorites are Alexander Stirling Calder's Shakespeare Memorial at 19th and the Parkway, the Aero Memorial by Paul Manship at 20th and the Parkway, and the dinosaurs depicted in the sculpture *Deinonychus* by Kent Ullbert at Logan Square.

And even if you wanted to miss the Swann Memorial Fountain—which you don't—you couldn't. Situated in Logan Square on the Parkway at 19th Street, this 11-foot-high work of art, designed by architect Wilson Eyre and sculpted by Alexander Stirling Calder, can be seen for miles.

You can find a full self-guided walking tour of the Parkway Museums District online at parkwaymuseumsdistrictphiladelphia.org. At the same website you'll find a 10.5-mile self-guided bike tour that includes the district and a scenic ride along the Schuylkill River.

Whether on foot or bike, start your tour off with a smile at Robert Indiana's *LOVE* sculpture at the spot that is popularly known as LOVE Park, but officially named JFK Plaza. (This is a prime photo-op property.) Stock up on tickets, maps, and other information at the Fairmount Park Welcome Center located at 1599 JFK Blvd.

Whatever your spiritual leanings, the Cathedral Basilica of Saints Peter & Paul (18th & the Parkway; 215-561-1313; cathedralphila.org) is well worth a visit simply to take in the architectural beauty of this 1864 landmark that was inspired by the Lombard church of San Carlo al Corso in Rome. The Mother Church of the Archdiocese of Philadelphia is open to the public daily for services and tours.

With so many major museums surrounding it, you might miss the galleries at the Moore College of Art and Design (20th & the Parkway; 215-965-4027; thegalleriesat moore.org). But this treasure exhibits some of the most exciting contemporary art from around the area and the world. And, best of all, it's free.

If you want to get from one place to another faster than your own two feet will carry you (or if the weather isn't conducive for an extended stroll), take the Phlash, a seasonal, distinctively purple trolley that connects almost 30 of the city's most popular tourist destinations. Cost is $2 each time you board. (For full information see the Tours chapter of this book.)

with the latest must-haves. It was also a place where the business suit and briefcase crowd bustled from meeting to meeting. But as dynamic as it was during the day, that's how dead downtown was after dark.

The restaurants were generally just places to grab a bite before curtain time at the theater. Otherwise, there was no reason to linger.

While the independent landmark department stores of those days are all gone, many great mom-and-pop boutiques have sprouted all around the city as well as stores sporting national household names. You'll find close to 80 shops as well as restaurants, accommodations, spas, and other upscale stuff along Rittenhouse Row (between 18th and Walnut Streets, from Broad to 21st Streets, between Spruce and Market). Historic Antique Row (which runs from Spruce to Lombard Streets, 9th to Broad Streets, and all included side streets from Spruce to Locust Streets) is a treasure trove of fabulous finds from vintage to ultra-valuable. Step under the can't-miss-it Chinese Friendship Gate at 10th and Arch Streets and you'll find yourself in the city's lively Asian-American enclave where you can browse shops featuring exotic wares as well as some wonderful (and usually quite economically priced) dining spots.

Architecture aficionados will love strolling the cobblestone streets—complete with "Franklin Lamps," electrified replications of 18th-century oil streetlights—in Society Hill (bounded by Walnut, Lombard, Front, and 17th Streets). Society Hill has the largest concentration of original 18th- and 19th-century architecture in the US. Queen Village, also adjacent to Independence Hall, is another area where architecture is one of the main attractions. Extending south from Lombard Street to Washington Avenue and east from the Delaware River to 6th Street, it is the place to go to see the three-century evolution of Philadelphia residences from modest row homes to elaborate Victorians to high-rise condos. You can see all of the above on the 100 block of Fitzwater Street. Included within the parameters of Queen Village is South Street, the city's most eclectic and eccentric shopping district, and Fabric Row (4th

Street from Bainbridge to Christian), the oldest and largest collection of shops of its kind, a mecca for those who love to sew and quilt.

Philadelphia's maritime past is celebrated at Penn's Landing, which runs for 10 blocks from Vine to South Streets in the Waterfront District. This waterside park is a popular local gathering spot, especially for free summer concerts, holiday season festivities, and winter ice skating. In addition to the Independence Seaport Museum, Penn's Landing is home to three historic vessels— the late-19th-century tall ship *Gazela* and mid-20th-century USS *Olympia*, a veteran of World War II and the Korean and Vietnam Wars, and the World War II and Cold War submarine *Becuna*.

Of course, this book can only offer a sampling of Philly's neighborhoods—for example, there's the "Great Northeast," where I was born (growing up, we never just said "Northeast" without the "Great"), North Philly (home of Temple University), East Falls . . . the list goes on and on. I apologize to the residents of those wonderful communities, but because of space constraints, I chose the areas that attract the greatest number of visitors.

i Center City Philadelphia's Jewelers Row, founded in 1851, is America's oldest Diamond District and remains one of the largest in the nation. Hundreds of independent shops 1 block from Independence Hall on Sansom Street (between 7th and 8th Streets) and on 8th Street (between Chestnut and Walnut Streets) offer fine jewelry at discounted prices.

Chestnut Hill

Far enough from the madding crowd of Center City, but just on its northwest boundary is the charming town of Chestnut Hill. With its tranquility and distinctive personality, this neighborhood is often viewed as a 'burb, even by the locals, but it is definitely situated within the city limits. Take a stroll along cobblestone-paved Germantown Avenue and pop in and out of the numerous specialty shops and art galleries. Stop for lunch at one of the restaurants and be sure to take home a loaf of freshly baked artisan bread.

Manayunk

Also located in the northwest part of the city, Manayunk has gone from working-class neighborhood to a heaven-on-earth for the hip. The name is Native American for "where we go to drink," and that's more fitting than ever since this neighborhood is a bastion of bars and nightclubs. It's also a great restaurant and boutique shopping destination, but parking is no picnic, so expect to pay for a valet.

Northern Liberties

North of Spring Garden Street to just south of Girard Avenue, bordered by the Delaware River on the east, Northern Liberties is very much an artists' community with numerous galleries and studios. It's also a fun dining destination for easygoing eateries and lively nightlife.

South Philly

The Eagles, Flyers, Sixers, and Phillies all play at the Sports Complex that is as much a part of South Philly's character as are the fantastic authentic Italian eateries in this neighborhood situated between the Delaware and Schuylkill Rivers. And even if you're a born-and-raised supermarket shopper, you'll want to spend some time soaking in the old-world sights, sounds, scents, and, of course, flavors of the historic and always colorful Italian Market (9th Street from Wharton to Fitzwater Streets), the oldest and largest (over 100 vendors) working outdoor market in the US.

University City

Young adults going grocery shopping in their pajamas, huddling over their computers in the coffee shops, or hustling from historic building to historic building . . . it must be a college campus. Actually this small section of West Philly is home to two, the University of Pennsylvania and neighboring Drexel University. These are true urban campuses bordered by student-friendly shops and casual dining spots. Truck food was popular here long before it became trendy, so look for curbside cuisine representing just about every culture.

i Comprising 63 regional and neighborhood parks throughout the city, Philadelphia's 9,200-acre Fairmount Park is the first and largest urban park in the world. Founded in 1855, Fairmount Park hosted the 1876 Centennial International Exhibition, the nation's first official World's Fair, which was held to celebrate the 100th anniversary of the signing of the Declaration of Independence.

THE 'BURBS

"Greater Philadelphia" is more than a description of their home city by its proud

Philly's Famous

Philly's neighborhoods and 'burbs boast numerous native sons and daughters who have made their mark on the worlds of art, entertainment, literature, sports, and other fields. Other legendary luminaries adopted the city as their home.

Philadelphians By Birth

Opera greats—Marian Anderson and Mario Lanza

Artists—N. C., Andrew, and Jamie Wyeth; Maxwell Parrish

Author Louisa May Alcott (*Little Women*)

Film director M. Night Shyamalan (*The Sixth Sense*)

Actors—John, Ethel, and Lionel Barrymore; Kevin Bacon; Will Smith; Grace Kelly (also Princess of Monaco); and Blythe Danner

Musicians—jazz greats Ethel Waters and Billie Holiday; soul diva Patti LaBelle; and rockers Pink and Joan Jett

Comedians—Bill Cosby, Tina Fey, Larry Fine (*The Three Stooges*), and W. C. Fields

Sports—basketball great Wilt Chamberlain and Rasheed Wallace

Philadelphians By Choice

Benjamin Franklin

Flagmaker Betsy Ross

Revolutionary War hero Thaddeus Kosciuszko

Pulitzer Prize– and Nobel Prize–winner Pearl S. Buck

Pulitzer Prize–winner James Michener

Lyricist Oscar Hammerstein II

and not-always-humble natives. It is the term used to designate the 5-county area that includes the city and its nearest and dearest suburbs. (Another, more tourist-focused name that's used for this combination of counties along with neighboring Pennsylvania Dutch Country is "Philadelphia and the Countryside.") More than just the offspring of city sprawl, these adjacent communities have played their own roles in US history and are destination-worthy all by themselves.

Bucks County

Located north of Philadelphia on the Delaware River, the boroughs, towns, and villages of Bucks County offer a countryside perspective on more than 3 centuries of history. William Penn made his home here (you can still visit). Later, so did turn-of-the-20th-century tile maker and leader in the arts and crafts movement, Henry Mercer; Pulitzer Prize–winning author James A. Michener; Pulitzer- and Nobel Prize–winning author Pearl S. Buck; and Academy Award–winning lyricist Oscar Hammerstein II. Today you will find a stunning array of art-oriented museums (particularly in the borough of Doylestown). For antiques and collectibles and contemporary arts and crafts, allot at least an entire day to browsing the shops and studios in the village of New Hope. Treat yourself to some riverside recreation with a float on a tube or just watch the river sparkle as you sit a spell with a cocktail or meal. And for little kids, there's no place more fun than Sesame Place theme park.

Chester County

The fertile rolling hills dotted with hundreds of dairy and produce farms, orchards, and vineyards make this county located southwest of Philadelphia look and feel more like country than 'burb. It shares the Brandywine River shoreline with neighboring Delaware, creating a dual-destination-worthy entity called the "Brandywine Valley." (The tiny township of Chadds Ford, once a part of Chester County, now part of Delaware County, is also included under the Brandywine Valley umbrella. Chadds Ford is where you can explore the works and legacy of three generations of the Wyeth family, widely regarded as among the greatest American artists.) Leave at least an entire day each for visits to the magnificent du Pont family estates, Longwood Gardens in Kennett Square, and Winterthur right across the Delaware state border. And armchair shopping aficionados

won't be able to resist a tour through their favorite kingdom of commerce, QVC, which is headquartered in West Chester.

i Kennett Square in southern Chester County is known as "the Mushroom Capital of the World" for good reason. The borough was the first place in the US to cultivate the fabulous fungi, and its farmers still grow more than half of the nation's supply.

Delaware County

Delaware County, south of Philadelphia, is an area that thrives on diversity, from its working-class-to-wealthy population, quiet residential communities to college campuses (there are 11 universities here) to sprawling commercial complexes, quaint to contemporary architecture, and busy main roads to woodland trails. Visit the historic towns of Media and Chadds Ford (see Chester County for more on Chadds Ford). Enjoy the great outdoors at Ridley Creek State Park, Scott and Tyler Arboretums, and The John Heinz National Wildlife Refuge at Tinicum.

i While visiting Delaware County, be sure to save room for lunch. Romano's Pizzeria & Italian Restaurant (246 Wanamaker Ave., Essington, 610-521-9010, romanostromboli.com), the reputed birthplace of the stromboli, is still serving up its dough-wrapped deliciousness in original, chicken, pizza, steak, and vegetarian versions.

Montgomery County

During the cruel winter of 1777–78, George Washington didn't find this area west of

Philly Vital Statistics

Climate: Philadelphia has four clearly defined seasons. Summers tend to be warm to hot—average temperatures are around 75°F but can climb to the mid-80s and above with high humidity in July and August. Winters can be moderate to cold—average temperature around 30°F, a little lower in January and February. Springs and falls are generally moderate, with average temperatures in the mid to upper 60s.

Higher Education: With more than 80 colleges, universities, and trade and specialty schools in the 5-county area, Philadelphia has the second highest concentration of advanced education institutions in the US, including some of the most prestigious names in medicine, business, and law. Five of the area's medical schools are affiliated with major hospitals.

The University of Pennsylvania, located in West Philadelphia, was ranked as the Best Undergraduate Business Program and one of the top graduate schools for engineering, law, and both research and primary care medicine for 2011 by *US News & World Report*. The magazine named two Delaware County institutions, Swarthmore and Haverford Colleges, as well as Bryn Mawr College in Montgomery County as among the top National Liberal Arts Colleges and Villanova University (Delaware County) as the Best Value Regional College in the US. In its 2010 rankings of Best Colleges, *Money Magazine* listed Swarthmore and Haverford.

Top Employers: Prior to World War II, the segments of manufacturing and distribution made up the backbone of the Philadelphia economy, but today "eds and meds"—educational and health services—and technology companies are its primary drivers. The Milken Institute, a nonprofit, nonpartisan think tank, named Philadelphia the second "most vibrant" life sciences cluster in the US. According to the definition of "life sciences organizations," which includes hospitals as well as medical research, pharmaceutical and biotech companies account for 15 percent of all economic activity and one out of six jobs in the Greater Philadelphia area.

Largest among the private employers is The University of Pennsylvania (including the University of Pennsylvania Health System). Other major health care employers (some of which are located in Delaware and New Jersey but employ large numbers of Philadelphia area residents) include Jefferson Health System, Christiana Health Care System, Catholic Health East, Crozer-Keystone Health System, Tenet Health Systems, and Children's Hospital of Pennsylvania (CHOP). Among the 15 leading pharmaceutical firms in the area are Astra-Zenica, Bristol-Myers Squibb, GlaxoSmithKline, and Wyeth.

Alcohol Laws: The legal drinking age is 21; closing time for most bars is 2 a.m. 7 days a week. Wine and spirits are sold only in state stores; beer and wine coolers are available at many beer distributors and delis.

Daily Newspapers: *The Philadelphia Inquirer/Daily News* (philly.com); daily circulation about 356,000, Sunday 518,000.

Taxes: City wage tax 4 percent, sales tax 8 percent, hotel tax 15.2 percent. No tax on clothing sales.

High Stepping

The Philadelphia Museum of Art is renowned for its stellar centuries- and genre-spanning collections, but not all the multitudes of tourists sprinting (or, more often, schlepping) up the 72-stone steps to its majestic Grand (East) Entrance are racing to see the Rembrandts or making a beeline for the Botticellis. Thousands of visitors each year seek to channel their inner champions by literally following in the footsteps of Rocky, panting their way to the top where they can raise their arms in the same triumphant pose modeled by the 10-foot bronze statue of the fictional fighter below. If you want to look cool, skip the sky-punching and pretend you're a local jogger. And if you want to be really cool, keep galloping through the doors to the galleries.

Philadelphia to be terribly hospitable when he and his Continental army troops camped at Valley Forge between battles with the British. You, however, will certainly find a warmer welcome both at the historic national park where Washington wintered and in the rest of Montgomery County no matter what time of year you visit.

The park itself is 3,500 acres of flora- and fauna-filled tranquility, with miles of Schuylkill (pronounced skool-kill, but often pronounced skoo-kill by the locals) River- and creekside trails. George Washington's headquarters building still stands, meticulously preserved and open for touring. Outside of the park is a busy 'burb with multiple personalities. For the ultimate shopping experience, give your credit card a workout at the super-upscale King of Prussia Mall. Or follow boutique- and brand-name-store-lined Lancaster Avenue/Route 30 as it wends its way through the "Main Line," a close to 10-mile stretch of quaint towns and villages in Montgomery, Delaware, and Chester Counties. Named for the Pennsylvania Railroad line that connected it with Philadelphia, the Main Line was the residential refuge of choice for many of the city's wealthiest families in the 19th and 20th centuries. It still is. If you get off the main road, you will drive past still-lived-in historic mansions and expansive estates on quiet, winding, tree-lined streets in towns with names such as Bala Cynwyd, Bryn Mawr, and Gladwyne, inspired by the language of their original Welsh settlers.

GETTING HERE, GETTING AROUND

Situated in the heart of the Northeast Corridor, Philadelphia is within a 5.5-hour drive of 40 percent of the country's population. From New York City, for example, you can get here in 2 hours, from Baltimore 90 minutes, and from Washington, DC, 3 hours.

Getting into most big cities, especially on the East or West Coast, is a migraine event, and getting around them is even worse. Not so with Philadelphia! Freeways into Center City keep traffic moving as smoothly as sleek ribbon (except during the expected rush-hour jams), with easy-to-see signage that makes sense. For those flying in, more than 25 airlines stage some 575 departures every day to 115 cities around the world. Just blocks from downtown, Amtrak's 30th Street Station's 11 train lines connect to every train destination in the nation.

Philadelphia is so ideally positioned that getting here by plane, car, bus, or train is hassle-free. Once you're here, you're in a walking city, with dozens of historic sites inside the compact, 25-block Center City grid. Visitors too rushed for a stroll through history can easily hail one of the ubiquitous taxis constantly cruising the streets—and if you prefer to drive yourself, the grid is easy to negotiate, with plentiful parking in every section of town.

GETTING HERE

By Car

If you're driving into Philadelphia, your route will be marvelously simple: Only a handful of major roadways lead into Philadelphia, and they connect with all surrounding regions.

When coming from the west it is best to use the PA Turnpike (I-76). You can exit the Turnpike at Valley Forge and pick up the Schuylkill Expressway (I-676), which runs along the Schuylkill River and will take you into Center City, Philadelphia. If you are coming from the north, you can use the Blue Route (I-476) and exit at the Schuylkill Expressway. From there, continue going east into Center City Philadelphia. If you are coming from the south, use I-95, which flows through Philadelphia and has many exits throughout the city.

> **i** In Philly-speak, I-676 is always called "the Schuylkill Expressway." I-476 is known as the "Blue Route."

An efficient network of roads has been in place in Philly for nearly 2 centuries: A number of roads into the city, 20 feet wide and built of crushed stone—complete with tollgates—were completed by 1794 to facilitate the movement of goods. By 1821 paved toll highways connected Philadelphia to New York City, Baltimore, the state capital at Harrisburg, Reading, Lancaster, and into New Jersey. Fifty years later, some 300 miles of paved roads served Philadelphia, and in the early 1900s, the Pennsylvania Turnpike became the first statewide superhighway in the country.

By Air

Located about 7 miles from Center City, Philadelphia International Airport (PHL; phl .org)—serves more than 25 passenger airlines and is a hub for Southwest.

At this writing, airlines served by PHL are:

Air Canada, (888) 247-2262
Air Jamaica, (800) 523-5585
AirTran Airways, (800) AIRTRAN
American Airlines and American Eagle, (800) 433-7300
British Airways, (800) 247-9297
Continental Airlines and Continental Express, (800) 525-0280
Delta Air Lines and Delta Connection, (800) 221-1212
Frontier Airlines, (800) 432-1359
Lufthansa German Airlines, (800) 645-3880
Midwest Airlines, (800) 452-2022
Southwest Airlines, (800) 435-9792
United Airlines and United Express, (800) 241-6522
USAirways and USAirways Express, (800) 428-4322
USA3000 and Charters, (877) 872-3000

Parking at the Airport
Parking is operated by the Philadelphia Parking Authority Airport Operations Division (215-683-9842; philapark.org).

i If you want to buy some souvenirs and just about anything else and grab a snack or full meal after landing or prior to boarding, the Philadelphia Marketplace Food & Shops (800-937-3340; philamarketplace.com) has more than 160 local and name-brand stores and eateries. Prices are comparable to other locations operating under the same name (e.g., Gap) in Greater Philadelphia including Philadelphia, Delaware, Chester, Montgomery, and Bucks Counties as well as Camden and Burlington Counties across the river in New Jersey.

Ground Transportation to Center City
If you have any questions, you may speak with a Ground Transportation Information representative by calling (215) 937-6958.

BY RAIL

SEPTA (Southeastern Pennsylvania Transportation Authority), (215) 580-7800—Airport R-1 regional rail line connects the airport with key stops in Center City, including University City, 30th Street (Amtrak), Suburban, and Market East Stations. Cost is $7 weekdays, $6 weekends.

BY TAXI

One-way cab fare to and from Center City is $28.50. An additional $1 per passenger ($3 maximum) after the first passenger will be charged on flat-rate trips between the airport and Center City for passengers over age 12.

This "Center City" area eligible for this rate encompasses Fairmount Avenue (most northern point) to South Street (most southern point) and Delaware River (most eastern point) to University City/38th Street (most western point).

There is a $10 minimum fare from the airport to any destination. All other fares are based on a $2.70 "flag drop" fee upon entry into the cab plus $2.30 per mile.

Aside from the flat airport rate, other taxi rates are based per trip, not per person. Most taxis can accommodate up to 3 passengers. In some cases certain vehicle types can accommodate 4 passengers. Most companies will accept credit cards, but it would be wise to check with the dispatcher or driver.

Cabs are always lined up outside of the airport, and they're also readily available in Center City. To ensure that you are using a reputable cab company, the Greater Philadelphia Tourism Marketing Corporation (GPTMC) recommends:

All City Taxi, (215) 467-6666
Capital, (215) 235-2200
City Cab, (215) 492-6500
Convention Cab, (215) 462-0200
Liberty Cab, (215) 389-8000
Olde City Taxi, (215) AIR-PORT (247-7678)
Quaker City Cab, (215) 728-8000
Yellow Cab, (267) 672-7391

CAR RENTAL

I-76, I-95, and I-476 offer direct access to Center City. If you're renting a car at the airport, you will find information phones at all baggage claim areas. On-site rental companies are:

Alamo, (800) 331-1212; alamo.com
Budget, (800) 527-0700; budget.com
Dollar, (800) 800-4000; dollar.com
Enterprise, (800) RENT-A-CAR; enterprise.com
Hertz, (800) 654-3131; hertz.com
National, (800) 227-7368; nationalcar.com

LIMO & SHUTTLE SERVICES

Some of the city's largest limo and shuttle services include:

All American Limo, (215) 535-5466; 535limo.homestead.com
American Limo, (484) 368-7041; americanlimosvc.com
Atlantic Sedan Services, (610) 659-8513; towncarforhire.com
BostonCoach, (610) 521-0500 or (800) 672-767; bostoncoach.com
CAR ONE Sedan & Limousine, (610) 266-9770 or (888) 550-CAR1 (2271)
Corporate Sedan Service, (215) 860-6564 or (888) 258-9555; sedanservice.com
Eagle Limousine & Motorcoach, (800) 669-5460; eagledrives.com
Global Limousine Network, (215) 334-7900 or (800) 727-1957; gogloballimo.com
King Limousine & Transportation Service, Inc., (800) 245-5460; kinglimoinc.com
Lady Liberty Shuttle, (215) 724-8888; ladylibertyshuttle.com
Transline Airport One, (215) 677-3544 or (800) 535-5466 (LIMO); aairport1.com
Tropiano Transportation Services, Inc., (800) 559-2040; www.tropianotransportation.com/shuttle

By Train

Amtrak (800-USA-RAIL; amtrak.com) operates rail service along the Northeast Corridor from Boston to Washington, DC, and other major cities in the US and Canada. You will come into the city at 30th Street Station, which is only a few minutes from Center City. It is also the hub for service to suburban destinations.

Thirtieth Street also offers Acela Express Service with trains departing every hour during peak morning and afternoon rush times. Acela also operates round-trip routes between New York and Boston with stops in between.

i Built in 1933, 30th Street Station is a work of art with its neoclassical, columned structure; intricately patterned, 90-foot-high ceilings; travertine tile walls; marble floors; and gorgeous art deco chandeliers. It is listed on the National Register of Historic Places. The station also has a large food court, shopping area, and car rental kiosks.

By Bus

For a super-easy, comfortable, and economical way to get to Philadelphia, take the bus. **Greyhound** (215-931-4075; greyhound .com), **Martz Trailways** (800-233-8604; martz trailways.com), and **Peter Pan** (800-343-9999; peterpanbus.com) will bring you into the Greyhound Bus Terminal at 10th and Filbert Streets, only a few blocks from City Hall.

Super-economy **Megabus** (877-GO2-MEGA or 877-462-6342; us.megabus.com) and **BoltBus** (877-BOLTBUS or 877-265-8287; boltbus.com) arrive and depart outside of 30th Street Station. **New Century Travel** (215-627-2666; 2001bus.com), another low-cost carrier, takes you to 55 N. 11th St., and **New Jersey Transit** (800-772-2287; njtransit .com) to 10th and Market Streets.

GETTING AROUND

On Foot

Once you're here, you're in a walking city, with dozens of historic sites inside the river-to-river Center City grid, modeled on the one designed by William Penn. "Walk! Philadelphia" signs throughout Center City make it easy to find your way around on foot. You can also look for uniformed goodwill ambassadors who are available to answer questions, give directions, and stay in radio contact with Philadelphia police to promote public safety.

Public Transportation

Philadelphia's major public transportation service is **SEPTA** (Southeast Pennsylvania Transportation Authority, 215-580-7800; septa .org), which has bus, subway, trolley, trackless trolley, high-speed rail, and commuter train (commonly referred to as regional rail) lines throughout the city and suburbs. Under the SEPTA umbrella are the Market-Frankford Elevated Train (affectionately called "The El"), which runs east and west on its Center City route, and the Broad Street Subway, which runs north and south along Broad Street. The El and Subway are most frequently used by commuters and students. For visitors, the bus and trolley components of SEPTA are the easiest and most convenient forms of public transit. Base price for all SEPTA lines except for regional rail is $2.

i Monday through Friday (except on holidays), SEPTA operates a special LUCY loop bus route that runs through University City from 30th Street Station to the University of Pennsylvania, Drexel University, University City Science Center, University of Pennsylvania Medical Center, Presbyterian Medical Center, The Children's Hospital of Philadelphia, Children's Seashore House, and VA Medical Center. Base fare is $2. Go to universitycity .org/getting_around/lucy or call (215) 580-7800 for schedule.

Cheap & Easy Rides

If you plan to see a good part of the city, forget the car and buy an **Independence Pass from SEPTA.** A 1-day pass, which costs $11 for an individual or $28 for a family (up to 5 people traveling together, with a minimum of 1, maximum of 2 individuals ages 18 or older), entitles you to unlimited rides on all of SEPTA's city transport lines. Independence Passes may be purchased at the Independence Visitor Center, from shop.septa.org, and at other convenient locations listed on the septa.org website.

From spring until early fall (dates vary depending on city budget), a purple trolley called **The Phlash** (215-389-TOUR; phillyphlash.com) allows you to hop on and hop off at or near almost 30 popular historical and cultural attractions along its loop through the city. The Phlash also offers direct connections to SEPTA and other major providers of city transit. The website has a map detailing every stop along the Phlash route along with a list of city garages that offer "Park & Ride" discounts. Service is about every 12 minutes from 10 a.m. to 6 p.m. Cost is $2 per person each time you board the trolley, or you can purchase an all-day Phlash pass for just $5 or family pass (2 adults and 2 children ages 6 to 17) for $10. Children under 5 and seniors ride free. You can purchase Phlash tickets at the Independence Visitor Center, located at 6th and Market Streets, or when getting on the trolley.

By Car

You'll be thanking William Penn again and again for his grid design as you cruise the streets of Center City. Although many of the side streets are narrow and one-way, you'll find that it only takes about 3 quick turns (left-left-left or right-right-right) to get back on course should you miss a turn anywhere within the 25 blocks between the Delaware and Schuylkill Rivers. Within this area, north/south streets are numbered and most east/west streets between Market and Lombard Streets in the Rittenhouse Square area have tree names such as Walnut, Spruce, and Pine. Even-numbered streets generally run south, odd-numbered streets run north. Broad Street (technically 14th Street) runs both north and south.

Every hotel and inn in the city either has its own garage or valet parking, or the desk staff can guide you to safe parking nearby. If you plan to park on your own, here are your options:

Non-metered On-street Spots

Before you park, read the signs to find out the hours and days that public parking is permitted, the length of time you can stay in the spot, and if there's a meter that has to be paid.

On-street Meters

Recently, the city has begun replacing traditional coin-only meters with multispace green meter kiosks that accept coins, cash, credit/debit cards, or **Smart Cards** (prepaid cards that are available in $10, $20, and $50 denominations). The kiosk will dispense a receipt, which you should display on your windshield. The current cost of meter parking in Center City is $2 per hour. You can purchase Smart Cards in advance from the Philadelphia Parking Authority (215-683-9600; philapark.org) or at any of close to 200 retail locations throughout the city, including Independence Center and many convenience stores.

Again, make sure you read the street signs. Metered parking is free or may be prohibited even at metered spots on specific times and/or days. And be careful too of the time; if your meter expires, you will be ticketed $36.

Parking Lots & Garages

The **Philadelphia Parking Authority** (215-683-9600; philapark.org) operates many off-street parking lots and garages throughout the city. Listed by location, they are:

CONVENTION CENTER/CITY HALL/GALLERY MALL

THE AUTOPARK AT CITY CENTER
15th & Arch Streets
Philadelphia, PA 19102
(215) 683-9812
Open: Mon to Fri 5:30 a.m. to 8 p.m.; Sat 7 a.m. to 4 p.m.

THE AUTOPARK AT 8TH & FILBERT
801 Filbert St.
Philadelphia, PA 19107
(215) 925-4305
Open: 24 hours a day, 7 days a week

THE AUTOPARK AT JEFFERSON
10th & Ludlow Streets
Philadelphia, PA 19107
(215) 683-9410
Open: 5 a.m. to 11 p.m. 7 days a week

THE AUTOPARK AT JFK PLAZA
15th & Arch Streets
Philadelphia, PA 19102
(215) 683- 9800
Open: 24 hours a day, 7 days a week

PHILADELPHIA GATEWAY PARKING GARAGE
1540 Vine St.
Philadelphia, PA 19102
Entrances on Spring and 16th Streets
(215) 246-0300
Open: 24 hours a day, 7 days a week

HISTORIC DISTRICT/WATERFRONT/OLDE CITY

THE AUTOPARK AT INDEPENDENCE MALL
5th & Market Streets
Philadelphia, PA 19106
(215) 683-9408
Open: 24 hours a day, 7 days a week

THE AUTOPARK AT OLDE CITY
2nd & Sansom Streets
Philadelphia, PA 19106
(215) 683-9407
Open: 24 hours a day, 7 days a week

PHILADELPHIA PARKING AUTHORITY (PPA)
8th & Chestnut Streets
Philadelphia, PA 19102
(215) 683-9413
Open: Mon to Sat 6 a.m. to 8 p.m.

Parkway/Museums

PPA
19th and Callowhill Streets
Philadelphia, PA 19130
(215) 683-9813
Open: 24 hours a day, 7 days a week

Private Parking Companies

Central Parking System, (215) 563-3650; parking.com; 48 lots throughout the city.

E.Z. Park, Inc., (215) 733-0700; ezparkinc .com; more than 20 lots throughout the city; website has a pull-down menu that allows you to enter your desired destination (e.g., Kimmel Center or Chinatown) to find the locations of their closest lots.

Parkway Corporation, (215) 569-8400; parkwaycorp.com; 51 lots throughout the city.

HISTORY

By the time William Penn first stepped onto the land called Pennsylvania in 1682, it already had been explored—decades earlier—by Dutch and Swedish colonists.

Back in 1623, a Dutch stockade and trading post were the only structures in the busy city we know as Philadelphia. The region still was a place of dense, deep green forests. Bears, foxes, and other wildlife were abundant, and the rivers were rich with fish. Most of the inhabitants were Lenni-Lenape Indians, a branch of the Delaware Tribe of the Algonquin Indians. Shawnee, too, were here, living in villages of 100 to 300 people along the Delaware River.

As treaties with Indians were signed mid-century, land was purchased and, beginning in 1643, Swedes, Dutch, Finns, and English settlers came and built cabins on the fertile farming land near the Delaware. The Indians were a presence—cordial neighbors, for the most part, trading with settlers for furs and tobacco.

William Penn, a Quaker, cleared the way for more organized settlement when he accepted the title to Pennsylvania in a land grant from King Charles II of England. Penn delegated the task of finding a site for Philadelphia, instructing his committee to find a spot with good river frontage, and Penn personally arrived to inaugurate and design the city in October 1682.

Using a rectangular grid pattern on just 1,200 acres, Penn planned the city streets between the Delaware and Schuylkill Rivers—a 22-by-8-block pattern, with a town square (now the location of City Hall) and four public squares. Penn had survived the terrible London fire of 1666 and knew well the perils of narrow streets lined with wooden buildings, so he laid out Philadelphia along broad boulevards. Wanting to treat European settlers and Native Americans equally, he specified that no city walls or neighborhood borders be used. Penn named east–west streets after trees and plants (though Sassafras was changed to Race Street for the horse-and-buggy races held there), with Front Street and subsequent numbered streets running parallel to the Delaware River. Penn's urban design was meant to facilitate future growth and served as the basic format for dozens of future cities across America.

In March 1683, Philadelphia was named capital of the colony of Pennsylvania. Because of the region's fertile lands and riverside location, Philadelphia's population multiplied quickly to 7,000 residents by the early 1700s—mostly Quakers, or "Friends," from England, with growing numbers of Scottish, Irish, and German immigrants. Before the American Revolution began, Philadelphia had become a strategic port and a major city.

THE REVOLUTIONARY WAR BEGINS

No city was more vital to American independence than Philadelphia. After the French and Indian War in 1763, when Britain began tightening the reins on trade in the colonies, Philadelphia—the economic and political center—was the hub of discontent over the new policies. With unpopular taxes also being imposed, and no colonial representation in the British Parliament, the buzz in the 1770s was for independence. Even Benjamin Franklin, who was loyal to King George III until well into the 1770s, became disenchanted and talked of the "capricious English policy."

King George sent troops to the colonies to help control unrest. In 1774 the First Continental Congress convened at Carpenters' Hall in Philadelphia. Instead of directly rejecting the British policies, Congress decided on a commercial boycott of British goods. But over the next 9 months, rebellion grew in Massachusetts, and in April 1775, the King's troops attacked Concord and "the shot heard 'round the world" proclaimed that the American Revolution had begun.

i One of the first major waves of immigrants into Philadelphia was the European farmers, eager to work the affordable land. Most were English, Scottish, and Germans—or, in the German language, Deutsch—which is why the farm families in the surrounding countryside are known as the "Pennsylvania Dutch."

Still, the colonies sent delegates to the Second Continental Congress in May 1775 to try to resolve the problems without going to war, meeting this time in Independence Hall (then the Pennsylvania State House). Though they were meeting for peace, they established a Continental army and named George Washington as commander-in-chief.

Congress met a third time on July 4, 1776, no longer hoping for a peaceful resolution. John Adams, Benjamin Franklin, Thomas Jefferson, Robert R. Livingston, and Roger Sherman were appointed to draft a Declaration of Independence. Jefferson wrote the first draft, presented to Congress on June 28, and a vote was called the afternoon of July 4. Nine of the 13 colonies voted to adopt the Declaration, and signatures were collected.

i Of all the signatures on the Declaration of Independence, the most flamboyant was that of John Hancock, who, legend says, signed with a flourish so "King George can read that without spectacles!" But, while Hancock's signature was indeed the largest and most ornate on the document, he probably didn't sign that way to make it easier for the monarch to make out. According to National Park Service historians, that's the way Hancock signed everything.

WASHINGTON'S RIVER RAID

The Revolutionary War came to Philadelphia, and British troops occupied the homes of the city's elite. It was 25 miles northeast of the city, however, in pastoral Bucks County, that George Washington turned the tide of the war.

Bucks County had been settled, along with Philadelphia, in the 1600s. Some of the first European settlers paddled up the

🔍 Close-up

Let Freedom Ring

John Adams wrote that four days after the signing of the Declaration of Independents, on July 8, 1776, bells rang throughout Philadelphia to summon some 8,000 patriots to hear the first reading of the Declaration of Independence by Colonel John Nixon. National Park historians say that probably among those bells was the one that hung in the tower of the Pennsylvania State House. This particular bell's inscription read, "Proclaim LIBERTY throughout all the Land unto all the inhabitants thereof." Aptly, it came to be known as the Liberty Bell and its state house home Independence Hall.

The bell was cracked long before it rang on that momentous July day. It had been commissioned by the Pennsylvania Assembly in 1751, to celebrate the 50th anniversary of William Penn's state constitution. The bell's inscription, a quote from Leviticus 25:10, was inspired by Penn's Quaker philosophies and his liberal position on Native American rights. It's believed that the crack appeared the first time the bell was rung, possibly because it was too brittle.

Despite this flaw, it is generally believed that the 3-foot-high, 2,080-pound, mostly copper behemoth sounded its E Flat note to summon citizens for special announcements and meetings before the war and as it progressed. (On the bell, Pennsylvania is spelled "Pensylvania." But that wasn't another flaw; at that time spelling wasn't as standardized as it is today and this version was acceptable.)

Weeks before the British occupied Philadelphia in October 1777, all bells were removed from the city to keep them from being melted down for cannonballs. The Liberty Bell was hidden under the floorboards of the Zion Reformed Church in Allentown, Pennsylvania, until after the war was over.

The Liberty Bell was permanently silenced after suffering a fatal injury when it was rung on George Washington's birthday in 1846. But, whether it did or did not ring on July 8, 1776, the bell has remained an important symbol of the quest for freedom for abolitionists, the women's suffrage movement, Civil Rights organizations, war protestors, Native Americans, and immigrants.

Today more than 2 million people per year visit the Liberty Bell Center at 600 Chestnut St. (between 5th and 6th), where this national icon is displayed on its original American elm yoke.

Delaware River, which forms the county's western boundaries, and stayed in what became the port town of Bristol in lower Bucks County. Others explored the river, establishing small settlements as they traveled north. With productive farmland and large agricultural stakes of those early families, Bucks County soon established itself as an enclave of the wealthy and genteel.

It also presented itself to George Washington as a strategic military outpost. His Long Island, New York campaign of 1776 had been disastrous, he had been forced to retreat into Pennsylvania, and he desperately needed a victory. The Delaware River was the barrier. If he could get across, he and his soldiers could position themselves for a surprise attack on the British in New Jersey.

The plan was for the 2,400 ragged soldiers to cross during the night of December 25. The river was clogged with ice; soon after they entered the river, the weather suddenly changed and the men were fighting sleet and blinding snow. Two supporting divisions didn't make it, but Washington and his men got across.

That crossing was pivotal to our winning the Revolution. Washington went on to surprise the British troops at Trenton, New Jersey, the morning of December 26, 1776—a huge victory that revitalized his troops and renewed the faith of Americans that liberty would prevail.

MORE PAPERWORK

Although the colonies had come together in the name of freedom, keeping them together was another matter. In 1781, the members of the Continental Congress passed the Articles of Confederation, a plan to define the governing powers of the federal government as an entity and the individual states. When the Articles proved to be weak and unsatisfactory, another general convention was called in Philadelphia to revise it. All of the states except for Rhode Island attended. When the delegates of the Constitutional Convention (also known as the Philadelphia Convention or the Grand Convention at Philadelphia) met, they realized the changes that were needed were so extensive they would have to draft a whole new document. The result was the US Constitution, which was ratified in 1788 and put into effect in 1789.

Following the war, Philadelphia continued its growth into a major industrial center. By the time the Civil War broke out, the city had become an important source of arms and financial support to the Northern war effort. True to its original principles of freedom, it also became a hotbed of abolitionist activity. Industry attracted another major wave of immigrants from all over Europe, the Caribbean, Latin America, and as far away as China, particularly in the late 19th and early 20th centuries. African Americans also came from the South to make new lives. All of them made—and continue to make—their own distinctive contributions to the city's culture.

i Truth or urban legend? Some historians believe that, after showing her friend George Washington how to make a five-point star with one scissor-cut, Betsy Ross went on to sew the first American flag—which, if true, means Old Glory was created using origami!

It would be nice if this brief history could conclude with a happily ever after scenario of brotherhood and harmony. The truth is, like any other major urban entity, Philadelphia struggles with its share of economic, political, and social concerns and conflicts. But the fundamental self-starter spirit and determination that made Philadelphia so dynamic in its early days are still evident in everything from its preservation of its historic treasures and renewal of its neighborhoods to its emphasis on higher learning and technological innovation to its efforts to create a downtown area as vibrant as the other great cities of the world.

INTO THE 19TH CENTURY

When we think of "Philadelphia" and "history," the images are of Revolutionary War

Renaissance Rebel

Although he was born in Boston, Philly definitely considers this Founding Father as one of its own hometown heroes. He is widely honored for his insatiable curiosity, razor-sharp wit, and creative genius. Sometimes he even shows up at city events to say a few words and nibble on a pretzel or cheesesteak. A printing apprentice, young Ben ran away to Philadelphia at 17 and, the next year, continued his printer's training in London. His publishing talents would serve him well, making him wealthy as a printer and publisher of the *Pennsylvania Gazette* and the annual *Poor Richard: An Almanack*. But Franklin was more than just a good businessman. His life was filled with accomplishments as an author, legislator, international diplomat, scientist (he documented the effects of electricity while flying a kite), inventor, economist, abolitionist, and, of course, signer of the Declaration of Independence. The only thing that could get him to stop working was his death at the age of 84. Many pithy quotes can be attributed to Benjamin Franklin, but one that probably best describes his overall philosophy of life was:

"If you would not be forgotten,

As soon as you are dead & rotten,

Either write things worth reading,

Or do things worth the writing."

battles, Ben Franklin strolling past sedate brick buildings, and women dressed like Betsy Ross. So much of our quest for independence happened in Philadelphia, it's only natural that we dismiss the rest of the city's history.

The Revolution wasn't Philadelphia's only trauma: Before 1800 the city experienced two yellow fever epidemics, the first in 1762. The second, in 1793, killed 10 percent of the city's people, with lesser recurrences over the next 5 years and outbreaks of malaria to come.

Still, the city grew. It served as the nation's capital from 1777 to 1788 (except during 9 months of British occupation), and again from 1790 to 1800. Residential areas spread west to Broad Street and along the river. Industry and culture made Philadelphia a thriving city; institutions such as the Pennsylvania Academy of the Fine Arts, founded in 1805, and, in 1809, the Walnut Street Theater, along with private academies such as Friends Select and Germantown Friends School, are still popular today.

The first mint in the country—in fact, the first building legislated by the US government—was built in 1792. George and Martha Washington donated their personal household goods to use in making coins, just to see the mint succeed. David Rittenhouse, for whom the fashionable Rittenhouse Square neighborhood is named, was the mint's first director and greatest champion. A second, larger mint was built in 1833, a third in 1901, and a fourth—the current mint, the largest in the world—opened in 1969.

Immigrants swelled the city in waves. Industrialization, hastened by navigable rivers and the nearby Eastern Seaboard, created a huge need for laborers. By 1850 Philadelphia had become one of the world's largest producers of iron machinery and tools, glass, furniture, ships, textiles, and publishing. English commoners brought their skills in the 1820s, followed by Irish fleeing the 1840s potato famine. In the 1870s, Germans and central Europeans came seeking peace and refuge. Later, from the 1880s to the 1920s, Italians, Russians, and Jews from Eastern Europe and African Americans from the South came for work.

Philadelphia again distinguished itself in the Civil War, becoming the first large city north of the Mason–Dixon line to become involved. Several regiments of Union infantry and cavalry were based here, and Philadelphia was a recruitment center for thousands of soldiers. Its industries were

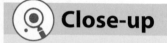

Close-up

Great Beginnings

A fun way to begin your Philly experience is to take a magical history tour with Mr. Ben Franklin as your genial guide at the **Liberty 360 3-D Show** at the PECO Theater in the Philadelphia Center (6th and Chestnut Streets, Philadelphia, PA 19106; 215-629-4026; historicphiladelphia.org). Surrounded by imagery and sound in the 360-degree, 3-D theater, you'll find yourself immersed in the stories of how some of the nation's most iconic symbols, including the bald eagle, the Statue of Liberty and, of course, the Liberty Bell, came to represent freedom and the American way of life. This 15-minute show is a dazzler and a lot of fun for the whole family. Cost is $6 for adults, $5 for seniors and children 12 and under; family four-pack is $20. Open daily beginning at 10 a.m.; closing hours are seasonal. Shows begin every 20 minutes.

If you want to explore the soul of Philadelphia while you're visiting its heart, put the **Philadelphia History Museum at the Atwater Kent** (15 S. 7th St., Philadelphia, PA 19106; 215 685-4830; philadelphiahistory.org) on your itinerary. Here you'll find exhibits (many hands-on), hundreds of artifacts (including the wampum belt that the Lenni Lenape Indians gave to William Penn in 1682), art, and multimedia presentations that trace 300 years of the city's growth and development. Open Tues through Sat, 10:30 a.m. to 4:30 p.m. $10 adults, $8 seniors, $6 students and teens.

Yahoo.com recently ranked **Franklin Square** (200 N. 6th St., Philadelphia, PA 19106; 215-629-4026; historicphiladelphia.org) as one of the top-five playgrounds in the US, so let the kids have a blast riding on the Liberty Carousel ($2.50 per person) or playing a round on Center City's only miniature golf course with its 18 Philly-themed holes ($9 for adults, $7 for children). Then just hang out and enjoy the scenery while munching on a SquareBurger or slurping a Cake Shake, an only-in-Philadelphia concoction featuring local ice cream and classic TastyKakes snack cakes. Franklin Square is open daily from 10 a.m. to 5 p.m., until 7 p.m. in spring and summer.

Philly Firsts

Did you know that Philadelphia's University of Pennsylvania claims to have built the world's first computer, named ENIAC, in 1946? If not, then read on to discover some other American firsts that happened in Philly:

First Capital of the US: 1790 to 1800

First Public Grammar School: Opened in 1689, now called the William Penn Charter School

First Public Library: Free Library of Philadelphia, founded by Benjamin Franklin in 1731

First Hospital: The Pennsylvania Hospital, cofounded by Benjamin Franklin in 1751. Also first medical (1765) and nursing (1850) schools

First University: University of Pennsylvania, founded in 1779

First Mint: 1792

First Art Museum and School: The Pennsylvania Academy of Fine Arts, 1805

First Zoo: 1874

primary suppliers of munitions, rifles, and uniforms for the army, and 11 warships were built in Philadelphia's Navy Yard. The city also was one of the first abolitionist centers.

Port activity soared after the Civil War, with cotton from the South supporting Philadelphia's huge textile industry. Like most cities, urbanization welcomed the 20th century; as the manufacturing sector boomed, agriculture became less prominent.

A MODERN, COSMOPOLITAN CITY

With advances in every occupational category following the Industrial Revolution, the need for skilled and unskilled labor, as well as professionals, was relentless.

One of the major immigrant groups as the 20th century unfolded was Latinos, who actually had been in Philadelphia since the 18th century; in colonial times, the port traded regularly with Puerto Rico and Cuba. As Caribbean and Latin American countries fought for their own independence in the 1800s, Philadelphia—the historic mecca for freedom fighters—was a destination for revolutionaries in exile.

Trade with Latin American countries focused on tobacco in the 1800s; as the 20th century loomed, Philadelphia's Spanish-speaking families clustered in new neighborhoods with other Latinos. The US government hired Mexican laborers to work on Philadelphia's railroads during World War II, and postwar prosperity brought a new Puerto Rican population for manufacturing and domestic service jobs.

Another major ethnic group was the Chinese, initially a "bachelor society" in America. Discriminatory laws prevented many from starting families or realizing their dreams and, as in other large cities, they worked in hand laundries and restaurants, gradually settling in Chinatown. Those restrictions were lifted during World War II, and Chinese citizens joined their neighbors in starting families and pursuing careers. Once a "red-light district," Philadelphia's Chinatown today is a thriving village in the heart of the city.

African Americans, too, came to Philly from the South, drawn by jobs before and after World War II. As the migration to the suburbs began in the 1950s, those jobs began leaving as well, and the need for urban renewal became clear in the 1960s. Those initiatives brought the loss of some significant architecture in Center City, but the overall outcome was widespread support of revitalization. Philadelphia would not be left to decay.

There have been more challenges in recent times: In the 1970s, Mayor Frank Rizzo was an icon among the city's working class, but his management style was, in the view of some, old-school. No Philadelphians can forget the firebombing a few years later, ordered by Mayor Wilson Goode, of an entire city block occupied by the armed radicals of Project MOVE. And in 1990, the city teetered on the brink of bankruptcy,

Still, Philadelphia grows and thrives. Its urban fabric meshes with the sprawl that stretches from Boston to Washington, DC—a region that has been settled for 300 years. At the same time, its open green spaces, from the immense Fairmount Park to bucolic Bucks County, rival any city's natural attractions.

In Philadelphia, the more things change, the more they stay the same: every Fourth of July, children who are descendants of the men who signed the Declaration of Independence gather at the new Liberty Bell Center, across from Independence Hall. There, at 2 p.m., the children tap the Liberty Bell 13 times, honoring their ancestors and patriots from the original 13 states. In Philadelphia, we still let freedom ring.

ACCOMMODATIONS

Over 35 million domestic travelers, more than half from the Mid-Atlantic region, visit the Greater Philadelphia area each year, generating more than $25 million per day, according to the Greater Philadelphia Tourism Marketing Corporation (GPTMC). Over the past decade, Philadelphia has experienced a 36 percent increase in total visitors and 63 percent more leisure travelers.

More than 80 percent of visitors to Philadelphia said they came for fun. For the past 6 years, Center City Philadelphia's Saturday night hotel occupancy has been more than 80 percent higher than that of Baltimore, Boston, and Washington, DC.

But don't worry, Philly has plenty of room—or should I say rooms—for everyone. You'll find them in the context of pretty much any accommodation ambience you prefer, whether it's a world-class upscale or economy hotel, gracious historic home, or intimate bed-and-breakfast. And don't assume that visiting a big city like Philadelphia requires a big bankroll. There are awesome overnight oases to fit any budget.

Unless otherwise stated, the listed hotels herein have at least a few wheelchair-accessible rooms, complimentary off-street parking, free wireless Internet, fitness center, and are nonsmoking properties. Pet-friendly accommodations will be noted.

Price Code

Prices represent average room "rack rate"—before any discounts—for a 1-night stay, double occupancy, in high season. Usually, you'll have to add the city's 15.2 percent hotel tax to the room rate, but some accommodations include the tax in their quoted rates; call to make sure. Tax rates may vary in areas outside the Philadelphia city limits.

$	Less than $100
$$	$100 to $150
$$$	$150 to $200
$$$$	$200 to $250
$$$$$	More than $250

HOTELS & MOTELS

Airport Area

ALOFT PHILADELPHIA
AIRPORT $$
4301 Island Ave.
Philadelphia, PA 19153
(267) 298-1700
starwoodhotels.com
One-hundred-thirty-six loft-style rooms feature 9-foot ceilings and large windows, oversize walk-in showers, 24/7 pantry, and minifridge. Free shuttle provides easy access to the airport located 0.5 mile away. Indoor pool, self-service car wash, meeting space/boardroom, on-premises lounge. Off-street parking costs $7 per night.

COURTYARD PHILADELPHIA AIRPORT $$-$$$

8900 Bartram Ave.
Philadelphia, PA 19153
(215) 365-2200
marriott.com

Take the free airport shuttle to this 152-room property, which features an indoor pool, on-premises restaurant, and meeting rooms.

EMBASSY SUITES PHILADELPHIA $$$$

9000 Bartram Ave.
Philadelphia, PA 19153
(215) 365-4500, (800) 362-2779
philadelphiaairport.embsuites.com

Located about 1 mile from Philadelphia International Airport, this all-two-room-suite hotel offers a host of amenities for both business and leisure travelers, including in-room refrigerator and microwave, on-site restaurant, heated indoor pool, whirlpool, made-to-order breakfast, and 24-hour airport shuttle service. Business center, meeting rooms, and boardroom suites are available.

FAIRFIELD INN PHILADELPHIA AIRPORT $$-$$$

8800 Bartram Ave.
Philadelphia, PA 19153
(215) 365-2254, (800) 228-2800
marriott.com/hotels

The twenty-four-hour complimentary shuttle makes it easy to come from and go to the airport located 0.5 mile away. Other amenities at this 97-room, 12-suite property include complimentary continental breakfast, swimming pool, and whirlpool.

FOUR POINTS BY SHERATON $$

4101A Island Ave.
Philadelphia, PA 19153
(215) 492-0400
starwoodhotels.com

Convenient to the airport (free 24-hour shuttle service) and Center City, this property features an outdoor pool, on-premises bar, and pet-friendly policy.

HAMPTON INN PHILADELPHIA AIRPORT $$$

8600 Bartram Ave.
Philadelphia, PA 19153
(215) 966-1300, (800) 426-7866
hamptoninn.com/hi/philadelphia-airport

Complimentary breakfast and access to the outdoor pool come with all 152 guest rooms, including 5 junior suites. Meeting rooms are available.

HILTON PHILADELPHIA AIRPORT $$

4509 Island Ave.
Philadelphia, PA 19153
(215) 365-4150, (800) 445-8667
hilton.com

A large swimming pool, heated whirlpool, pool table, and video arcade are among the leisure amenities at this 331-room and suite, 2-restaurant property. Business services include audiovisual equipment rental and secretarial service.

PHILADELPHIA AIRPORT MARRIOTT $$$$-$$$$$

1 Arrivals Rd.
Philadelphia, PA 19153
(215) 492-9000, (800) 682-4087
marriott.com

Just a sky bridge walk to the airport, the 414-room, 5-suite property has an on-site restaurant, indoor pool and whirlpool, pet-friendly policy, and meeting rooms. Wireless Internet is available for a fee; on-site parking is $17 daily.

RAMADA INN AT THE PHILADELPHIA INTERNATIONAL AIRPORT $$
76 Industrial Hwy. (Route 291)
Essington, PA 19029
(610) 521-9600, (800) 277-3900
ramada.com

This 292-room, high-rise property is the bargain of the airport hotels yet offers a host of amenities including free 24-hour shuttle service, heated seasonal outdoor pool, on-site restaurant and lounge, and meeting spaces.

RENAISSANCE PHILADELPHIA $$–$$$
500 Stevens Dr.
Philadelphia, PA 19113
(610) 521-5900
marriott.com

This 52-deluxe-suite hotel boasts the largest pool in the area. There's also a cocktail lounge on-site.

SHERATON SUITES PHILADELPHIA AIRPORT $$$
4101 B Island Ave.
Philadelphia, PA 19153
(215) 365-6600, (800) 325-3535
starwoodhotels.com

This pet-friendly hotel features recently updated 2-room suites, an indoor heated pool and whirlpool, on-site eateries, and meeting rooms. Limited airport transportation is free; parking and high-speed Internet for separate fees.

Avenue of the Arts & Convention Center

ALEXANDER INN $$–$$$
12th and Spruce Streets
Philadelphia, PA 19107
(877) Alex-Inn (253-9466)
alexanderinn.com

Antique Row is only 1 block away and the Avenue of the Arts 2 from this classy yet comfy turn-of-the-20th-century accommodation. Speaking of the arts, that's what this B&B is all about with its original stained-glass windows, carved oak moldings, and marble floors. A plethora of paintings and 48 art-deco decor guest rooms are among the architectural details that make this a one-of-a-kind getaway. A bountiful breakfast buffet and complimentary all-day snack bar are included. Discounted parking is available in a nearby lot.

COURTYARD PHILADELPHIA DOWNTOWN $$$$
21 N. Juniper St.
Philadelphia, PA 19107
(215) 496-3200
marriott.com

Just across the street from City Hall, this 489-room (including 21 suites) hotel, built in 1926, was formerly City Hall Annex. Guests have access to the indoor pool and whirlpool, on-site restaurant, meeting rooms.

CROWNE PLAZA HOTEL PHILADELPHIA DOWNTOWN $$$–$$$$
1800 Market St.
Philadelphia, PA 19103
(215) 561-7500, (888) 303-1746
cpphiladelphia.com

A multilingual staff will greet you at this 445-guest-room, 2-suite hotel. Some smoking rooms and business centers are available. The outdoor rooftop pool offers sweeping city views. Valet parking costs $33 per night.

DOUBLETREE HOTEL
PHILADELPHIA $$
237 S. Broad St.
Philadelphia, PA 19107
(215) 893-1600
doubletree1.hilton.com

Located in the heart of the city's cultural district on the Avenue of the Arts, this 432-room (including 8 deluxe suites) hotel features a multilingual staff; rooftop atrium pool with sundeck, whirlpool, and walking track; racquetball courts, and on-premises dining. Self-parking costs $25, valet $29.

FOUR POINTS BY SHERATON
PHILADELPHIA CITY
CENTER $$$-$$$$
1201 Race St.
Philadelphia, PA 19107
(215) 496-2700
starwoodhotels.com

The Convention Center is just steps away from this 92-room hotel. Paid parking with third-party valet or at 30th Street Train Station is available.

HAMPTON INN PHILADELPHIA
CENTER CITY $$
1301 Race St.
Philadelphia, PA 19107
(215) 665-9100
hamptoninn.hilton.com

Adjacent to the Pennsylvania Convention Center, this 250-room hotel has a multilingual staff, pool, complimentary hot breakfast, some smoking rooms, a swimming

pool, business services, and meeting rooms. Self-parking $24, valet $27.

HILTON GARDEN INN PHILADELPHIA
CENTER CITY $$-$$$
1100 Arch St.
Philadelphia, PA 19107
(215) 923-0100
hiltongardenphilly.com

Adjacent to the Pennsylvania Convention Center, this 279-room-and-suite property offers a heated indoor pool and whirlpool, in-room fridge and microwave, and on-premises restaurant. Paid parking is available at the Convention Center.

HOLIDAY INN PHILADELPHIA—
HISTORIC DISTRICT $$$-$$$$
400 Arch St.
Philadelphia, PA 19106
(215) 923-8660
holidayinn.com

Three hundred sixty-four rooms and suites are within walking distance of all major city attractions and the Convention Center. Amenities include a multilingual staff, on-site pub and restaurant, and rooftop pool. Use of off-site health/fitness center costs $12.

HYATT PHILADELPHIA AT THE
BELLEVUE $$$$$
Broad and Walnut Streets
Philadelphia, PA 19102
(215) 893-1234
philadelphia.bellevue.hyatt.com

Located on the Avenue of the Arts, this luxurious 172-guest-room (including 16 suites) hotel is one of the best-known buildings in Center City. A plethora of upscale amenities includes mahogany furnishings with luxe linens, marble baths, concierge service, on-site salon and spa, business center, on-site restaurants and upscale boutiques (think Tiffany & Co. and Nicole Miller), access to the connecting 93,000-square-foot fitness center, and business facilities. Self-parking is $27, valet $37.

i The Bellevue-Stratford Hotel, as it was called for more than a century and a half, has been a Philadelphia fixture since 1904. Built in the grand French Renaissance style and offering the finest amenities of its day, its celebrity-studded clientele (including every US president from Theodore Roosevelt through Ronald Reagan) earned it the nickname the "Grand Dame of Broad Street." In the 1970s, the hotel closed, then changed ownership several times until it was restored and reopened as the Hyatt Philadelphia at the Bellevue in 1996 and has regained its status as a city icon. The beautiful building is also listed in the National Register of Historic Places.

LE MÉRIDIEN $$–$$$
1421 Arch St.
Philadelphia, PA 19102
(215) 422-8200
starwoodhotels.com
Originally a YMCA, this new 10-story Georgian Revival-style structure, located less than 1 block from the Convention Center, houses 202 luxury guest rooms. Amenities include an on-premises restaurant and bar. Valet parking is available for $38 per night.

LOEWS PHILADELPHIA HOTEL $$$$$
1200 Market St.
Philadelphia, PA 19107
(215) 627-1200
loewshotels.com/hotels/philadelphia

It's impossible to miss this 581-room-and-suite luxury hotel with its 27-foot-high, red, illuminated PSFS (for Philadelphia Savings Fund Society, this 1932 building's original inhabitant) sign that can be seen from 20 miles away. Features include special kids' amenities, on-premises spa and dining, a heated lap pool, and full-service concierge. Pets are welcome. Overnight parking costs $36.

PHILADELPHIA MARRIOTT DOWNTOWN $$$$$
1201 Market St.
Philadelphia, PA 19107
(215) 625-2900, (800) 320-5744
marriott.com
This expansive, 23-floor hotel has 1,332 rooms with an indoor pool, concierge, on-site salon and spa, upscale restaurant and lounge, and business facilities. On-site parking is about $43 per night.

RESIDENCE INN PHILADELPHIA CENTER CITY $$$$$
1 East Penn Sq.
Philadelphia, PA 19107
(215) 557-0005, (800) 331-3131
marriott.com
Designed for relocations, temporary housing, or corporate housing, this centrally located, extended-stay accommodation has 269 one- and two-bedroom suites with fully equipped kitchens and offers a complimentary buffet breakfast and grocery service. Valet parking is $42 per day.

RITZ-CARLTON PHILADELPHIA $$$$$
10 Avenue of the Arts
Philadelphia, PA 19102
(Broad Street)
(215) 523-8000, (215) 851-8000
ritzcarlton.com/hotels/philadelphia

This 303-room (including 36 suites and full-floor penthouse) Center City jewel prides itself on extraordinary personal and extravagant amenities including in-room massage services (or, if you prefer, treatments at the on-premises, full-service spa), twice-daily housekeeping, babysitting services, on-site upscale shopping (think Tiffany's), and restaurants. Valet parking costs $48 per day.

i Follow a rose petal–strewn path to a steaming floral-fragranced tub illuminated by scented candles while fluffy slippers, chilled champagne, and rich chocolate truffles await you in the bedroom. And it was all set up for you by your personal Bath Butler, an optional service at the Ritz-Carlton Philadelphia. A Sleep Engineer is also on hand to help you choose the most comfy pillow from 7 offered on the Slumber Menu, and a Technology Butler will come to your rescue should your computer get cranky.

RODEWAY INN $$–$$$
1208 Walnut St.
Philadelphia, PA 19107
(215) 546-7000
choicehotels.com

From the outside, the building located 5 blocks from Philly's Old City attractions looks like a charming Victorian row house, but inside it is a very contemporary 32-room hotel with all of the requisite modern amenities. The continental breakfast is free at this family-owned accommodation, and use of a nearby gym with sauna, Jacuzzi, and pool is available for a small fee. Cost for parking is $10.50 (no in and out).

i In preparation for hosting the 2000 Republican National Convention, Philadelphia nearly doubled its Center City hotel rooms from 6,000 to 11,000, and boosted airport rooms to 4,500.

TRAVELODGE PHILADELPHIA $–$$
1227 Race St.
Philadelphia, PA 19107
(215) 564-2888
travelodge.com

One of Center City's best deals and located across the street from the Convention Center, this budget-conscious accommodation offers a complimentary continental breakfast and multilingual staff. There is no on-premises parking, but there is a pay-to-park lot nearby.

Old City

**BEST WESTERN INDEPENDENCE PARK
   HOTEL** $$$–$$$$
235 Chestnut St.
Philadelphia, PA 19106
(215) 922-4443, (800) 624-2988
independenceparkinn.com

From the outside, you'd never know this 36-room accommodation, housed in an 1856 building listed on the National Register of Historic Places, is a chain hotel. Inside, the high ceilings, sweeping staircase, columns, large fireplace, and period furnishings are also non-chain-like. Amenities include marble baths; complimentary serve-yourself breakfast (you can make your own waffles), afternoon tea and snacks, and ample meeting space. There is no on-premises parking, but there is a pay-to-park lot around the corner.

COMFORT INN DOWNTOWN/ HISTORIC AREA $$–$$$
100 N. Columbus Blvd.
Philadelphia, PA 19106
(215) 627-7900, (800) 689-1714
choicehotels.com

Centrally located less than 1 mile from Penn's Landing and 2 from the heart of the Old City attractions (the hotel provides free transport to the historic district, business district, and convention center), this 185-room hotel offers free continental breakfast, some smoking rooms, lobby bar, and meeting facilities. Parking is available for $23.

HYATT REGENCY PHILADELPHIA $$$$
200 S. Columbus Blvd.
Philadelphia, PA 19106
(215) 928-1234
pennslanding.hyatt.com

This 22-story, 350-room (including 13 suites) hotel offers beautiful views of the Delaware River and city skyline. Amenities include glass-enclosed pool, river-view pool and sauna, 24-hour business center, on-site restaurants and bars, and on-premise car rental. Overnight self-parking in an adjacent lot is $21, valet $29.

OMNI HOTEL AT INDEPENDENCE PARK $$$$$
401 Chestnut St.
Philadelphia, PA 19106
(215) 925-0000
omnihotels.com

This city-sophisticated hotel has 150 elegantly furnished guest rooms (3 of which are suites) furnished with marble baths. There's an indoor pool and on-site spa, multilingual concierge, kid-centric amenities, and wonderful views of Independence National Historic Park. Nearby self-parking costs $24, valet $34.

PENN'S VIEW HOTEL $$$–$$$$
14 N. Front St. (Front and Market Streets)
Philadelphia, PA 19106
(215) 922-7600, (800) 331-7634
pennsviewhotel.com

Listed on the National Register of Historic Places and an architectural award-winner, this family-owned boutique hotel with wonderful river views is housed in an 1828 building and its 2 neighbors. Some rooms have a marble bath, Jacuzzi, and fireplace; meeting rooms are available; on-premises renowned wine-centric restaurant. Continental breakfast is included. Parking is available in a nearby lot for $21.

SHERATON SOCIETY HILL $$$$$
1 Dock St. (2nd and Walnut Streets)
Philadelphia, PA 19106
(215) 238-6000
starwoodhotels.com

Three hundred sixty-five room-and-suite property features indoor heated pool and whirlpool, 4 on-site dining options, pet-friendly amenities, babysitting and concierge services, and access to private Club Lounge (offering complimentary breakfast and hors d'oeuvres) option for $30. Wireless Internet is available for $9.95 per day, valet parking for $38.40. There is no on-site self-parking.

Rittenhouse Row

FOUR SEASONS HOTEL $$$$$
1 Logan Sq.
Philadelphia, PA 19103
(215) 963-1500
fourseasons.com/philadelphia

This 8-story hotel across the street from the beautiful fountain on Logan Square does its

Society Hill

Although it is undeniably one of the most affluent neighborhoods in Philadelphia, Society Hill was not named for the wealthy, well-connected, high-society inhabitants. It is actually named after the 18th-century Free Society of Traders, a company chartered by William Penn in 1682 to boost the colony's commercial development. Looking at the preserved and restored 18th- and early-19th-century buildings, you'd never know that, by the mid-19th century, Society Hill had lost its luster and, in fact, had begun a decline that would continue until the 1950s when the city, state, and federal governments launched one of the first urban renewal programs. While that program protected the neighborhood's historic row homes, unfortunately, many of the early commercial structures were demolished to make way for the 31-story Society Hill Towers apartment building designed by famed architect I. M. Pei as well as some low-rise buildings, modern townhomes, and parks.

famous name proud with 364 guest rooms (96 of which are suites) furnished in Federal period style. It is an example of understated elegance. Amenities include twice-daily housekeeping service, marble bath, kid-friendly amenities, complimentary house car service for transportation within the downtown area, indoor pool, courtyard garden with waterfall, acclaimed white tablecloth restaurant, and intimate cafe with piano lounge. Overnight valet parking is $49.

HOTEL PALOMAR
  PHILADELPHIA   **$$$–$$$$**
117 S. 17th St. (corner of S. 17th and Sansom Streets)
Philadelphia, PA 19103
(215) 563-5006, (888) 725-1778
hotelpalomar-philadelphia.com
Environmentally conscious visitors will appreciate the eco-friendly orientation of this first LEED Gold Certified luxury hotel in the heart of Center City Philadelphia. Striking art deco appointments, sumptuous

furnishings, and original artwork create a one-of-a-kind ambience in its lobby and 194 guest rooms (including 19 spa rooms and 17 suites). Amenities include in-room spa services, pet-friendly accommodations, a contemporary-classy restaurant and lounge, and meeting facilities. Valet parking is available for $37 per night.

HOTEL WINDSOR   **$$$**
1700 Benjamin Franklin Pkwy.
Philadelphia, PA 19103
(877) 784-8379, (215) 981-5678
thewindsorsuites.com
Spacious studios and 1-bedroom suites with fully equipped kitchens are perfect for luxury overnight or extended stays. Amenities include rooftop pool, 2 on-site restaurants, and marble baths. Some rooms offer separate living areas; guests also are invited to use the rooftop pool with skylight views, 24-hour concierge, and meeting rooms. Valet parking is available for a fee.

LATHAM HOTEL $$$
135 S. 17th St.
Philadelphia, PA 19103
(215) 563-7474, (877) LATHAM1
lathamhotelphiladelphia.com

Built in 1907, this European-style boutique hotel has retained its historic charm from the gorgeous wood-paneled, marble lobby to its 139 Victorian-gracious guest rooms. Valet parking is $32 per day.

RADISSON PLAZA-WARWICK
   HOTEL PHILADELPHIA $$$$$
1701 Locust St.
Philadelphia, PA 19103
(215) 735-6000, (800) 333-3333
radisson.com

Listed on the National Register of Historic Places, the 301-room Warwick built in 1926 just off Rittenhouse Square is an elegant example of gracious English Renaissance style. The lobby alone with its soaring ceiling, glittering crystal chandelier, and elaborate woodwork is a work of art. Amenities include a multilingual staff, granite bath, dedicated pet-friendly floor ($50 deposit, $10 per night), restaurant, and lounge. Valet parking is $30; prices at off-premise parking in 2 nearby Chancellor Street lots range from $12 to $30.

THE RITTENHOUSE HOTEL $$$$$
210 W. Rittenhouse Sq.
Philadelphia, PA 19103
(215) 546-9000, (800) 635-1042
rittenhousehotel.com

This multiple-award-winner is Philadelphia at its posh and pampering best, offering 98 spacious guest rooms (including 11 suites) furnished in mahogany and upscale amenities including marble baths; 24-hour concierge; twice-daily maid service; complimentary use of on-premises spa and town car for transportation within Center City; and four dining spots, including 2 of Philly's top white-tablecloth restaurants. Some suites feature kitchen, washer/dryer, and whirlpool tub. Pets are welcome ($50 fee) and, for $15, they'll even walk Fido for you. Overnight valet parking costs $30.

RITTENHOUSE 1715, A BOUTIQUE
   HOTEL $$$$$
1715 Rittenhouse Square St. (between
17th and 18th Streets, between Locust
and Spruce Streets)
Philadelphia, PA 19103
(877) 791-6500, (215) 546-6500
rittenhouse1715.com

You'll need the specific location of this tiny 23-room-and-suite charmer because it's tucked away on a quiet side street right off Rittenhouse Square. Amenities include marble baths, 24-hour concierge, and continental breakfast. Parking at the lot on 17th and Chancellor Streets is $20 overnight.

SOFITEL PHILADELPHIA $$$$$
120 S. 17th St. (17th and Sansom)
Philadelphia, PA 19103
(215) 569-8300
sofitel.com

Amenities at this European-inspired, 306-room-and-suite hotel include marble baths, pet-friendly accommodations, an on-site currency exchange, on-premises upscale French restaurant, and a lounge with nightly entertainment. Valet parking is $36 per night.

WESTIN PHILADELPHIA $$$$$
99 S. 17th St. at Liberty Place
Philadelphia, PA 19192
(215) 563-1600
starwoodhotels.com/westin

Next door to the Shops at Liberty Place, the Westin offers 239 rooms and 19 suites with kid- and pet-friendly amenities, sauna and restaurant and lounges. In-room wireless is available for $9.95 per day. Overnight self-park is $33, valet $45.

University City

THE HILTON INN AT PENN $$$$$
3600 Sansom St.
Philadelphia, PA 19104
(215) 222-0200, (800) HILTONS
theinnatpenn.com
Located at the center of the UPENN campus and a few blocks from Drexel University, this 238-room Hilton features a multilingual staff, meeting facilities, in-room spa services, on-premise restaurant, and wine bar. Valet parking is available for $35 overnight.

SHERATON UNIVERSITY CITY
**   HOTEL $$$$–$$$$$**
36th and Chestnut Streets
Philadelphia, PA 19104
(215) 387-8000
starwoodhotels.com/sheraton
This 332-room-and-suite accommodation on the University of Pennsylvania campus and a few blocks from Drexel University recently underwent a multimillion-dollar renovation, giving it a fresh, more contemporary look and feeling. There's an outdoor pool, on-site restaurant and lounge, and car rental service. Pets are welcome.

Chestnut Hill

CHESTNUT HILL HOTEL $$$
8229 Germantown Ave., Chestnut Hill
Philadelphia, PA 19118
(215) 242-5905, (800) 628-9744
chestnuthillhotel.com

Located 9 miles northwest of Center City but still within the city limits, Chestnut Hill has the personality of a lovely suburb with a main street (i.e., Germantown Avenue) that features blocks of boutique shops and independently owned restaurants. In colonial times and through the Civil War era, Philly residents considered this neighborhood to be a "summer hausen" or vacation spot. It's still a great getaway destination, and this 1864 36-room hotel is located right in the middle of everything. Amenities include complimentary parking and continental breakfast, 3 on-site restaurants, and adjacent farmers' market.

Montgomery County

Visitors come from all over the world to visit Valley Forge National Park and the King of Prussia Mall, the East Coast's largest retail shopping mall with more than 400 name-brand department stores, boutique shops, and restaurants from the Cheesecake Factory to Morton's The Steak House.

BEST WESTERN THE INN AT
**   KING OF PRUSSIA $$**
127 S. Gulph Rd.
King of Prussia, PA 19406
(610) 265-4500
bestwesternpa.com
Amenities include in-room refrigerator, heated outdoor pool and hot tub, multilingual staff, complimentary continental breakfast.

COMFORT INN VALLEY FORGE $–$$
550 W. Dekalb Pike, US 202 N
King of Prussia, PA 19406
(610) 962-0700
comfortinn.com

This 121-room familiar-name accommodation offers free breakfast with hot waffles, business center, and smoking rooms.

CROWNE PLAZA VALLEY FORGE $$$$$
260 Mall Blvd.
King of Prussia, PA 19406
(610) 265-7500
cpvalleyforge.com
Deluxe 225-room (including 5 suites) hotel offers on-site dining and meeting facilities.

DOLCE VALLEY FORGE $$–$$$
301 W. Dekalb Pike
King of Prussia, PA 19406
(877) 851-5551, (610) 337-1200
dolce-valley-forge-hotel.com
This recently redesigned hotel offers 327 rooms and suites, 3-season, outdoor heated pool and whirlpool, on-site restaurant, and pub with billiards.

FAIRFIELD INN PHILADELPHIA VALLEY FORGE/KING OF PRUSSIA $$$
258 Mall Blvd.
King of Prussia, PA 19406
(610) 337-0700
marriott.com
Located directly across from the King of Prussia Mall and less than 2 miles from Valley Forge National Park, this 5-floor, 80-guest-room accommodation offers complimentary visits to connected Bally Total Fitness Center with indoor pool, sauna, whirlpool, running track and free weight area; complimentary deluxe continental breakfast; and in-room minifridge.

HAMPTON INN PHILADELPHIA/ KING OF PRUSSIA $$$
530 W. Dekalb Pike (Rt. 202)
King of Prussia, PA 19406
(610) 962-8111
hamptoninn3.hilton.com
Basic, clean, and comfortable with 148 rooms and suites, some smoking; complimentary hot breakfast or breakfast to go; multilingual staff.

HOLIDAY INN EXPRESS HOTEL & SUITES $$
260 N. Gulph Rd.
King of Prussia, PA 19406
(800) 972-2796, (610) 768-9500
hiexpress.com
You can walk or take the complimentary shuttle to the King of Prussia Mall from this 155-room property. The breakfast buffet is free and two restaurants—one upscale and one casual—share the parking lot.

BED-AND-BREAKFASTS & HISTORIC INNS

Staying at a historic or homey bed-and-breakfast or inn can be quite romantic. But if you truly "want to be alone," like Greta Garbo, you may want to keep a few things in mind. In some cases, the owners live on the premises. I, for one, like that because it means that I get the chance to talk to them about the area and get their "insiders" views on hidden treasures. Often, they're also interesting people, and it's just plain fun to get to know them.

Breakfast is also usually a social occasion. Some bed-and-breakfasts and inns serve guests at a traditional dining room table. Other setups are more intimate with individual tables. Either way, you can interact with the other guests as much—or as little—as you prefer (as long as you're willing to offer a simple smile and "Good morning" to your breakfast mates). You may also want to ask in advance if a full meal is served or if you'll be serving yourself continental style. Also be sure to tell your hosts about any dietary restrictions you may have; most will be happy to accommodate your particular needs or preferences.

If you're an adult who would prefer to relax in a child-free environment, many accommodations can oblige. On the other hand, if you're a parent, you should ask the operator if the bed-and-breakfast or inn is child-friendly (many welcome children over a specific age).

Some historic accommodations have some guest rooms with shared bathrooms. Be sure to check on the website of the property of your choice or ask the host before booking.

If climbing flights of steps, bags in hand, might present a problem, either ask if the innkeeper has a ground-floor room or elevator, although the latter is rare. Wheelchair access and other necessary special needs amenities may also be an issue, particularly in historic homes.

Who wants to work on vacation? If you insist on it, make sure the accommodation has Internet access—either in-room or in a public space.

Many bed-and-breakfasts and inns have resident dogs or cats (some even have big birds such as free-range cockatoos). If you have allergies to or fear of any of the above furred and feathered friends, ask if there are any on the premises before you book.

Today, the majority of boutique properties are smoke-free. Many owners will charge you a fee (often a hefty one) if they have to clean the smell of cigarettes out of your room. Although it's not a common thing, some also have a no-alcohol policy. Since you are in their "home" (even if they don't live there), it's only polite to comply.

Some bed-and-breakfasts and inns require 2-night minimum stays on weekends and/or holidays. Be sure to ask if you're planning on visiting during any of those times.

Center City/Avenue of the Arts

LA RESERVE CENTER CITY BED AND BREAKFAST $-$$
1804 Pine St.
Philadelphia, PA 19103
(215) 735-0582, (800) 354-8401
lareservebandb.com
If you're surprised to find such modest prices in the heart of Center City, only 3 blocks from Rittenhouse Square, join the club. No, I mean really. Two beautifully preserved, mid-19th-century, 4-story town houses make one gracious accommodation. Breakfast is served in the formal dining room and there's a vintage Steinway in the parlor that guests are welcome to play. Wireless service is available throughout the house. Overnight garage parking is available at 1740 South St. (between 17th and 18th Streets) for $20.

Old City

MORRIS HOUSE HOTEL $$$-$$$$
225 S. 8th St.
Philadelphia, PA 19106
(215) 922-2446
morrishousehotel.com
Just a 2-block walk from Independence Hall, this 1787 National Register of Historic

Places–listed home combines class and convenience, featuring 15 beautifully restored guest rooms. (As a nod to modern times, wireless is available in every room.) Continental breakfast and afternoon tea by the dining room fireplace are included—room service is available upon request. Park in the public garage across the street (entrance is on 8th Street, between Walnut and Locust Streets) and you'll get a 15 percent discount off the regular $25 overnight fee with validation from the hotel.

THE THOMAS BOND HOUSE $$–$$$
129 S. 2nd St.
Philadelphia, PA 19106
(215) 923-8523
thomasbondhousebandb.com
This National Register of Historic Places–registered 1769 town house, located across the street from Welcome Park, features 12 restored guest rooms. If posh is your preference, ask for the Dr. Thomas Bond Jr., Elizabeth Benson Chew Bond, or Dr. Thomas Bond Sr. Rooms, all of which have Chippendale period furnishings, oriental rugs, and whirlpool tubs. Continental breakfast is available on weekdays; on weekends full breakfast is served. Children over 10 are welcome. Park next door at the Ritz parking garage for $18 per day.

i In Welcome Park, an "outdoor museum" dedicated to William Penn built on the site of his 1699–1701 city residence, the "Slate Roof House," you'll find a statue of Philly's founder that is a miniature of the one that sits atop City Hall. The park is named for William Penn's ship *The Welcome*.

University City

CORNERSTONE BED & BREAKFAST $$–$$$
3300 Baring St.
Philadelphia, PA 19104
(215) 387-6065
cornerstonebandb.com
Built in 1870, this mansion has retained its regal demeanor with dramatic 12-foot-high ceilings and original mahogany staircase and stained-glass windows. Have breakfast by the fireplace—continental on weekdays, full on weekends. Of the 7 guest rooms, 2 are suites; the Continental has a jetted tub. All rooms have wireless Internet. Check the website for on-street parking instructions.

i For a list of gay-owned lodgings and businesses in Philadelphia, go to visitphilly.com/gay-friendly-philadelphia or philadelphia.gaycities.com.

SPRUCE HILL MANOR $$
3709 Baring St.
Philadelphia, PA 19104
(215) 472-2213, (866) 521-2975
sprucehillmanor.com
This 1879 Victorian mansion is a real beauty with its original oak and mahogany woodwork, stained glass, antique furniture, and landscaped lawns and gardens. Half of the 6 guest rooms are suites, including the crystal chandelier–adorned First Floor Eakins Library with original working fireplace (minimum occupancy is 3) and Tiffany-Parrish Suites with oriental rugs and antique rosewood bed. All rooms include all natural/organic breakfast, kitchenettes, concierge service, wireless Internet, and free parking. Children over 9 are welcome.

Youth Hostels

Students over 18 looking for a clean, amenity-filled accommodation will want to check out the city's youth hostels. These two accommodations are members of Hostelling International (hihostels.com). You'll share a dorm (unless you are able to get a semiprivate or private room) and a bathroom, but you can't beat the prices. Both are air-conditioned, feature kitchen and laundry facilities, provide linens (no sleeping bags, they spread bedbugs!), free foosball, and other games.

Apple Hostels in Old City (32 Bank St.; 215-922-0222; applehostels.com). Chartered for students and foreign travelers (ID verification is required for both). Choose from men's or women's, couples-only, or semiprivate dorms; a few private rooms are available. All guests share common bathrooms. Free pub crawls, $2 walking tours, and other activities. Park at garage located on 2nd Street between Chestnut and Walnut Streets; overnight cost is $18.

Chamounix Mansion (West Fairmount Park, 3250 Chamounix Dr.; 215-878-3676; 800-379-0017; philahostel.org). Immerse yourself in Philadelphia history in this grand, antique-filled 1850 mansion nestled in magnificent Fairmount Park. Chamounix (pronounced *CHAM'-ah-nee*) offers 2 dorm-style rooms plus a limited number of smaller rooms to accommodate couples and families. There's ample free parking, and the hostel provides free bikes to explore the park.

Bucks County

*BARLEY SHEAF FARM ESTATE & SPA $$$$$
5281 Old York Rd.
Holicong, PA 18928
(215) 794-5104
barleysheaf.com

Some of the most famous names from 1930s Hollywood, Broadway, and the literary world played and stayed at this 1740 stone manor house, then home to Pulitzer Prize–winning playwright George S. Kaufman. Now, 15 lush, whirlpool-and-fireplace suites offer celebrity-worthy overnighters, especially when you add en-suite spa treatments. Cooked-to-order breakfast is included. Ask about wine-pairing dinners (four courses $65, six for $85).

BLACK BASS HOTEL $$$–$$$$$
3774 River Rd.
Lumberville, PA 18933
(215) 297-9260
blackbasshotel.com

Aside from its 8 recently renovated suites, this circa-1745 (and reputedly haunted) riverside spot welcomes pets in its Baxter Suite cottage, with a fenced-in yard and Jacuzzi.

DOYLESTOWN INN $$$
18 W. State St.
Doylestown, PA 18901
(215) 345-6610
doylestowninn.com

Historic downtown Doylestown lies right out your front door when you stay at this very lovely inn, actually a trio of buildings, 2 of which were built in 1871. All 11 guest rooms

Destination Doylestown

They say good things come in small packages, and whoever "they" are, they must have been thinking about Doylestown, the county seat of Bucks County. Within its 15.5-square-mile area, this historic township, founded in 1765 and incorporated in 1838, has some of the Philadelphia suburbs' finest cultural attractions. Sadly, the establishment that gave the township its name, Doyle's Tavern, is now a Starbucks. Other downtown historic buildings have been preserved on the outside and converted into contemporary boutique shops on the inside. Well worth a day trip or, better yet, an overnighter, Doylestown is also home to the castles of early-20th-century tile artist Henry Chapman, now museums of American life and global art, as well as the home-turned-museum of author James A. Michener. See the "Attractions" chapter for further details.

are located on the 3rd floor, but don't worry, there's an elevator to take you and your bags up with ease. Continental breakfast, wireless access, and parking are complimentary. There's also a charming boutique bar for coffee, spirits, and light snacking on the premises. Limited accommodations are available for children.

OLD HARGRAVE HOUSE B & B   **$$$**
50 S. Main St.
Doylestown, PA 18901
(215) 348-3334
hargravehouse.net
Another very special getaway spot in Doylestown's Historic District, this early-19th-century accommodation features 7 large rooms, 4 with fireplaces, 5 with 2-person jetted tubs. Full breakfast is served and off-street parking is free.

New Hope

INN AT BOWMAN'S HILL   **$$$$$**
518 Lurgan Rd.
New Hope, PA 18938
(215) 862-8090
theinnatbowmanshill.com

Remember the L'Oreal commercials that affirmed even though their products cost a little more "You're worth it"? Well, the same can be said for this gorgeous, gracious getaway tucked away about 2 miles south of downtown New Hope right next to the 100-acre Bowman's Hill Wildflower Preserve, which is itself a Certified Wildlife Habitat. All 6 guest rooms and suites in the Main House, attached Tower Suite, and Carriage House have 2-person whirlpool baths, heated towel racks, and fresh flowers; some have private porches. Other amenities include a hot tub and cooked-to-order, multicourse breakfast and optional in-room massage.

PORCHES ON THE TOWPATH   **$$–$$$**
20 Fisher's Alley
New Hope, PA 18938
(215) 862-3277
porchesnewhope.com
Overlooking the peaceful Delaware Canal with its towpath that's popular for strolling and bicycling, this whitewashed-brick, mid-19th-century, Federal-style home has 12 distinctive main house and 2-story carriage house guest accommodations (prices

Little Village, Big Shopping

Think of a mimosa on a beautiful morning—sunny, bubbly, and sweet. That's the way I see New Hope. Even though it's clearly a retail-driven village, it still has an undeniable charm that draws me in every time. Situated along the Delaware River and Canal, New Hope is a very pretty place, one that makes you want to grab a bite to eat or a glass of wine (there are plenty of great places where you can do one, the other, or, better yet, both) and enjoy the tranquil water views. It is also a historic town, with roots and architecture that date back to the 18th century. And while its "downtown" consists of only 4 streets, you can—and should—spend an entire day or even an entire weekend browsing the more than 100 shops that feature the works of local and global artists and artisans. If that's not enough to set your credit card smoking, you'll find more similar-style shops and restaurants 5 miles south in Lahaska, where Peddler's Village has been giving visitors 70 additional reasons to linger in the New Hope area.

for several of the latter can jump to $$$$). Full breakfast is served inside or on the wraparound porch. Off-street parking is free.

Chester County/Brandywine Valley

HARLAN LOG HOUSE   **$$–$$$**
205 S. Fairville Rd.
Chadds Ford, PA 19317
(610) 388-1114
bbonline.com/pa/harlan

It's not fancy, but this 250-year-old Quaker homestead listed on the National Register of Historic Places is an authentic piece of the past tucked away on 5 acres of tranquility. Two suites on separate floors feature sitting rooms and wood-burning fireplaces.

KENNETT HOUSE BED &
   BREAKFAST   **$$$**
503 W. State St.
Kennett Square, PA 19348
(610) 444-9592, (800) 820-9592
kennetthouse.com

Situated a short 2-block walk from the heart of Kennett Square, this 1910 Arts and Crafts–designed mansion offers 3 rooms and 1 suite that come with wireless access and full breakfast with locally sourced ingredients. Children 10 and over are welcome.

i It took 10,000 pieces of glass hand-fired in 260 colors to make "Dream Garden," a 15-foot by 49-foot mosaic mural that was created in 1916 by renowned Philadelphia artist Maxwell Parrish and Louis Comfort Tiffany and produced by the Tiffany Studios for the lobby of the Curtis Publishing Building at 601–45 Walnut St. (call 215-238-6450 if you want to see this masterpiece called "one of the major artistic collaborations in early-20th-century America.")

Delaware County/Brandywine Valley

HAMANASSETT B&B &
  CARRIAGE HOUSE   **$$$–$$$$**
115 Indian Springs Dr.
Media, PA 19063
(877) 836-8212, (610) 459-3000
hamanassett.com
The address says Media, but this circa-1856 (plus 1896 additions) English country manor is actually located 5 miles south in Chester Heights. Whatever . . . it's still only 15 minutes from Longwood Gardens, 20 from Winterthur, and 8 from Chadds Ford. Posh rooms, some with fireplaces, all with wireless access, come with elegant full breakfast by the fire on antique silver, crystal, and china in the formal dining room. Hamanassett is also home to the Brandywine Cooking School, which offers intimate, daylong classes for $200 per person (specially priced overnight packages are also available).

RESTAURANTS

Man does not live by cheesesteaks alone. Even if that man happens to be a Philadelphian. At last count (2009), the Greater Philadelphia area has 680 restaurants. More than half of them fit the category of "fine dining." You'll find dress-up-and-paint-the-town grand ones with elaborate and even avant-garde menus and find-me-if-you-can holes-in-the-wall that the locals love (and prefer to keep their own little secret).

Philly certainly has more than its fair share of nationally celebrated chefs. But just as exciting is finding the innovative up-and-comers who are currently cooking their way to stardom. And if you need any proof of the city's diversity, check out the plethora of multicultural menus that thrive in every neighborhood.

All restaurants listed have nonsmoking policies, so you needn't be bothered by cigarette and cigar smoke, and unless we've indicated otherwise, all restaurants honor major credit cards. If wheelchair accessibility is a requirement, keep in mind that some dining spots are located in older houses and other buildings that might not be able to accommodate your needs. To be sure, call or check the website of the establishment of your choice prior to your visit.

It's up to you whether you're up for a budget-busting blowout, some extremely economical eats, or something in the middle. To help you find just the right place at just the right price, we've included a code using dollar signs to indicate how much you'll spend on average for a dinner entree without tax (8 percent), tip, or beverage.

Price Code

$	Less than $10
$$	$10 to $20
$$$	$20 to $30
$$$$	$30 to $50
$$$$$	More than $50

If you read my restaurant recommendations, you'll see that there are quite a few BYOBs listed. With more than 200 of them (and more opening just about every day), it's no wonder that Philadelphia is often referred to as the "BYOB capital of North America." And there's good reason. Under the commonwealth of Pennsylvania's Quota Law, the only way to obtain a liquor license is by purchasing an existing one and, since the number of restaurants far exceeds the number of existing licenses, it's a seller's market. The Pennsylvania Liquor Control Board reports that licenses have sold for up to $400,000. But even if you bring your own bottle, keep in mind that you'll have to buy it at a Pennsylvania state-operated Wine & Spirits Store (commonly referred to as a "state store") so you may have to be flexible in your selection and be prepared to pay the state-set prices. Also, be sure to ask about your restaurant selection's policy on corkage fees. For a list of the city's BYOBs, go to visitphilly.com/restaurants-dining/byob-bring-your-own-bottle.

CENTER CITY/OLD CITY

*ALMA DE CUBA $$$–$$$$
1623 Walnut St.
Philadelphia, PA 19102
(215) 988-1799
almadecubarestaurant.com

This is the place where I first fell in love . . . with the mojito (classic version, please). Tingle your taste buds with ceviche tasting. Vaca Frita (fried cow) . . . no, really . . . is a wonderfully crispy skirt steak with black beans and tomato escabeche. Enjoy the delectable and cool to look at Chocolate Cigar with dulce de leche ice cream.

AMUSE $$–$$$
Le Méridien Hotel
1421 Arch St.
Philadelphia, PA 19102
(215) 422-8201
starwoodhotels.com

This new kid on the block (or should I say in the city?) is very sleek, very chic, and very French onion soup topped with a trio of cheeses, beef bourguignon, steak frites, and even a tongue-in-cheek "le hamburger." The one thing it isn't is very stuffy.

i Just about every major national steak house you can name has an outpost in Philadelphia, including Morton's (mortons.com), Ruth's Chris (ruthschris.com), Del Frisco's (delfriscos.com), and Capital Grille (thecapitalgrille.com). But don't overlook the numerous excellent native-born bastions of beef such as Barclay Prime (barclayprime.com).

BUDDAKAN $$$
325 Chestnut St.
Philadelphia, PA 19106
(215) 574-9440
buddakan.com

A larger-than-life golden Buddha presides over the communal table at this high-concept, yet surprisingly not exceptionally high-priced (for Center City Philadelphia anyway) restaurant with its lavish European-accented Asian cuisine. If you don't want to mingle, you can sit at your own table. Don't miss the truffle-scented edamame ravioli or desserts, often an afterthought in Asian restaurants, but definitely not here. The chocolate bento box is a stunner and the 5-space dippable doughnuts a fun finish.

i A perfect time to try out that hot new or just plain pricey restaurant that makes your budget balk is during September's Restaurant Week, when more than 100 of the city's elite eateries offer special 3-course prix fixe lunches and/or dinners at seriously discounted prices. (215) 440-5500; centercityphila.org.

CAPOGIRO GELATO $
Midtown Village
119 S. 13th St.
Philadelphia, PA 19107
(215) 351-0900
capogirogelato.com

This family-owned operation produces the real thing—made from scratch every morning in traditional flavors such as stracciatella and exclusive seasonal sensations using local produce, hormone-free dairy products, herbs, and spices in some surprising combinations (think lemon opal basil and rosemary honey goat's milk). Other locations are at

Rittenhouse Square, 117 S. 20th St. (corner of 20th and Sansom), (215) 636-9250; **University City**, 3925 Walnut St., (215) 222-0252; **Passyunk Scoop Shop** (South Philadelphia), 1625 E. Passyunk Ave., (215) 462-3790.

CHIFA $$–$$$
707 Chestnut St.
Philadelphia, PA 19106
(215) 925-5555
chifarestaurant.com

Can Peruvian and Cantonese cuisine find happiness on the same menu? They can when the matchmaker is Food Network Iron Chef Jose Garces. Here ceviche cheerfully shares the spotlight with bao buns and empanadas with red curry.

✳CITY TAVERN $$$–$$$$
138 S. 2nd St. at Walnut Street
Philadelphia, PA 19106
(215) 413-1443
citytavern.com

The First Continental Congress made Philadelphia's City Tavern, opened in 1773, its first, though unofficial, meeting place from 1774 to 1777. The Second Continental Congress members made it their regular Saturday night dinner spot; some members ate there every evening. It was George Washington's restaurant of choice when he wined and dined visiting dignitaries. Thomas Jefferson (whose favorite sweet potato and pecan biscuits are still on the menu) called it "the most genteel tavern in America." Although the original building was burned in 1834 and demolished 20 years later, in 1948 Congress commissioned a historically accurate reproduction of the historic City Tavern. The authentic-right-down-to-the-china-flatware-and-glassware-patterns new City Tavern opened in time for the nation's Bicentennial celebration in 1976. And it has been serving sophisticated, 18th-century-inspired fare ever since. Since 1994, multiple-award-winning chef Walter Staib has been the guiding force behind City Tavern's renaissance as a gathering spot for locals as well as a must-see (and eat) for visitors. His menus are based on such colonial era–inspired recipes as West Indies Pepper Pot Soup (later to be generally known as Philadelphia Pepper Pot Soup), honey-glazed roasted duckling, and pastry-lidded turkey potpie. If the dinner prices are a bit too rich for your budget, the same menu is available at lunchtime for less.

THE CONTINENTAL RESTAURANT & MARTINI BAR $$–$$$
138 Market St.
Philadelphia, PA 19106
(215) 923-6069
continentalmartinibar.com

It looks like a '50s diner both inside and out, but you certainly wouldn't find Korean pork tacos and crab pad thai on an Eisenhower-era menu. Brunch is traditionally tasty with jam-packed omelets and cinnamon flapjacks. While the martinis are fun, the bar also makes a mean Singapore Sling, Gin Rickey, and other retro cocktails.

FORK $$$
306 Market St.
Philadelphia, PA 19106
(215) 625-9425
forkrestaurant.com

Chef Terence Feury makes his own charcuterie. That should give you some idea of how serious he is about putting out great food. The ambience is cool, contemporary, and comfortable. Light dishes—at light prices—are also available.

Close-up

24-hour Dining

It's midnight and suddenly you must, must, MUST have a stack of pancakes or an omelet, a burger and milk shake, or a basket of fried chicken and fries (and don't forget the scrapple; diners do it best). Breakfast and lunch items are usually $, dinner items $–$$. Well, in Philly, you can satisfy your craziest cravings 24/7 at any one of the city's renowned diners:

CENTER CITY

Little Pete's $–$$
219 S. 17th St. (at Chancellor)
Philadelphia, PA 19103
(215) 545-5508

Midtown II $–$$
122 S. 11th St. (at Sansom Street)
Philadelphia, PA 19107
(215) 627-6452
midtown2restaurant.com

Midtown III $–$$
28 S. 18th St. (between Market &
Chestnut Streets)
Philadelphia, PA 19103
(215) 567-5144

SOUTH PHILADELPHIA

⁕Melrose Diner $–$$
1501 Snyder Ave. (at South 15th
Street)
Philadelphia, PA 19145
(215) 467-6644

Oregon Diner $–$$
302 Oregon Ave. (at 3rd Street)
Philadelphia, PA 19148
(215) 462-5566
oregondinerphilly.com

DELAWARE COUNTY/MAIN LINE

Minilla's Diner $–$$
320 W. Lancaster Ave.
Wayne, PA 19087
(610) 687-1575
minellasdiner.com

**FOUNTAIN RESTAURANT AT
  FOUR SEASONS HOTEL** $$$$–$$$$$
1 Logan Sq.
Philadelphia, PA 19103
(215) 963-1500
fourseasons.com/philadelphia
Check out any best restaurant list from *Zagat* to *Bon Appétit* and you'll find the French-inspired Fountain. The food is as elegant as the surroundings, and that's pretty impressive. There's also a beautiful tasting menu with or without wine. Afternoon tea is also a glorious return to civility.

⁕FRANKLIN FOUNTAIN $
116 Market St.
Philadelphia, PA 19106
(215) 627-1899
franklinfountain.com
Did you know that there's a Philadelphia-style vanilla ice cream? Yup. It's generously speckled with real vanilla bean and, unlike French vanilla, has no eggs. Get some at this family-owned reproduction of a 1900 soda fountain either plain, in a super sundae, in a float, or sandwiched between two hot waffles. It—and all of the other flavors—are

Close-up

What the Truck?

In general, Philadelphia is a fast-paced city full of serious eaters, and the culinary scene has adapted to keep pace with lifestyles of an on-the-go population. Food trucks, mobile carts, and even tricked-out tricycles have become de rigueur all over the city—you'll find them camped out near university campuses, idling on the corners of the business district, and dishing up great street eats in local parks. Although a few proprietors have actual brick-and-mortar locations with traditional contact information, many mobile eateries utilize social media to broadcast their location, menu changes, and specials. But remember, most food trucks are cash-only so give your plastic a break and make sure you hit the ATM before hopping in line.

Comfort food—more specifically, soul food—is enjoying a comeback, and **Denise's Soul Food** (30th & Market Streets; 215-424-7022), **Jamaican D's** (1700 Spring Garden St.; 215-668-5909), and Vendy Award (annual food truck awards) winner **GiGi** and **Big R's Caribbean Soul Food** (38th & Spruce Streets; 610-389-2150) specialize in Caribbean and American soul food. Jerk chicken, rice and beans, and a slew of side dishes are popular.

Most people know tacos are the perfect street food—portable, tasty, and conducive to eating on the go. Several food truck operators are catching on to the taco craze as well, finding ways to stuff just about anything into a tortilla shell—from spicy pulled pork to cheesesteak-style rib eye. Newcomer **Honest Tom's Taco Truck** (267-767-4168; @HonestToms) is a local favorite with fish tacos and simple breakfast tacos getting top billing from loyal patrons. **Taco Loco** (South 4th Street & Washington Avenue), **Tacos Don Memo** (3800 Sansom St.; @tacosdonmemo), and Vendy Award People's Choice winner **Cucina Zapata** (31st Street & Ludlow Street; @Cucina_Zapata) are also dishing up delicious tacos around the city.

Philadelphia has a diverse cultural tapestry, and the city's food choices not only reflect it but celebrate it as well. Culinary diversity is not just limited to traditional restaurants—mobile food carts were among the first to offer food that accurately represented the population. Famous for their "Hangover" breakfast sandwich with spicy sriracha (served *bánh mì*-style on a soft baguette), Vietnamese food truck **Bui's** (248 S. University Ave.; 856-630-7269) is—surprise—a favorite among nearby university students. Korean meets Japanese at appropriately-named **KoJa** (38th Street & Sansom Street; kojagrille.com; 267-322-9925), which serves fusion fare but is most popular for its bulgogi (marinated barbecued meat), which is served in pork, chicken, and even cheesesteak form.

City-dwellers also have an affinity for Middle Eastern food as well, and **Falafel Truck** (NE corner 20th & Market Streets) and **King of Falafel** (South 16th Street

& JFK Boulevard) battle for falafel supremacy in busy Center City. The decision seems to be split when it comes to choosing a favorite—both serve extremely tasty food. However, the owner of Falafel Truck has made a name for himself with his no-nonsense service that can come off as brusque if you aren't familiar with the ordering process. The only choice you'll get is "chicken" or "no chicken"—referring to the enormous falafel platters.

Always dreamed of roaming the streets of Paris in search of the perfect bistro? You don't have to cross the pond because mobile eateries like **La Copine Brunch Cart** (la-copine.com; @PhilaCopine) prove that you don't have to dine at a white-linen restaurant to enjoy elevated food. **La Dominique** (33rd & Market Streets) and **The Creperie** (13th & Norris Streets; 215-778-4771) serve a variety of expertly crafted sweet and savory crepes.

The Dapper Dog (2nd & Poplar Streets; 203-887-8813; thedapperdog.org; @the dapperdog) and **Renaissance Sausage** (renaissancesausage.com; @TheSausage Truck) have figured out a way to dish up dogs and sausages with a twist. The Dapper Dog, much to the delight of midnight munchers, is open ridiculously late; check the website and Twitter for updates.

For the health-conscious and those seeking lighter fare, **Fresh Fruit Truck** (37th & Spruce Streets) is a great option that serves fresh-cut fruit and smoothies (they are not advertised but can be made). **Produce Truck** (43rd & Walnut Streets) is a produce stand on wheels and an excellent alternative to a traditional grocery store and much lighter on the wallet as well.

Just about everyone loves an ice cream truck, but what about an ice cream tricycle? **Little Baby's Ice Cream** (littlebabysicecream.com; @LittleBabysIC) specializes in artisanal ice cream in creative flavors like Earl Grey sriracha and birch beer vanilla bean. If more traditional sweets are your thing, **Sweet Box Cupcakes** (1600 John F. Kennedy Blvd.; 215-237-4647; @SweetBoxTruck) and **Sugar Philly Truck** (38th & Walnut Streets; 267-940-7473; sugarphillytruck.com; @sugarphilly) often sell out of their decadent cupcakes and *macarons* respectively.

Magic Carpet (34th & Walnut Streets; 215-334-0948; magiccarpetfoods.com) has been dishing up vegetarian world cuisine for over 25 years, which is a testament to the quality of the food. On any given day, expect to find Indian, Middle Eastern, and Greek fare on the menu.

Hemo's (36th & Spruce Streets) found its niche in crafting simple, well-made sandwiches like grilled chicken, cheesesteaks, and chicken cheesesteaks, but the owner is renowned for his famous (and secret) "Hemo sauce." No one knows the secret, but everybody slathers it on their sandwiches.

homemade (and so is the decadently rich hot fudge).

![i] **April's "Dining Out for Life"** may just be the busiest restaurant night of the year in Philly. That's when more than 200 of the region's most popular restaurants donate 33 percent of the cost of each meal to local organizations fighting HIV and AIDS. (877) EAT-4LIFE, diningoutforlife.com.

LACROIX $$$$$
210 W. Rittenhouse Sq.
Philadelphia, PA 19103
(215) 790-2533
rittenhousehotel.com

Although celebrated chef Jean-Marie Lacroix has retired from his eponymous restaurant, the commitment to excellence that earned it such accolades as "World's Best Hotel Dining Rooms" by *Gourmet* magazine and the "Wine Spectator Award of Excellence" carries on. If you're planning to pop the question, you won't find a more romantic spot. In addition to a la carte entrees, there are 5-course ($75) and 8-course ($95) tasting menus.

✳LE BEC FIN $$$$–$$$$$
1523 Walnut St.
Philadelphia, PA 19102
(215) 567-1000
lebecfin.com

Arguably Philadelphia's most famous white tablecloth restaurant when it was owned and manned by Chef Georges Perrier, this feast of French cuisine and style has maintained its award- and accolade-winning standards in food and service under new owners, Nicolas Fanucci and Chef Walter Abrams. For the full experience choose one of Chef Abram's 3- or 4-course prix fixe lunches or a 4- or 8-course

dinners. Or you can dine on a la carte fare downstairs at Chez Georges.

MATYSON $$$
37 S. 19th St.
Philadelphia, PA 19103
(215) 564-2925
matyson.com

One of Philly's best BYOBs has an ever-changing menu of seasonal specialties with an emphasis on stellar seafood (lobster-stuffed skate wing, nori-crusted ahi tuna) and irresistible desserts (coconut cream pie with chocolate ganache). Every week, the restaurant offers a different 3-course lunch and 5-course dinner tasting menu based on a seasonal ingredient or theme.

MONK'S $$–$$$
264 S. 16th St.
Philadelphia, PA 19102
(215) 545-7005
monkscafe.com

Moules et frites (mussels and fries)? What else would you expect to find in a "Belgian Beer Emporium"? Well, there really are other selections including burgers, chicken, salmon, even rabbit, but with 8 different kinds of mussels on the menu, why stray from tradition?

MORIMOTO $$$–$$$$
723 Chestnut St.
Philadelphia, PA 19107
(215) 413-9070
morimotorestaurant.com

If your budget allows, let Masaharu Morimoto show you why he is one of Food Network's most revered "Iron Chefs" with an *omakase* or multicourse tasting of his favorite dishes (begins at $80). The lunch version is a bit smaller, but $20 lighter on the budget. You can also order sushi, sashimi, or one of the chef's innovative Asian entrees a la carte.

ℹ Whether you don't know your Chianti from your Chardonnay or are a bona fide oenophile, you can explore the worlds of wines, beers, and food pairings at 2-hour tastings at The Wine School, which holds classes at various locations in the city and on the Main Line (800-817-7351; vinology .com).

∗MOSHULU $$$
Penn's Landing
401 S. Columbus Blvd.
Philadelphia, PA 19106
(215) 923-2500
moshulu.com
The food is good; the restaurant itself even better on the oldest 4-masted sailing ship still in the water. During World War I, the *Moshulu* (pronounced *Mo-shoeloo*) sailed the seas on the American side; during World War II, it was captured by the Germans. Now the century-old tall ship reigns over the Delaware River in elegant 19th-century splendor. Sit outside on one of the multilevel outdoor decks with views of the city-scape. The 3-course weekend brunch ($35) is an extra-special treat.

PUMPKIN RESTAURANT, CAFE, AND MARKET $$$
1713 South St. between 16th and 18th Streets
Philadelphia, PA 19146
(215) 545-4448
pumpkinphilly.com
This tiny treasure serves up farmers' market finds in truly innovative ways. It's a real find.

The cafe serves breakfast all day ($)—mmm, Nutella and banana panini. BYOB. Cash only.

VETRI $$$$
1312 Spruce St.
Philadelphia, PA 19107
(215) 732-3478
vetriristorante.com
Called "possibly the best Italian restaurant on the East Coast" by Mario Batali and "probably the best Italian restaurant in America" by esteemed food writer Alan Rich, you might expect this dining spot, the brainchild of James Beard Award–winning, *Food & Wine* magazine–acclaimed chef Marc Vetri would be bigger than life. Just the opposite. While certainly city-sophisticated, this homemade-pasta-centric dining spot has a rustic, laid-back ambience. Don't miss the heirloom tomato and burrata lasagna or guinea hen breast stuffed with prosciutto.

ℹ If you want to sample Marc Vetri's food at less than his eponymous restaurant's prices, try Osteria in nearby Fairmount (640 N. Broad St.; 215-763-0920; osteriaphilly.com; $$–$$$), an easygoing eatery that specializes in thin-crust pizza in varieties that range from the traditional margherita to the innovative pistachio pesto, mozzarella, and mortadella.

CHESTNUT HILL

MCNALLY'S TAVERN $–$$
8634 Germantown Ave.
Philadelphia, PA 19118
(215) 247-9736
mcnallystavern.com
Don't look for a sign; there's just a small plaque on the front of the green door so

Soft Pretzels

Philadelphia adopted the European twisted treat long ago and it is still a favorite on city streets and in mom-and-pop shops dotted all over town. If you should find yourself needing a boost of energy in the form of a carb-laden snack, **Miller's Twist** (51 N. 12th St., Philadelphia, PA 19107; 717-669-6409; millerstwist.com) in Reading Terminal Market offers a variety of buttery, slightly salty Amish-style pretzels; traditional twists and sticks and a host of pretzel dogs are available. For the pretzel purists, **Philly Soft Pretzel Company** (multiple locations; 1532 Sansom St., Philadelphia, PA 19195; 215-569-3988; phillysoftpretzelfactory.com) serves up traditional pretzels in all their wheat-y goodness fresh out of the oven. Chewy and slightly doughy, pretzels from this bakery chain are generally thought to be the real deal. Speaking of real deals, **Center City Pretzel Company** (816 Washington Ave., Philadelphia, PA 19147; 215-463-5664) is an authentic pretzel bakery specializing in traditional Philly pretzels only. You'll find no pretzel dogs, pretzel bites, or fancy mustards at this late-night hot spot—just amazing old-fashioned pretzels crafted in true Philly style. Those in the know make sure to arrive just after the place opens at midnight to get their hands on the first batch out of the oven and, at a mere 35 cents apiece, you can afford to satisfy your inner pretzel glutton.

look for the bench and single coach light instead. Go for the signature "Schmitter," a monster meal of sliced steak, grilled salami, tomatoes, fried onions, and special sauce jammed between two halves of a Kaiser roll.

CHINATOWN

LEE HOW FOOK $–$$
219 N. 11th St.
Philadelphia, PA 19107
(215) 925-7266
leehowfook.com
This family-owned BYOB serves Cantonese classics such as pan-fried noodles with beef and black bean sauce; salt-baked shrimp, scallop, and squid; and a host of hot pots. If you're looking for some heat, the Szechuan selections won't disappoint.

**RANGOON BURMESE
RESTAURANT** $–$$
112 N. 9th St.
Philadelphia, PA 19107
(215) 829-8939
phillychinatown.com/rangoon.htm
Start with thousand layer bread with potato or chicken curry dip, then on to fiery chili chicken or a fierce-sounding but really mild-mannered "pagan" beef with coconut peanut sauce.

✳RAY'S CAFE & TEA HOUSE $–$$
141 N. 9th St.
Philadelphia, PA 19107
(215) 922-5122
rayscafe.com
If you think that Chinese food has to be full of MSG and salt, you'll change your mind after eating at Ray's. On this menu, the

🔍 Close-up

The Best Food at Reading Terminal Market

At 120-year-old **Reading Terminal Market** (51 N. 12th St., Philadelphia, PA 19107; 215-922-2317; readingterminalmarket.org), over 100 vendors gather under one roof to offer fresh produce, meats, seafood, ice cream, fresh-cut flowers, Amish baked goods, and specialty and ethnic foods. As one of the nation's busiest markets, it hosted approximately 6.3 million visitors in 2011—on average, up to 120,000 patrons visit the market every week. It's impossible to experience and sample what the market has to offer in just one visit; from garden-fresh produce to prepared foods to confections, it's easy to see why people keep coming back to this heavily trafficked market. Be sure to check out these highlights.

Bassetts Ice Cream (215-925-4315): As the nation's oldest ice cream company, family-owned Bassetts has been crafting super-premium ice cream for over 150 years. By far, the most popular flavor is the signature Gadzooks—chocolate ice cream studded with peanut butter brownie pieces, chocolate chunks, and caramel swirl.

Dutch Eating Place (215-922-0425): Sidling up to the counter for breakfast or lunch promises a homey, comforting Pennsylvania Dutch–style meal like blueberry pancakes, corned beef hash, or a juicy burger fresh off the griddle. While your waist may not be, a sweet tooth is satisfied by the famous apple dumpling drizzled with heavy cream.

Flying Monkey Bakery (215-928-0340): Treat yourself to a sweet treat from this popular bakery, whose decadent *Pumpple*, a mile-high confection with whole apple and pumpkin pies baked into cake layers, consistently sells out; arrive at the market early to score a slice. A host of cupcakes (try the lavender one), whoopee pies, and sugary goodies fill the glass display case and have garnered a huge following.

Sang Kee Peking Duck (215-922-3930): At this outpost of Sang Kee's Chinatown locale, juicy Peking duck and steamed dumplings make for a delicious, affordable meal. Steaming bowls of noodle soup are belly-filling and satisfying.

Tommy DiNic's (215-923-6175): Monstrous, delicious sandwiches are worth tolerating the always-long lines guaranteed to be packed with tourists and hungry lunch-breakers alike. The juicy roast pork sandwich with sharp provolone is a thing of beauty.

---

flavor comes from fresh ingredients, lightly tweaked to give them their Asian accent. Carnivores will find plenty of dishes to make them happy, but try some of the ingenious tofu and Chinese mushroom creations and I'll bet you won't miss the meat.

VIET THAI $–$$
907 Race St.
Philadelphia, PA 19107
(215) 627-8883
phillychinatown.com/vietthai.htm

The exotic menu here has subtitles so you won't accidentally order the crispy fried frog (unless, of course, you want to). A big bracing bowl of pho is only $5.50. Or order a hot pot for 2.

i The neighborhood may be called "Chinatown," but it's really a diverse community of pan-Asian cultures including Thai, Vietnamese, Malaysian, and Burmese.

MANAYUNK

JAKE'S AND COOPER'S WINE BAR $$-$$$
4365–67 Main St.
Philadelphia, PA 19127
(215) 483-0444
jakesrestaurant.com

White tablecloth fancy? Pizza cafe casual? You don't have to decide until you walk in the front door of this dual-personality dining spot. For more than 20 years, white tablecloth Jake's, with owner/chef Bruce Cooper at the helm, has been a Main Street mainstay serving contemporary American cuisine. Now Cooper has added a big brick oven to his open kitchen and designed a cool cafe that features a collection of creative, crisp-crusted pizzas—ever have one topped with pulled pork and gouda or short rib and horseradish cream? (Gayout and MSN listed Cooper's pizzas as among the 10 best in the country.) And don't miss Jake's seasonal mac and cheese (a recent summer combination was corn and crab) and its grilled steak and chop selections.

TOMMY GUNN'S AMERICAN BARBEQUE $-$$
4901 Ridge Ave. (Main Street)
Philadelphia, PA 19128
(215) 508-1030
tommygunns.net

Sure you can get Memphis- or Texas-style Q here, but when in Philly . . . the main attraction is "Philly-style" barbecue, which is more a designation of cut (more meat on each bone) and finish (grilled after smoking). Meats are coated with "secret" rub, smoked for 3 to 4 hours, grilled, and finished with house recipe sauce. Pair with spicy collard greens, Carolina slaw, or, if you dare, deep-fried mac and cheese.

NORTHERN LIBERTIES

BAR FERDINAND $$
1030 N. 2nd St.
Philadelphia, PA 19123
(215) 923-1313
barferdinand.com

Hot and cold tapas and small plates are the mainstays of this Spanish-inspired eatery. I crave the calamari rellenos (squid stuffed with shrimp, leeks, and sage brown butter). For a real taste of this restaurant's specialties, try the $35 fixed price Chef Tasting Menu and come and get some extra Spanish flavor on First Friday live flamenco dancing nights.

*HONEY'S SIT 'N EAT $-$$
800 N. 4th St.
Philadelphia, PA 19123
(215) 925-1150
honeys-restaurant.com

Clearly, Honey's is a Jewish deli with its latkes, bubby's brisket, bagels and lox, and corned beef on rye. So what are burritos, fish tacos, chicken-fried steak, and grits doing on the menu? Somehow they just belong. Cash only.

SOUTH PHILLY

*CRÊPERIE BEAU MONDE $–$$
Northwest Corner of 6th and Bainbridge
Streets
Philadelphia, PA 19147
251-592-0656
creperie-beaumonde.com

My favorite brunch is the smoked salmon Breton-style buckwheat crepe at this charming little South Philly spot. Or maybe my favorite is the one with andouille sausage or coquilles St. Jacques. For dessert, a sweet crepe with chestnut crème—*c'est manifique*!

DANTE & LUIGI'S
CORONA DI FERRO $$–$$$
762 S. 10th St.
Philadelphia, PA 19147
(215) 922-9501
danteandluigis.com

One of the oldest existing Italian restaurants in the US, this 1899-founded pasta-centric dining spot situated in 2 converted town houses makes a gravy (aka red sauce) that's worthy of Momma. Parking in this neighborhood is tough, so take advantage of the valet option. Also pay cash and save yourself a 3.5 percent service charge.

MARIGOLD KITCHEN $$$
501 S. 45th St.
Philadelphia, PA 19104
(215) 222-3699
marigoldkitchenbyob.com

Chef Robert Halpern, an alumnus of Ithaca, New York's iconic Moosewood Restaurant, and company demonstrate a true respect for their ingredients while creating whimsical interpretations of such homestyle classics as chicken and waffles and pork and beans. For brunch ($$), go for the "Elvis-style" crème brûlée french toast.

THE RESTAURANT SCHOOL AT
WALNUT HILL COLLEGE $$–$$$$$
4207 Walnut St.
Philadelphia, PA 19104
(215) 222-4200
walnuthillcollege.edu

Be among the first to sample a world of lovingly prepared selections from America's future culinary stars at any of the school's four themed restaurants: International Bistro ($$$) for a 3-course, European-style menu; American Heartland ($$) for farmhouse-fresh favorites made with contemporary flair; The Great Chefs ($$$$$) for 5 courses of fine dining specialties created by the city's most famous chefs exclusively for the school; and Italian Trattoria ($$) for a different regional pasta dish each night. Don't miss a hand-crafted treat from the Pastry Shop, where students turn out everything from tortes to tarts, croissants to cheesecakes.

BUCKS COUNTY

*MARSHA BROWN $$$$
15 S. Main St.
New Hope, PA 18938
(215) 862-7044
marshabrownrestaurant.com

Laissez les Bontemps Rouler, y'all. Marsha Brown's a real Louisiana girl who knows her Creole cooking. And she has fashioned her family recipes into some very sophisticated Southern fare at her gorgeous restaurant housed in a 125-year-old stone church complete with stained-glass windows, carved wood accents, and a sweeping golden staircase. Order the gumbo ya ya, jambalaya, seafood court-bouillon (Louisiana bouillabaise), and you're in New Orleans. Consider the fabulous 3-course prix-fixe ($69).

South of the Border in South Philly

South Philly may be famous for its Italian Market, but peppered among the pasta palaces are a number of great Mexican dining spots that range from home-style to haute.

Dos Segundos Cantina $$–$$$
931 N. 2nd St., Northern Liberties
Philadelphia, PA 19123
(215) 629-0500
cantinadossegundos.com
Slow-cooked goat, suckling pig, ceviches of the day, vegan fajitas, and tequila flights. Sure they have burritos, but there's so much more of Mexico to savor.

Los Caballitos Cantina $–$$
1651 E. Passyunk Ave.
Philadelphia, PA 19148
(215) 755-3550
cantinaloscaballitos.com
Choose a chilaquiles tortilla casserole or huevos a la Mexicana breakfast or costillitas with barbecued pork ribs or enchiladas placeras, corn tortillas filled with roasted chicken, chicken chorizo, and all kinds of other yummy stuff. Lots of vegetarian and vegan options, too.

Paloma Mexican Haute Cuisine $$$–$$$$
763 S. 8th St.
Philadelphia, PA 19147
(215) 928-9500
palomafinedining.com
Chef-owner Adán Saavedra and wife, Barb Cohan-Saavedra, add a French twist to upscale Mexican cuisine. Think bronzino with habañero-chardonnay sauce, smoked salmon Napoleon with pablano peppers and jalapeño marinade, and wild mushroom flan with cilantro pesto.

Ralph's Italian Restaurant $–$$
760 S. 9th St.
Philadelphia, PA 19147
(215) 627-6011
ralphsrestaurant.com

George Washington didn't eat here, but Frank Sinatra did as well as Teddy Roosevelt, heavyweight boxing champion Rocky Marciano, and a long list of other celebrities. The Dispignos (fifth generation) who operate this century-old eatery say that it is "the oldest family-owned restaurant in the country." Whatever you do, order the broccoli rabe as an appetizer or a side. No Italian meal is complete without it.

✳ Sabrina's Cafe $-$$
(2 locations)
Italian Market
910 Christian St.
Philadelphia, PA 19147
(215) 574-1599
Fairmount/Art Museum
1804 Callowhill St.
Philadelphia, PA 19130
(215) 636-9061
sabrinascafe.com
Get in line. It's worth it for the best breakfast and brunch in Philly. Both of these BYOB locations are tiny and no-frills, but your patience will be richly rewarded with the apple and sharp cheddar omelet, "Barking Chihuahua" Breakfast Burrito, and stuffed caramelized challah french toast.

White Dog Cafe $$$-$$$$
University City, 3420 Sansom St.
Philadelphia, PA 19104
(215) 386-9224
whitedog.com
More than 25 years ago, long before the word *locavore* found its way into the language, social activist Judy Wicks was sourcing her ingredients whenever possible from nearby farms, the best organic and sustainable producers on the East Coast, and American wineries and breweries. A local culinary entrepreneur (he owns numerous other eateries including Moshulu) carries on Wicks's mission at this award-winning University City landmark.

(Q) Close-up

Philly Food Fight

If you want to read, go to the library! Menu boards are for tourists, and you don't want to hold up the line and get between a Philadelphian and his cheesesteak. Just remember to say whether you want yours "wit" (Cheez Whiz and fried onions). Don't want Whiz? You can also ask for provolone, but do it quickly. What's a hoagie? Some call them subs, heroes, or torpedoes, but in Philly, don't call these meat-, cheese-, and veggie-stuffed sandwiches dressed with a little oil and a sprinkle of Italian herbs on fresh-baked Italian rolls any name but hoagie. Here are the best places to find your sandwich of choice!

CHEESESTEAKS

Geno's Steaks $
1219 S. 9th St.
Philadelphia, PA 19147
(215) 389-0659
genosteaks.com

Jim's Steaks $
Four locations in Philly and the 'burbs
jimssteaks.com

Pat's King of Steaks $
9th Street (at Wharton and Passyunk Avenues)
Philadelphia, PA 19147
(215) 468-1546
patskingofsteaks.com

Tony Luke's $
39 E. Oregon Ave.
Philadelphia, PA 19148
(215) 551-5725
tonylukes.com

HOAGIES

Chickie's Italian Deli $
1014 Federal St. (South Philly)
Philadelphia, PA 19147
(215) 462-8040
chickiesdeli.com

Primo Hoagies $–$$
Multiple locations throughout Philly and the 'burbs
primohoagies.com

Sarcone's Deli $–$$
Two locations:
734 S. 9th St. (South Philly)
Philadelphia, PA 19147
(215) 922-1717

2100 S. Eagle Rd., Newtown (Bucks County)
Newtown, PA 18940
(215) 860-9500
sarconesdeli.com

MARTINE'S RIVERHOUSE RESTAURANT $$$$
14 E. Ferry St.
New Hope, PA 18938
(215) 862-2966
martinesriverhouserestaurant.com
The menu categories are deceptively simple: The "salmon" is glazed with spiced fig and red wine jam, the "chicken" Latin-spiced with a black bean coconut sauce. Add in the river views and you have a destination for dining.

SINE'S 5 & 10 CENT STORE $
236-240 W. Broad St.
Quakertown, PA 18951
(215) 536-6102
sines5and10.com

For over a century, this real old-fashioned soda fountain has been serving up no-fuss breakfasts, sandwiches, and homestyle dinners (Mom's meatloaf, anyone?), along with ice cream specialties. Kids will also love the more than 200 model airplanes and operating train.

SPRIG AND VINE $$
450 Union Square Dr.
New Hope, PA 18938
(215) 693-1427
sprigandvine.com

One hundred percent vegan, 0 percent boring. Meat eaters—leave your preconceptions behind. This is anything but rabbit food. Try the curry cauliflower steak or miso-barbecue eggplant. You won't miss the meat. Brunch is an even bigger wake-up call.

THE TALKING TEACUP $–$$
301 W. Butler Ave.
Chalfont, PA 18914
(215) 997-8441
thetalkingteacup.com

Set in a lovingly restored 250-year-old farmhouse, this anything-but-snooty tearoom is family friendly (there's even a kids' tea). Everything—from the scones to the sandwiches to the sweets—is homemade.

i You can sample the specialties of the county's fertile fields and artisans of edibles on a 5-hour guided tour, including transportation and lunch, with a Feast With Food Tour. Book the Mixed Bag of Bucks Tour for the maximum delectable diversity. (215-598-2979; buckscountyfoodtours .com).

CHESTER COUNTY

GEORGES' $$–$$$$
503 W. Lancaster Ave.
Wayne, PA 19087
(610) 964-2588
georgesonthemainline.com

Georges Perrier may no longer own Le Bec Fin, but his suburban dining spot keeps him in the local spotlight. This Main Line restaurant represents his interpretation of casual. With its wide range of selections and price points, it's really hard to categorize this menu that includes everything from sandwiches (albeit fancy ones) and brick-oven pizzas ($$) to upscale (and priced that way, too) entrees including $45 steaks ($$$–$$$$). It's a good place for lunch, too ($$).

GILMORE'S $$$
133 E. Gay St.
West Chester, PA 19380
(610) 431-2800
gilmoresrestaurant.com

Former Le Bec Fin chef de cuisine Peter Gilmore creates European-inspired entrees such as crab meat in shrimp mousse and truffled-mushroom-puff-pastry-wrapped chicken Wellington. For dessert, go for the baked Alaska—a sophisticated take on a classic.

MUSHROOMS CAFE $
Brandywine River Antiques Market—The White Barn
878 Baltimore Pike (Route 1)
Chadds Ford, PA 19317
(610) 388-2000
brandywineriverantiques.com/
mushrooms.html

Located in the heart of the "Mushroom Capital of the World," this little eatery is the best place to experience the versatility of these fabulous fungi. Start with the house sampler of mushrooms three ways—in soup, stuffed, and in a dip with pita. Move on to the grilled portobello sandwich. Of course, you can order one of the fungus-free items on the menu, but why would you? (All kinds of mushrooms are available by the pound for take-home, too.)

TALULA'S TABLE $$$$$
102 W. State St.
Kennett Square, PA 19348
(610) 444-8255
talulastable.com

This cute, European-style gourmet market offers more than 100 artisan cheeses and an impressive selection of charcuterie, sandwiches, daily-baked breads and pastries, and small-batch specialties such as organic fried chicken, pulled pork enchiladas, lamb kebabs, and more for eat-in at the communal farm table or takeout (picnic anyone?).

> **i** A great place for a picnic that is known only to the neighbors is Anson B. Nixon Park (just north of downtown Kennett at North Walnut just off State Street; 610-444-1416; ansonbnixonpark.org), 100 acres of ponds, streams, centuries-old beech groves, 3 miles of walking trails, disc golf, and free summer concerts.

DELAWARE COUNTY

**SUSANNA FOO GOURMET
  KITCHEN** $$–$$$
555 E. Lancaster Ave.
Radnor, PA 19087
(610) 688-8808
susannafoo.com/gourmet-kitchen-home

Mongolian-born, two-time James Beard Award–winning chef Susanna Foo offers her distinctive Asian-French fusion cuisine for dining in or takeout. Don't miss her bento box lunches, delectable dumplings, or sushi and sashimi sampler.

TEIKOKU $$–$$$
5492 West Chester Pike
Newtown Square, PA 19073
(610) 644-8270
teikokurestaurant.com

Japanese and Thai specialties serenely share a menu in this surprising find on busy Route 3. Stunning in its simplicity both in decor and food preparation, this garden-inspired oasis serves impeccably fresh sushi and sashimi and a wide range of Asian delicacies from sashimi to sate, tempura to pad thai. It's also a great way to discover the nuances of sake with a flight of 3 or 5 different types.

MONTGOMERY COUNTY

ARPEGGIO $–$$
542 Springhouse Village Center
909 Sumneytown Pike
Spring House, PA 19477
(215) 646-5055
arpeggiobyob.com

In summer, sit out on the patio and in winter inside with the 2-sided fireplace at this intimate BYOB as you enjoy the global menu that includes everything from kebabs to teriyakis, parmesans, and Florentines. The wood-fired oven also turns out more than 25 varieties of thin-crusted pizzas prepared with daily-made dough.

SHANACHIE IRISH PUB AND
  RESTAURANT $$–$$$
111 E. Butler Ave.
Ambler, PA 19002
(215) 283-4887
shanachiepub.com

Irish-born Gerry Timlin and partner Ed Egan offer a true taste of the Emerald Isle with traditional specialties, including corned beef and cabbage, potato boxty, and coddle. Belly up to the bar and stick around for the live entertainment every Wednesday through Saturday.

NIGHTLIFE

I remember when at the end of the workday, the mass exodus of commuters out of Center City would leave it an after-dark ghost town. Now you'll find a lively nightlife offering creative cocktails, live entertainment, and ample opportunity to dance the night away.

BARS & LOUNGES

Center City/Old City

✳CUBA LIBRE RESTAURANT AND RUM BAR
10 S. 2nd St.
Philadelphia, PA 19106
(215) 627-0666
cubalibrerestaurant.com
With its Latin floor shows and salsa dancing after dinner hours on weekends and Old Havana ambience, you know you've come to the right place for rum—more than 75 varieties of it including a house-labeled brand. And what better use of rum than to make mojitos that feature fresh-pressed sugarcane juice (*guarapo*) and the Mexican mint-like herb called *hierba buena*? The Nuevo Latin menu by super-chef Guillermo Pernot is also excellent.

FRANKLIN MORTGAGE & INVESTMENT COMPANY
112 S. 18th St.
Philadelphia, PA 19103
(267) 467-3277
thefranklinbar.com
If you're tired of bartenders who just slosh your drink into a glass while keeping one eye on the game on the TV, you're ready for this classy, clubby pre-Prohibition paragon of potables where mixology maestros fashion froufrou-free classics with respect and artistry.

LUCY'S HAT SHOP BAR & LOUNGE
247 Market St.
Philadelphia, PA 19106
(215) 413-1433
lucys215.com
Two large bars with dueling DJs plus great drink specials make this one of Center City's most popular places to party.

ROUGE
205 S. 18th St.
Philadelphia, PA 19103
(215) 732-6622
rouge98.com
There's no better way to pass the time: Watch the passersby on Rittenhouse Square while sipping a blueberry lemonade (don't be fooled into thinking this is a granny drink; it's made with Blueberry Pearl vodka) or a root beer float (the vanilla is cognac) at this hot

French bistro's sidewalk cafe. Pair your potent potable with a nice artisan cheese plate.

STANDARD TAP
901 N. 2nd St.
Philadelphia, PA 19123
(215) 238-0630
standardtap.com

A true showcase for local brews (you'll find more than 20 of them) along with some pretty upscale tavern food such as duck confit salad and chicken pie.

SWANN LOUNGE
Four Seasons Hotel
1 Logan Sq.
Philadelphia, PA 19103
(215) 963-1500
fourseasons.com

Cozy couches, baby grand piano—it's rich, regal, and romantic. So what's a Philly cheesesteak spring roll doing on the bar menu? Bursting a few perceptions of pretension, we presume.

10 ARTS BISTRO LOUNGE
Ritz-Carlton Rotunda
10 Avenue of the Arts
Philadelphia, PA 19102
(215) 523-8273
10arts.com

This Ritz-y concept, credited to nationally renowned chef Eric Ripert, is about as posh as you can get, but the drinks menu is anything but intimidating. Among its "Perfect 10" cocktails ($15) you might find a heady duet of hibiscus and prosecco, watermelon daiquiri, or blood orange old-fashioned. The nibbles are top rate, too, especially the warm soft pretzel with cheddar cheese, jalapeño jam, and Dijon mustard.

TEQUILA'S BAR AT LOS CATRINES
1602 Locust St.
Philadelphia, PA 19103
(215) 546-0181
tequilasphilly.com

More than 75 tequila varieties give the "liquid chef" at this unassuming gathering place unlimited options to come up with creatively complex-flavored cocktails. On the way in, note the spooky yet symbolic mural in the entryway so you won't think you've had too many on your way out.

BREWERIES, BREWPUBS & TAVERNS

Center City/Old City

*MCGILLIN'S OLDE ALE HOUSE
1310 Drury St.
Philadelphia, PA 19107
(215) 735-5562
mcgillins.com

Open since 1860, McGillin's Olde Ale House is the oldest continuously operating tavern in Philadelphia. Over the years, the clientele has been studded with stars including Will Rogers, Tennessee Williams, Vincent Price, the Marx Brothers and, more recently, Robin Williams, Will Ferrell, and the list goes on. Despite its long history, though, this pub keeps it fresh with a wide variety of today's best regional microbrews and imports.

NODDING HEAD BREWERY & RESTAURANT
1516 Sansom St., 2nd Fl.
Philadelphia, PA 19102
(215) 569-9525
ripsneakers.com/nodding

From the easy-drinking, light-tart Ich Bin Ein Berliner Weisse to the dark chocolaty stick-around-and-sip-it-slowly grog, these micros are masterfully made.

YARDS BREWING COMPANY
901 N. Delaware Ave.
Philadelphia, PA 19123
(215) 634-2600
yardsbrewing.com

The *New York Times* rated Yards' Philadelphia Pale Ale as one of the best in the country. Further proof of the brewery's growing following is the fact that it has had to move into progressively larger quarters—4 in a little over 10 years—to keep up with demand. Don't miss the distinctive Ales of the Revolution, a collection of 3 beer re-creations based on the original recipes of George Washington, Thomas Jefferson, and Ben Franklin. Free tours of the 100 percent wind-powered brewery are available on Saturday.

Manayunk

MANAYUNK BREWERY & RESTAURANT
4120 Main St.
Philadelphia, PA 19127
(215) 482-8220
manayunkbrewery.com

If you're a Philly native, you know that "Schuylkill Punch" has never been something that has been drunk with great relish (the name is a reference to the city's sometimes suspicious-smelling and tasting drinking water). But these clever brew masters have given the name a new lease on life by bestowing it upon their luscious raspberry lager. Relax outside on the deck overlooking the infamous Schuylkill itself.

Chester County/Delaware County

IRON HILL BREWERY
3 W. Gay St.
West Chester, PA 19380
(610) 738-9600
30 E. State St.
Media, PA 19063
(610) 627-9000
(Other locations are listed on the website)
ironhillbrewery.com

Sample the malty Vienna Red Lager, the hoppy Ironbound Ale, and the traditional Belgian Ale-of-the-Month. As for the food, make sure you get a bowl of the ale and onion au gratin soup and, if you're under the legal age or just not a beer aficionado, a mug of the house-made root beer will hit the spot. There's an extensive gluten-free menu as well.

VICTORY BREWING COMPANY
420 Acorn Ln.
Downingtown, PA 19335
(610) 873-0881
victorybeer.com

How can you resist trying a beer that its brewers describe as "menacingly delicious," or one that's poetically positioned as "a swirling dynamo of flavor, with a steady calm of satisfaction at its heart"? Free tours are offered on Friday.

DANCE CLUBS

If you never thought of Philadelphia as sexy, you might be surprised that after dark, this prim colonial lady ditches her dowdy dowager duds, slips on the stilettos, and goes for the glam.

Center City/Old City

BRASIL'S
112 Chestnut St.
Philadelphia, PA 19106
(215) 413-7000
brasilsnightclub-philly.com
Pure Latin even to the salsa lessons offered for the price of a $5–$10 cover charge on Wednesday, Friday, and Saturday nights. Great drink specials on those same nights.

FLUID NIGHTCLUB
613 S. 4th St.
Philadelphia, PA 19147
(215) 629-3686
fluidnightclub.com
A disco-style dance club offering an eclectic mix of electronica, funk, house, soul, trip hop, trance, progressive, drum 'n bass, jungle, break beat, hip-hop, rock 'n' roll, and punk rock.

i Don't want to sit at the bar with the rest of the riffraff? Then opt for European bottle service, but only if you have the budget to back it up. For the price of a full bottle or two (a couple of hundred dollars or more apiece is not a stretch and some clubs have a minimum number), you can have your own VIP seating area, dedicated hostess, and all the mixers and garnishes you could want to design your own cocktails. Liquor lockers are also often available for rental to make sure you don't have to waste a drop even after you've decided to call it a night. If you BYOF (bring your own friends), check out the per-drink price, then figure out if bottle service might be a reasonable alternative. Reservations for this service are often required, so call or check the website before you just stop on by.

i For a listing of gay and lesbian clubs, check out the following website: philadelphia.com/nightlife/gay.

JAZZ & BLUES CLUBS

Center City/Old City

CHRIS'S JAZZ CAFE
1421 Sansom St.
Philadelphia, PA 19102
(215) 568-3131
chrisjazzcafe.com
Tickets are generally $10 ($5 for students)—from $15 to $20 for headline performers.

✳WARMDADDY'S
1400 S. Christopher Columbus Blvd.
Philadelphia, PA 19147
(215) 462-2000
warmdaddys.com
Southern-style blues, zydeco, rhythm and blues, and soul every night of the week. Shows are usually around $15. To really get you in the mood, start with a soulful Southern dinner, maybe fried chicken and waffles, low-country catfish, or shrimp and grits ($$). Or come for the Sunday Jazz Brunch ($$$).

West Philly

WORLD CAFE LIVE
3025 Walnut St.
Philadelphia, PA 19104
(215) 222-1400
worldcafelive.com
Actually two venues in one, this University City hosts live musical artists that run the gamut from rock to jazz, folk to world music, comedy to children's concerts in its downstairs bistro music hall and upstairs at its street level cafe. Tickets for regular concerts are usually around $25 ($15 for students); for

kids' performances they are $13 ($8 for the young'uns).

COMEDY CLUBS

COMEDYSPORTZ
2030 Sansom St.
Philadelphia, PA 19103
(877) 98-LAUGH
comedysportzphilly.com
Comedy is a team sport at this family-friendly improv club. You call out the topics and award the points for the players who make you laugh the most. Tickets are $15 ($12 for students and seniors).

LAFF HOUSE
221 South St. (between 2nd and 3rd Streets)
Philadelphia, PA 19147
(215) 440-4242
laffhouse.com
Headliners and rising stars from around the country make this comedy club their home away from home while enjoying the brotherly love of Philly fans.

SPORTS BARS

Center City/Old City

BUFFALO BILLIARDS & METROPOLITAN LOUNGE
116 Chestnut St.
(215) 574-7665
Philadelphia, PA 19106
buffalobilliards.com
Two floors, 2 bars, 9 billiard tables ($8 for one person, $12 for two), 16 HDTVs.

CAVANAUGH'S RITTENHOUSE
1823 Sansom St.
Philadelphia, PA 19103
(215) 665-9500
cavsrittenhouse.com
Twenty HDTVs show every game you could possibly want to see. Look for half-price pub food and discounted drink specials.

Manayunk

BAYOU BAR & GRILLE
4245 Main St., Manayunk
Philadelpha, PA 19127
(215) 482-2560
bayoubar.com
Sixteen TVs, $1 drink specials, and "Best of Philly" award-winning buffalo wings.

South Philadelphia

✳CHICKIE'S AND PETE'S CRAB HOUSE AND SPORTS BAR
1526 Packer Ave.
Philadelphia, PA 19145
(215) 218-0500
chickiesandpetes.com
Ride the free "Taxi Crab" on game days from the stadium for some spirited celebration or some liquid consolation. Seafood is the star, and rumor has it that Jon Bon Jovi loves the lobster pizza.

West Philadelphia/University City

CAVANAUGH'S
119 S. 39th St. (at Sansom Street)
Philadelphia, PA 19104
(215) 386-4889
cavssportsbar.com
Get there early for a laid-back libation from the international beer collection or join the college crowd for an evening of unbridled energy.

Wandering the Wine Trails

The Philly area has a wealth of wineries—almost 20 between the Brandywine and Bucks County Trails. Among these operations are many national and international award-winners. Many of the tasting rooms are housed in historic buildings, which make the visit even more fun. Most welcome picnickers (or they serve food themselves) and host special events throughout the year. Among the varietals available along the trails are Cabernet Franc, Chambourcin, Chardonnay, Merlot, Pinot Gris, Pinot Noir, Port, Riesling, Sauvignon Blanc, Syrah, Traminette, Vidal Blanc, Vignoles, and native Cayuga and Niagara. Each winery also creates its own distinctive blends, some make not-too-sweet spiced apple wines (warm it on a cold winter day and your house will smell heavenly) and some delightful dessert Rieslings and Cabernet Franc ice wines. Maps of both trails and contact information for the individual wineries are included on the websites. Call in advance about tasting fees.

Along Route 1 in Southern Chester County near Longwood Gardens and Kennett Square are 8 wineries that make up the Brandywine Wine Trail (866-390-4367; bvwinetrail.com). The Bucks County Wine Trail (buckscountywinetrail.com) has 9 participants.

WINE BARS

IL BAR
Penn's View Hotel
14 N. Front St.
Philadelphia, PA 19106
(215) 922-7800
pennsviewhotel.com

You can't help but be impressed by the "cruvinet," the largest wine preservation and dispensing system in the world, which allows this oenophile's oasis to keep an ever-changing collection of 120 bottles on tap at any given time. Order by the 3-ounce tasting glass, 5-ounce regular glass, or 5-variety flight or bottle. The ambience is pleasantly posh, as a wine bar should be.

MOVIES/THEATERS

LANDMARK THEATERS
Ritz Five, 214 Walnut St. (between 2nd and 3rd Streets), Philadelphia, PA 19106

Ritz East, 125 S. 2nd St. (between Walnut and Chestnut Streets, Front and Second Streets), Philadelphia, PA 19106

Ritz at the Bourse, 400 Ranstead St. (on 4th Street between Market and Chestnut), Philadelphia, PA 19106
(215) 925-7900 for all 3 theaters
landmarktheatres.com

RAVE MOTION PICTURES (FORMERLY THE BRIDGE CINEMA DE LUX)
40th and Walnut Streets
Philadelphia, PA 19104
(215) 386-0869
ravemotionpictures.com
Six screens.

Manayunk

UNITED ARTISTS MAIN STREET 6
3720 Main St.
Philadelphia, PA 19127
(215) 482-6138
regmovies.com

South Philly

UNITED ARTISTS RIVERVIEW PLAZA STADIUM 17
1400 S. Columbus Blvd.
Philadelphia, PA 19147
(215) 755-2353
regmovies.com

King of Prussia/Montgomery County

UNITED ARTIST KING OF PRUSSIA STADIUM 16 & IMAX
300 Goddard Blvd.
King of Prussia, PA 19406
(610) 337-0282
regmovies.com

SHOPPING & SERVICES

There's no sales tax on clothing in Pennsylvania! Now that I've got your attention, let's get to some of the places you can splurge on the latest (and cutting-edge) fashions that come straight from the runway or from some avant-garde artist's fevered imagination (see South Street). Your home can get a whole new lease on life courtesy of Philly's couture decor. In Old City/Center City, you'll find a number of shopping meccas that will appeal to all ages, preferences, and budgets. There are upscale boutiques on Rittenhouse Row, store after store of sparklers on Jewelers Row, valuable and vintage finds on Antique Row, and the fabulously funky South Street (celebrated as "the hippest street in town" in a hit song of the '60s).

A short drive beyond Center City, you'll find a bounty of boutiques lining the historic cobblestone streets of the highly strollable neighborhoods of Manayunk and Chestnut Hill. Then, of course, you don't want to miss the must-do destinations of King of Prussia Mall in Montgomery County and Peddler's Village in New Hope, Bucks County.

In this chapter, I have organized the shops by geographical locations (e.g., major shopping districts such as "Jewelers Row" and "Chestnut Hill"). Keep in mind that, to make it easier to pursue your own areas of interest, some shopping categories such as "Antiques" and "Kidstuff" are explored in chapters of their own.

PHILADELPHIA COUNTY

Center City

THE BELLEVUE
Broad & Walnut Streets
Philadelphia, PA 19102
(215) 875-8350
bellevuephiladelphia.com
In addition to being the site of the upscale Park Hyatt Hotel and such renowned fine dining establishments as The Palm, this gorgeous, French Renaissance–style, circa-1904 landmark also features a few selected shops such as Polo Ralph Lauren (215-985-2800), Teuscher Chocolates of Switzerland (215-546-7600), Tiffany & Co. (215-735-1919),

Vigant Italian Handbags (215-735-5057), and Williams-Sonoma (215-545-7392).

THE BOURSE
111 S. Independence Mall East, Ste. 900
Philadelphia, PA 19106
(215) 625-0300
bourse-pa.com
The shops in here are few, but they're really cool and really Philly. Best of Philadelphia (215-629-0533) is a great place to pick up a city souvenir, from an inexpensive magnet to full gift basket; Destination Philadelphia

✳9th Street Italian Market

If there's any shopping spot that screams "Philadelphia," it's this oldest and largest working outdoor market in the US. A landmark for more than a century, it is a must-visit destination not only for anyone who loves to cook but also for everyone who loves to eat. More than a century old, this market has maintained its authenticity thanks in large part to the family-owned businesses that have remained here for many generations. And while a multitude of cultures, including Asian and Latin, have brought their own flavors to the mix, the accent is still very much on the Italian.

Save at least half a day to savor the Italian Market experience. Better yet, save a whole day. You'll need it to take in the more than 40 produce vendors; 4 cheese shops; 7 meat and 4 each of seafood and poultry markets; 2 pasta manufacturers; 3 bakeries, including one that bakes the city's best Italian bread, another the best cannoli; 3 spice houses; and 2 coffee and tea purveyors. Also, look for the little shops that sell linens and handmade lace, lingerie, shoes, and luggage.

Don't miss the best Italian bread at Sarcone's Bakery, the hard-to-find ingredients at the Spice House, the natural house-made sausage at D'Angelo Bros., the more than 400 varieties at DiBruno Bros. House of Cheese, the 900 varieties of handmade pastas at Talluto's, the porchetta at A. Esposito Inc., the cannoli at Isgro Pasticceria, or the utensil utopia that is Fante's Kitchen Wares Shop.

The market is open Tues through Sat from 9 a.m. to 5 p.m. and Sun from 9 a.m. to 2 p.m. Be sure to check the website for parking recommendations. Information: South 9th Street; Wharton to Fitzwater Streets; phillyitalian market.com.

(215-574-8286) for imprinted sportswear and accessories; Out of Left Field (215-925-0413) for licensed hometown sports apparel and other items; and Vision Graphics (215-627-0279) for color and black-and-white Philly-themed prints. If you're hungry, there are more than a dozen different options ranging from salad to cheesesteaks in the food court.

THE SHOPS AT LIBERTY PLACE
1625 Chestnut St.
Philadelphia, PA 19192
(215) 851-9055
shopsatliberty.com

Another nice food court with some shops that represent a good mix of upscale apparel and accessory stores for men, including Jos. A. Bank (215-563-5990) and Les Richards (215-751-1155), and for women, including Ann Taylor Loft (215-557-9181) and Bella Turka (215-557-9050), which features a small but exclusive collection of jewelry from around the world.

Fabric Row

(South 4th Street between South and Catharine Streets; southstreet.com)

Head House Square

In 1745, farmers began gathering in the area around South 2nd Street from Pine to Lombard Streets to sell their produce, meats, and other homegrown and homemade products at an open-air shed known as "the shambles" (a reference to the English word for "butcher shop" or "meat stalls"). To differentiate it from the other surrounding trade areas, this place of commerce became known as "New Market." In 1805, a 3-story, stone firehouse called the "Head House" was built for the volunteer fire department—believed to be the first in the nation. Over time, the firehouse, attached market shed, and adjacent park became known as "Head House Square." Today, the Head House itself is a community center and the site of many special events throughout the year including the environment-oriented GreenFest Philly in September and Good Food, Good Beer, and the Rest is History tasting of local restaurant specialties in July. The shambles, which was demolished in 1950 but rebuilt in the early '60s, remains the site of a covered open-air farmers' market on Sat and Sun from early May to the week before Christmas. It is operated by the nonprofit Food Trust, an organization dedicated to making fresh foods accessible and affordable to all (thefoodtrust.org/php/head house). Head House Square was declared a National Historic Landmark in 1966. The Head House vendors only accept cash, food stamps, and WIC/Senior Citizen vouchers. Check the website for parking recommendations. Information: 2nd and Lombard Streets; thefoodtrust.org.

At the turn of the 20th century, many of the Jewish immigrants who came to Philadelphia settled in what is now South Philadelphia. Many of them were highly skilled tailors and seamstresses who were only able to scratch out a living by taking jobs in sweatshops making fine garments for the upper class. Others became peddlers who sold fabric remnants and sewing supplies from pushcarts. As the years passed, a number of these peddlers were able to open storefronts from which to sell their wares. And while the area is anything but glamorous, you can still get some great buys on a wide array of sewing staples at the shops that remain from those days and some newer ones that are keeping up the garment trade tradition.

CRAWFORD'S FINE MILLINERY
764 S. 4th St.
Philadelphia, PA 19147
(215) 922-7515
Not all of the shops on Fabric Row are geared toward do-it-yourselfers. Tim Crawford makes some of the coolest, most artistic hats you'll find anywhere.

MAXIE'S DAUGHTER
724 S. 4th St.
Philadelphia, PA 19147
(215) 829-2226
The fabrics are nicely arranged, clean, and well kept, and the staff is extremely helpful. If you're making a wedding dress, this a good place to come for materials and guidance.

*WILBUR VINTAGE

716 S. 4th St.
Philadelphia, PA 19147
(215) 413-5809
wilburvintage.blogspot.com

Oh-so-fabulous wood and embroidered shoes from the '30s and '40s, Jean-Paul Gaultier jackets, '60s dresses with psychedelic Pucci-like prints . . . you have to go here.

i While in Philly, you may hear references to The Gallery at East 9th and Market Streets (215-625-4962; galleryatmarketeast.com) as a shopping destination. There's an interesting story behind this 5-block-long, 4-story-high mall, not all of it happy. The Gallery was opened in 1977 and expanded in the early '80s as part of a major urban renewal program to revitalize the once-dynamic Market Street retail corridor. Anchored by some of the city's most respected department stores, it was constructed to be a magnet for both city and suburban shoppers. Over the years, those anchors have been replaced by retailers such as Kmart and Burlington Coat Factory and, while there are still more than 100 stores that are a combination of mall standards and independents, it never really lived up to its original promise and, unfortunately, is not on my recommended list.

Jewelers Row

(One block from Independence Hall on Sansom Street between 7th and 8th Streets and 8th Street between Chestnut & Walnut Streets.)

Whether you're looking for the engagement or other custom ring of your dreams, a statement-making necklace or bracelet, or a watch that quietly communicates your taste and status, you'll find hundreds of jewelers offering deeply discounted prices in Philly's famous diamond district, the oldest (established 1851) and one of the largest in the nation. A number of these shops have been owned and operated by generations of the same family for more than a century. Many of the jewelers are certified by the Gemological Institute of America (GIA). Shops along the row are generally open 7 days a week.

CAMPBELL & COMPANY

702 Sansom St.
Philadelphia, PA 19106
(215) 627-4996
campbelljewelers.com

There's no commissioned sales staff at this more-than-60-year-old family-owned shop—just the owners, Ed and Richard Campbell. With their design skills and goldsmiths and diamond centers working right on the premises, the Campbells have the ability to create custom, one-of-a-kind pieces.

FRANK G. SCHAFFER

Jewelry Designer/Gem Cutter/Gem Dealer
708 Sansom St., Rm. 200
Philadelphia, PA 19106
(215) 925-2591
fgsgems.com

Schaffer's shop is a treasure trove of emeralds, rubies, and other colored gemstones, many unusual, some quite rare. He cuts them himself to enhance each stone's natural beauty and value and keep prices reasonable.

Living Legends

All of the elaborate, independently owned department stores are gone—demolished or converted into offices—but we feel fortunate that Macy's has preserved the retail tradition that was begun in 1876 by Philadelphian John Wanamaker when he opened his eponymous department store that was the first in the city and one of the first in the nation. In addition to operating from the regal circa-1911 building that housed Wanamaker's until it became a Hecht's (later Macy's) in 1965, Macy's has also carried on some of the original store's most beloved symbols, such as the 2,500-pound bronze eagle in the marble-arched Grand Court ("Meet me at the Eagle" is still a familiar refrain for people seeking a rendezvous point) and the 1904 St. Louis World's Fair Pipe Organ, the largest playable instrument in the world and listed as a National Historic Landmark. Grand Court Organ concerts are performed twice a day, Mon through Sat, at the Center City Macy's (1300 Market St.; 215-241-9000; visitmacysphiladelphia.com).

And it wouldn't be the holidays in Philadelphia without the Christmas Pageant of Lights (simply referred to as "The Light Show") that, thanks to Macy's, has remained a treasured tradition for more than 50 years. This animated, music-accompanied display, which tells the stories of The Nutcracker, Frosty the Snowman, and The Magic Christmas Tree, features almost 100,000 colored LED lights. Macy's has also restored another decades-old Philly holiday attraction, the "Dickens Village," a 6,000-square-foot, 26-scene animated walk-through depiction of the Christmas classic.

RIA SMITH DESIGNS
709 Sansom St., 2nd Fl.
Philadelphia, PA 19106
(215) 574-8900
riasmithdesigns.com

Her background as a painter, sculptor, and graphic artist gives Ria Smith the skills to translate her unique artistic point of view into wearable silver and gold art, including her signature Fire and Water reversible heart design. At her Jewelers Row studio and showroom, Smith also conducts open-to-the-public, 1-day classes in basic jewelry-making ($75 to $100).

SAFIAN & RUDOLPH JEWELERS
701 Sansom St. (corner of 7th & Sansom)
Philadelphia, PA 19106
(215) 627-1834
phillydiamonds.com

Family-owned and operated for more than half a century, Safian & Rudolph has more than 1,000 engagement ring mountings, wedding bands, and anniversary rings in stock in designs from traditional to contemporary in platinum, white, or yellow gold. Prices are discounted at 30 percent to 50 percent off retail.

STEVEN SINGER JEWELERS
739 Walnut St.
Philadelphia, PA 19106
(215) 627-3242
ihatestevensinger.com

This is probably the most fun place to buy a diamond. Sales personnel don't push; they prefer to offer information about a potentially intimidating purchase in a non-intimidating way.

SYDNEY ROSEN COMPANY
712–714 Sansom St.
Philadelphia, PA 19106
(215) 922-3500
sydneyrosen.com

More than 60 years ago, Sydney Rosen launched his business from a tiny 2nd-floor shop (furnished with just a desk and a safe) on Jewelers Row. Today his sons, David and Steven, both GIA-graduate gemologists, operate what they describe as "the area's largest diamond and fine jewelry showroom." If it isn't, there aren't many that are larger.

i Prior to becoming a diamond destination, the area now known as "Jewelers Row" was the place where builder and architect Thomas Carstairs constructed 22 look-alike dwellings between 1799 and 1820 to provide affordable housing. Then dubbed "Carstairs Row," these buildings were the first row homes in the country.

Rittenhouse Row

(Between the Avenue of the Arts and 22nd Street from Market to Pine; rittenhouserow .org)

Home Furnishings
DWR (DESIGN WITHIN REACH) STUDIO
1710 Walnut St.
Philadelphia, PA 19103
(215) 735-3195
dwr.com

You may not have access to designer showroom furnishings, but they do.

MANOR HOME
210 S. 17th St.
Philadelphia, PA 19103
(215) 732-1030
manorhg.com

This shop offers an unparallel selection of crystal, china, and flatware from around the world and a gorgeous collection of Judaica. Believe it or not, you can also find a nice selection of lovely gifts for under $100.

Children's Apparel & Accessories
CHILDREN'S BOUTIQUE
1702 Walnut St.
Philadelphia, PA 19103
(215) 732-2661
echildrensboutique.com

European and domestic designer clothing lines (think Ralph Lauren, Little Marc Jacobs, Juicy Couture) for children of all ages, design-your-own sweaters, even a $600 ride-on race car.

Men's Apparel & Accessories
✳BOYDS
1818 Chestnut St.
Philadelphia, PA 19103
(215) 564-9000
boydsphila.com

Always one of Philadelphia's premier menswear stores featuring more than 70 top designers from around the world, Boyds now offers fashion-forward lines for women.

HENRY A. DAVIDSEN MASTER TAILORS & IMAGE CONSULTANTS
1701 Spruce St., 2nd Fl.
Philadelphia, PA 19103
(215) 253-5905
henrydavidsen.com

Custom-made professional and casual menswear at affordable prices. They'll also assess and accessorize your current wardrobe and handle weekly maintenance such as dry cleaning and repair.

Women's Apparel & Accessories
MAXSTUDIO
1616 Walnut St.
Philadelphia, PA 19103
(215) 545-6003
maxstudio.com

Gwyneth Paltrow, Katie Holmes, and Angelina Jolie have been seen sporting the dramatic, sometimes even eye-popping footwear from this fashion-forward designer.

SOPHY CURSON
19th and Sansom Streets
Philadelphia, PA 19104
(215) 567-4662
sophycurson.com

Although this elite shop has been a Philly landmark since 1929, the designer day, cruise, and evening styles feature the cream of contemporary from the understated to the avant-garde.

SOUTH STREET

(Most people gravitate in the area called the South Street/Head House District that runs between 2nd and 4th Streets between Front and 10th Streets; southstreet.com)

The people-watching is almost as much fun as popping in and out of this eclectic (to put it mildly) collection of more than 300 shops and restaurants. If you're a night owl, many of them are open until midnight. But be sure to check their opening times; some don't greet visitors until noon.

Chestnut Hill

(chestnuthillpa.com)

Named a 2010 "Distinctive Destination" by the National Trust for Historical Preservation and one of the "Top Urban Enclaves" by Forbes.com, this historic community, tucked away in the northwest corner of Philadelphia, is easily accessible from the city by car, train, or bus. It is best known for its carefully preserved 19th- and early-20th-century architecture, flower-bedecked sidewalks, and tree-shaded, cobblestoned Germantown Avenue, which is lined for blocks by more than 125 boutique shops and eateries (don't be alarmed if you see a chain store or two—this neighborhood is vehemently mom-and-pop). Be sure to pop into the courtyards "hidden" behind the storefronts— there are treasures to be found.

✳BAKER STREET BREAD COMPANY
8009 Germantown Ave.
Philadelphia (Chestnut Hill), PA 19118
(215) 248-2500
bakerstreetbread.com

I absolutely crave the multigrain, rosemary focaccia, and apricot pistachio that are handmade daily at this award-winning bakery.

⊕ Close-up

✳South Street's "Magic Gardens"

1022 AND 1024 SOUTH ST.

In the 1960s, Philadelphia-born mosaic artist Isaiah Zagar and his wife, Julia, decided to settle down on South Street. Distressed by the destitute condition of many of the buildings in the neighborhood, they began to purchase and renovate them. As he had done in other parts of the world—and to great critical and public acclaim—Isaiah began to work his magic on the inside and outside walls of many of these buildings, creating works of art inspired by his family, their travels, the community, and current events that deeply affected him.

Zagar's "Magic Gardens" was a mammoth undertaking, an almost half-a-city-block-long indoor gallery and outdoor labyrinth, fully covered in colorful mosaic images made primarily from pieces of "found" objects including shards of ceramic, glass bottles, and mirrors. Philadelphia's Magic Gardens is open all year for self-guided or guided tours. You can download the map of Zagar's 55 South Philadelphia murals at phillymagicgardens.org.

Make sure you leave plenty of time to experience the one-of-a-kind phenomenon that is Philly's South Street. After all, where else can you buy occult oils, powders, sachets, rituals, and floor washes to change your luck and life; get a tattoo and/or body piercing (ears are only the beginning); find a custom-made stained-glass window; and cop a kosher cupcake all on the same street? For the exact locations where you can find these and other surprising shops, the following are my suggestions for getting a taste of the area that has been celebrated in legend and song as "the hippest street in town."

Crash Bang Boom
528 S. 4th St.
Philadelphia, PA 19147
(215) 928-1123
crashbangboomonline.com
For years, the building with the gigantic ants crawling all over it was called "Zipperhead." Under its new name, it still caters to the punk culture with everything from apparel to accessories (handbags decorated in skulls or hearses?), even special effects hair dye. You don't want to miss this extreme side of South Street culture.

Eyes Gallery

402 South St.
Philadelphia, PA 19147
(215) 925-0193
eyesgallery.com

Julia Zagar's shop is as interesting on the inside as it is on the outside. Look for decorative and wearable art: one-of-a-kind handmade furniture, jewelry, folk art, ceramics, and masks from around the world. There is also an entire gallery of decor and wearable items dedicated to Mexican artist Frida Kahlo.

Harry's Occult Shop

1238 South St.
Philadelphia, PA 19147
(215) 735-8262
harrysoccultshopinc.com

Ask for a free consultation to guide you through any ritual or get a reading to reveal your needs ($15–$25—walk-ins are welcome). After your how-to, you can purchase the items—from quartz crystals to crystal balls, talismans to tarot cards—to carry out the instructions at home.

Homemade Goodies by Roz

510 S. 5th St.
Philadelphia, PA 19147
(215) 592-9616

Roz Bratt makes kosher, nondairy cupcakes (10 varieties) as well as traditional challah, muffins, scones, cakes, and cookies.

Tiffany City (two locations)

343 South St.   623 S. 3rd St.
Philadelphia, PA 19147   Philadelphia, PA 19147
(267) 408-5688 for both locations
tiffanycitylighting.com

Visit both shops to find a truly impressive (and affordable) collection of reproductions of the spectacular stained-glass designs of Louis Comfort Tiffany and original works by contemporary designers. You can also have stained-glass windows custom-made for your home.

EL QUETZAL
8427 Germantown Ave.
Philadelphia, PA 19118
(215) 247-6588
el-quetzal.com

This gallery-like shop reflects an artist's perspective on retail with beautiful displays of clothing, jewelry, and home decor.

HERBIARY
7721 Germantown Ave.
Philadelphia, PA 19118
(215) 247-2110
theapothecarygarden.com

Like the old apothecary gardens of colonial times, this shop has medicinal gardens growing both in front of and behind the building. Inside you'll find a wide selection of body- and soul-soothing herbal and floral extracts, essential and infused oils, teas, and other natural remedies. Check the website for the schedule of classes and workshops.

MONKEY BUSINESS
8624B Germantown Ave.
Philadelphia, PA 19118
(215) 248-1835
greentreecommunityhealth.org

Don't look for ambience; it's more basement-like than boutique. But don't waste time judging, just dive in and snag yourself some truly upscale wearables. Open since 1955 and staffed by volunteers, the store benefits the Green Tree Community Health Foundation.

THE NICHOLS BERG GALLERY
8611 Germantown Ave.
Philadelphia, PA 19118
(206) 380-4070
nicholsbergart.com

Having outgrown their home studio, print artists Scott Nichols and Steve Berg took this spot in Chestnut Hill to give themselves and local emerging artists a space in which to work and display their art.

O'DOODLES
8335 Germantown Ave.
Philadelphia, PA 19118
(215) 247-7405
odoodles.com

No matter how old you are, you can't walk by this window without smiling and being drawn inside to immerse yourself in a time before kids had to plug in to get their imaginations going. The selection of board games is enormous.

✳WINDFALL GALLERY
7944 Germantown Ave.
Philadelphia, PA 19118
(215) 247-6303
windfallgallery.com

Need a great gift that will make you feel as warm and fuzzy buying as giving? You'll find a collection of handmade jewelry, folk art, home decor, and other items made by more than 250 artisans in the US, Canada, and Fair Trade organizations around the world.

Manayunk

Manayunk's Main Street could well be called Philadelphia's "Home Furnishings" Row because, with more than 20 stores dedicated to furniture and decor, the town bills itself as having "the largest concentration of furniture stores on one street in the entire East Coast." But you deserve some decking out, too. So you should also visit this National Historic District's over 50 boutiques and, when you need a nutrition break, one of its 30 eateries from casual to upscale.

i Main Street, Manayunk, is the only street named Main in the city of Philadelphia.

ARTESANO
4446 Cresson St.
Philadelphia, PA 19127
(866) 939-4766
artesanoironworks.com
Custom, hand-forged iron architectural pieces, including doors, balconies, gates, stair rails and outdoor railings, lighting; hardware including door knockers and fireplace screens; sculptures; and other art are displayed in an early-20th-century warehouse. (Cresson Street is a block off and parallel to Main.)

CARSON WOOD FURNISHINGS
3791 Main St.
Philadelphia, PA 19127
(215) 482-6701
carsonwood.com
Great prices on imported teak furniture for indoor and outdoors.

D.I.G.S.
4319 Main St. (corner of Main and Cotton Streets)
Philadelphia, PA 19127
(215) 482-0315
Even though many of the furnishings and decorative items are on consignment, they definitely aren't toss-aways from Grandma's attic. This shop was created by an award-winning professional interior designer for her peers (thus the name, an acronym for Designer Inventory Goods Store) as well as for the public.

GREAT ESTATE CONSIGNMENT
701 County Line Rd.
Bryn Mawr, PA 19010
(484) 380-2174
greatestateconsignmentshop.com
This is the place to come for upscale home furnishings and decorative pieces.

GREENE STREET CONSIGNMENT SHOP
848 W. Lancaster Ave.
Bryn Mawr, PA 19010
(610) 519-0878
greenestreetconsignment.com
Now you can afford the brands you love. There are also locations in Center City (South Street), Manayunk, Chestnut Hill, and West Chester.

✳MARIA FE'S, MOMMIE'S & AT HOME
117 E. King St.
Malvern, PA 19355
(610) 407-4570 for Maria Fe's, (610) 407-4545 for Mommies & At Home
Much of the merchandise still has its original tags on, so you can see how much you're saving on top-of-the-line fashions for women, kids, and the entire home.

WAYNE WOMEN'S EXCHANGE
185 E. Lancaster Ave.
Wayne, PA 19087
(610) 688-1431
The handcrafted children's toys and clothing are worth a visit to this nonprofit shop.

BUCKS COUNTY

New Hope

From an industrial mill town of a century ago, the little village of New Hope, located in Bucks County about an hour north of Center City Philadelphia, became a focal point and inspiration for a group of Impressionist painters that were part of the "New Hope School of Art." Today, the area remains a vibrant center for artists who specialize in media from visual to wearable. They work and sell their wares in early-20th-century farmhouses, barns, and paper and gristmills that have been converted into studios and shops. New Hope is an easily negotiable town with only four major streets—Main Street, North and South; Bridge Street; Ferry Street; and Mechanic Street. Plus there are countless side streets and alleyways tucked back from the busy thoroughfares. New Hope's economy is largely based on tourism, so you can be sure you'll find plenty to see and do. In this section, I'll be concentrating on the shopping opportunities. But in other chapters you'll read more about the historical, performing arts, outdoor recreational, and just plain fun attractions you'll find here. For your convenience, I have categorized the stores by their street and numerical locations.

i Every Tuesday and Saturday in New Hope, Bucks County's largest and oldest market comes to life, with hundreds of local vendors selling everything from produce to pajamas, baby clothes to bonsai trees, and gourmet food items to golf clubs. Begun as a produce auction in 1860, the 30-acre outdoor Rice's Market (6326 Greenhill Rd.; 215-297-5993; ricesmarket.com) now draws thousands of people, both locals and visitors, each week for its vast and varied selection and bargain prices.

BUCKS COUNTY GALLERY OF FINE ART
77 W. Bridge St.
New Hope, PA 18938
(215) 862-5272
buckscountygalleryart.com
Bronze, wood, and steel original, limited-edition, and commissioned sculptures for indoor and outdoor display as well as oil, water, and pastel paintings.

COCKAMAMIES
6 W. Bridge St.
New Hope, PA 18938
(215) 862-5454
cockamamies.com
Herb Millman and John Dwyer are experts in art deco; they are authors of two books on the subject and appear as resident lighting experts for QVC. In their shop you'll find hand-picked examples of the finest in furniture, lighting, and other home decor and accessory items in this distinctive artistic style.

GARGOYLES
15 N. Main St.
New Hope, PA 18938
(888) GARGOYLE (427-4695)
Really. They're really cool, and everybody should have at least one.

✳LOVE SAVES THE DAY
1 S. Main St. (corner of Bridge and Main)
New Hope, PA 18938
(215) 862-1399
Vintage doesn't even begin to describe the merchandise that ranges from old prom gowns to Beatles memorabilia, KISS masks to superhero collectibles. Don't miss this shop!

Close-up

Door to Door Delights

Peddler's Village was built as a retail destination almost 50 years ago, but it's not a mall. It really is a 42-acre village with old-fashioned brick pathways that lead you past the beautifully decorated windows of 70 specialty shops (and 6 restaurants) that sell, as you would expect, family apparel, jewelry, and home decor items. But what you might not expect are the ones that sell kaleidoscopes, over 400 hot sauces, and Black Forest cuckoo clocks.

Peddler's Village hosts 11 festivals and special events throughout the year, including the January through April Quilt Competition; late April/early May Strawberry Festival; June Fine Art and Contemporary Crafts Show; July Celebration of Freedom; September/October Scarecrow Competition and Festival; November Apple Festival, Gingerbread House Competition and Display (until January 1) and Grand Illumination; December Christmas Festival.

PLEASE NOTE: Your GPS may tell you that the shops in Peddler's Village (peddlers village.com) are in New Hope, but they're really in Lahaska located about 4.5 miles west of New Hope (go west on West Bridge Street/PA 179 then follow 179 W, turn left onto US 202 S, and continue for about 3.5 miles).

NEW HOPE LEATHER
7 N. Main St.
New Hope, PA 18938
(215) 862-4455
newhopeleather.com

If I start to name the brands of shoes they sell here, there won't be any room to list any other fun places to shop. All I'll say is that if you're looking for a brand, it's here. That goes for bags, too, including adorable hand-painted ones by Anuschka.

THREE CRANES GALLERY
82 S. Main St.
New Hope, PA 18938
(215) 862-5626

Actually 2 galleries featuring more than 25 local and international artists. The first offers unusual global home decor items including furniture, hand-carved wooden dragons, and tapestries. The second offers wearable art. Three Cranes also specializes in Tibetan singing bowls, statues, ritual items, and all kinds of other not-found-everywhere stuff.

CHESTER COUNTY

A TASTE OF OLIVE
26 S. High St.
West Chester, PA 19382
(610) 429-0292
atasteofolive.com

The walls are lined with stainless-steel drums called fusti, which are filled with extra-virgin olive oils and balsamic vinegars from small farmers and artisans from around the world. Taste one or taste them all, choose the ones you like, and they'll fill, cork, and seal a bottle for you.

i Whether or not you're a collector of Byers' Choice famous hand-made caroling collectible figurines, you must visit its headquarters' factory and retail store (4355 County Line Rd., Chalfont, PA 18914; 215-822-6700; byers choice.com). You'll stroll a meticulously designed life-size London Street, its shop windows filled with Christmas-themed tableaux year-round, including a collection of nativities from around the world. Also, observe the artists at work from a perch above the factory floor.

✳THE MUSHROOM CAP
114 W. State St.
Kennett Square, PA 19348
(610) 444-8484
themushroomcap.com

You're in the mushroom capital of the world, so what are you going to bring back as souvenirs for your friends? That's right ... a bottle of mushroom "potpourri," fragrant with horse and poultry manure mixed with straw, hay, and other cool stuff. It's the medium that mushrooms grow in, and you really can buy it. Better yet, pick up some white, shiitake, portobello, maitake, or oyster mushrooms fresh from this family farm or pickled, made into pasta sauce, or dried into highly snackable chips. Make sure you visit the exhibit that will show you how these fabulous fungi are formed.

THOMAS MACALUSO RARE AND FINE BOOKS
130 S. Union St.
Kennett Square, PA 19348
(610) 444-1063

If you're looking for a rare title, you'll find more than 20,000 covering all subjects, some for as cheap as $20. The shop also carries 5,000 antiquarian engraved or lithographed maps and prints, autographs, and other historic items.

MONTGOMERY COUNTY

✳KING OF PRUSSIA MALL
160 N. Gulph Rd.
King of Prussia, PA 19406
(610) 265-5727
kingofprussiamall.com

Bloomingdales, Lord & Taylor, Nordstrom, Neiman Marcus . . . with an all-star lineup of anchors like this, more than 400 shops, boutiques, and restaurants, and "more pure retail space than any attraction in America," the word "mall" doesn't come close to adequately describing this singular shopping experience. Other high-profile residents include Gucci, Hermès, Coach, and Burberry. But you don't have to be Paris Hilton to be able to shop here. There are also plenty of moderately priced mall favorites for us regular folks. For mid-retail refueling, you'll find a slew of eateries inside and on the outside perimeter of the mall. Among them are Cheesecake Factory, Legal Sea Foods, Maggiano's Little Italy, Morton's Steakhouse, and fast-food, snack, and coffee shops around every corner of every corridor.

i With 3 million square feet of retail space, the King of Prussia Mall is large enough to accommodate 5 of the Great Pyramids. If you walked every corridor and aisle, it would be the equivalent of walking across Manhattan.

MISCELLANEOUS SHOPPING & SERVICES

The following shops and services are listed by category, geographical, and alphabetical order.

Day Spas & Services

CENTER CITY/"BURBS

ADOLF BIECKER SPA/SALON (THREE LOCATIONS)
The Rittenhouse Hotel
210 W. Rittenhouse Sq., Third Floor
Philadelphia, PA 19103
(215) 735-6404

508 W. Lancaster Ave.
Strafford, PA 19087
(610) 687-4750

138 S. 34th St.
Philadelphia, PA 19104
(215) 418-5550
adolfbiecker.com
Give yourself the gift of a body mask, aromatherapy wrap, or Caribbean body scrub for $90 or a customized facial for $100. Packages for her include "The Energizer," consisting of Caribbean body scrub, aromatherapy massage, and customized facial; for him the "Men's Club" with steam, body, and scalp massage, manicure, haircut, and gourmet lunch—each costs $255.

BLUE MERCURY APOTHECARY & SPA (TWO LOCATIONS)
Rittenhouse Square
1707 Walnut St.
Philadelphia, PA 19103
(215) 569-3100

Suburban Square
42 St. James Place
Montgomery County
Suburban Square, Ardmore, PA 19003
(610) 642-5400
bluemercury.com
Customized facials ($65 to $220), massages ($50 to $180), and salon services plus high-end branded skin care and cosmetics.

BODY KLINIC DAY SPA
2012 Walnut St.
Philadelphia, PA 19103
(215) 563-8888
thebodyklinic.com
Custom signature facials and massages begin at $100, body wraps at $90. Get a "TBK" package including massage, facial, and manicure for only $99 or splurge on a full-day (6-hour) package including mineral salt body polish, mineral clay pack for the back, full-body massage, brunch, spa pedicure and manicure, signature facial, and eyebrow shaping for $465. Couples massage (go for the guided massage for some take-home skills) is a specialty.

DUROSS & LANGEL
1218 Locust St.
Philadelphia, PA 19107
(215) 592-SOAP
durossandlangel.com
Honest, small-batch-made products for care of hair and body. They'll custom-blend 100 percent natural body balms for head to toe

(including lips and fingertips) smoothing and soothing and body and soul healing.

RACHEL D'AMBRA SPA & SALON
10 Avenue of the Arts
Philadelphia, PA 19102
(215) 523-8000
ritzcarlton.com

Skip lunch; relax with a 50-minute Tranquility Massage ($105) or refresh and energize with a 25- or 50-minute Tachyon Cocooning ($75 to $125).

RESCUE RITTENHOUSE SPA LOUNGE
255 S. 17th St.
Philadelphia, PA 19103
(215) 772-2766
rescuerittenhousespa.com

Treat yourself to a TLC time-out whether you have only a half-hour (a Zoom Groom Facial is only $65) or a full day (a multiservice total pampering package for $270).

TERME DI AROMA
32 N. 3rd St.
Philadelphia, PA 19106
(215) 829-9769
termediaroma.com

Stop in for a quick pick-me-up chair massage ($15) or relax under healing hands for a whole hour aromatherapy massage ($80). The Plaisir Des Sens Stone Facial, which means "pleasure of the senses," combines sensory, chakra, volcanic stone, aqua jade, and color gem therapies ($135 for 1.5 hours). Multiservice packages range from $150 to $275.

DELAWARE COUNTY

AME
111 Waynewood Ave.
Wayne, PA 19087
(610) 995-2631 (AME1)
amesalonandspa.com

Pronounced ah-may, this Main Line spa offers a Toxic Meltdown treatment (beginning at $115) that may sound like a nasty tantrum but is really a dynamic duo of alpha-hydroxy body polish and aromatherapy wrap.

HARMONIA HEALING ARTS SPA
411/413 E. Lancaster Ave.
Wayne, PA 19087
(610) 688-1007
harmoniaspa.com

Where else but on the Main Line would you find pearl or gold therapy body treatments ($150)? Or take a soak fit for a queen in a Cleopatra milk bath. For a romantic getaway, go for the couples package including his and hers therapeutic massages and facials.

ANTIQUES

For many years, Philadelphia's Antique Row—spanning Spruce to Lombard, 9th to Broad, later extended to 10th and 11th Streets from Spruce to Locust Streets—was "the" place to shop for vintage treasures. Quite frankly, the row has seen better days and not all of it is quite as well kept as it used to be, but there are still a number of stalwart shopkeepers who remain, among them some who continue to operate highly reputable, esteemed, generations-old businesses. If you are planning to visit Antique Row, keep in mind that the majority of the shops don't open until 11 a.m. Not all are open every day, so check before you go.

ANTIQUE ROW

ANTIQUE DESIGN
1102 Pine St.
Philadelphia, PA 19107
(215) 629-1812
Antique stained glass and leaded windows and doors are specialties. They also do custom work and restore existing pieces.

CLASSIC ANTIQUES
922 Pine St.
Philadelphia, PA 19107
(215) 629-0211
classicant.com
Eighteenth- and 19th-century French and English antiques are the specialties here.

DEJA VU COLLECTIBLES
1038 Pine St.
Philadelphia, PA 19107
(215) 991-9895
dejavucollectibles.biz
Remember your Chatty Cathy doll . . . your My Little Pony collection . . . the Little Golden Books your parents used to read to you (or you used

to read to your kids)? They're all here as well as vintage china tea sets and doll clothes (or you can have some custom-made for your favorite friends). You can even get your doll or stuffed animal carefully cleaned and/or repaired.

i Although it is not an antiques shop, SOTA Spirit of the Artist (1022 Pine St.; 215-627-8801) is a boutique I would recommend you visit because owner Frank Burkhauser sells decorative and functional items handmade from a very select group of American crafters. Another is Show of Hands (1006 Pine St.; 215-592-4010) for one-of-a-kind and limited-edition arts and crafts by juried artisans.

M. FINKEL & DAUGHTER
936 Pine St. (corner of 10th and Pine)
Philadelphia, PA 19107
(215) 627-7797
samplings.com
Since 1947, this 2-story shop has been internationally renowned for its extensive

selection of antique samplers, needlework, and silk embroideries from the 17th through mid-19th centuries.

UHURU FURNITURE & COLLECTIBLES
1220 Spruce St.
Philadelphia, PA 19107
(215) 546-9616
apedf.org

A Fundraising Project of the African People's Education and Defense Fund, dedicated to preserving health, education, economic development, and human rights for the black community, Uhuru is a great place to find antiques from the late 1800s through the 1930s and great retro furniture and other finds from the '50s, '60s, and '70s.

Philadelphia Antiques Show

Antiques buffs from around the world have gathered each year for half a century for the 4-day spring Philadelphia Antiques Show (The Navy Yard, Philadelphia Cruise Terminal at Pier One, 5100 S. Broad St.; philaantiques.com), one of the longest-running antiques shows in the country and considered by many as the premier American antiques and decorative arts show in the country. Proceeds are donated toward patient care at Penn Medicine facilities. On the same days, another major event, The 23rd Street Armory Antiques Show (22 S. 23rd St., between Market and Chestnut Streets; barnstar.com/philfall .htm), is held. The show provides free shuttle service to the Philadelphia Antiques Show so you can experience the best of both.

PHILADELPHIA

Rittenhouse Row

CALDERWOOD GALLERY
631 N. Broad St.
Philadelphia, PA 19123
(215) 546-5357
calderwoodgallery.com

Serious collectors of early- to mid-20th-century French decorative arts will find a stunning collection of French deco, Art Nouveau, Modernist, and '40s furniture and other home decor items from the period's most respected designers.

FREEMAN'S
1808 Chestnut St.
Philadelphia, PA 19103
(215) 563-9275
freemansauction.com

At more than 30 in-house auctions each year, Freeman's sells fine American, European, and Asian furniture, art, rare books and prints, fine jewelry, and silver.

H. A. EBERHARDT & SON INC.
2010 Walnut St.
Philadelphia, PA 19103
(215) 568-4144
eberhardts.com

Originally founded in Europe prior to 1869 and moved to America in 1888, this family-owned business is described by its owners as "Philadelphia's largest antiques dealer" and "America's oldest restorers" of antique ceramic china, porcelain, crystal, glassware, metal, and art. For sales, the shop specializes in Asian and European porcelains.

NIEDERKORN SILVER
2005 Locust St.
Philadelphia, PA 19103
(215) 567-2606
niederkornsilver.com
Whether you're a serious collector or are just looking for a special gift, this shop has it.

SCHWARZ GALLERY
1806 Chestnut St.
Philadelphia, PA 19103
(215) 563-4887
schwarzgallery.com
Third-generation owner Robert D. Schwarz continues the family tradition of being a premier dealer of 19th- and 20th-century American paintings, with an emphasis on, but not limited to, Philadelphia area artists including Thomas Eakins and the Wyeths.

Center City/Old City

*ARCHITECTURAL ANTIQUES EXCHANGE
715 N. Second St.
Philadelphia, PA 19123
(215) 922-3669
architecturalantiques.com
This is truly a one-of-a-kind shop featuring architectural artifacts rescued from French and Belgian castles, churches, saloons, and pubs, primarily from the Victorian period but also a number from the late 1700s through the 1930s. The accents and furnishings also run the gamut from colonial, French, and English to Art Nouveau, art deco, and Gothic.

MODERNE GALLERY
111 N. Third St.
Philadelphia, PA 19106
(215) 923-8536
modernegallery.com
If art deco is your passion, here are 4 floors of the best of America and France. You'll also find exclusive works of Wharton Esherick, George Nakashima, and Sam Maloof.

VINTAGE INSTRUMENTS
507 S. Broad St.
Philadelphia, PA 19147
Guitar Shop Inquiries: (215) 545-1000
Violin Shop Inquiries: (215) 545-1100
vintage-instruments.com
With an inventory that ranges from vintage guitars (particularly Martin and Gibson), banjos, mandolins, and 19th-century woodwinds and brass to concertinas, lutes, and melodeons, this appropriately named store definitely lives up to its description as "America's largest and most eclectic shop specializing in old and antique musical instruments." Open weekdays only.

South Philly

SOUTH STREET ANTIQUES MARKET/ ANTIQUARIAN'S DELIGHT
615 S. 6th St.
Philadelphia, PA 19147
(215) 592-0256
You'll have fun digging for treasure at this 25-vendor indoor mall, and even if you don't strike gold, you're sure to find a bit of nostalgia to nab or a wonderful piece of kitsch to covet. It's open Wed through Sun.

i Give your credit card a good workout for a good cause at Philadelphia AIDS Thrift (514 Bainbridge St.; 215-922-3186; phillyaidsthrift.com), a nonprofit that distributes its proceeds to local organizations fighting HIV/ AIDS. The wearable, decorative, and just plain fun merchandise is wide ranging and well chosen.

Chestnut Hill

ANTIQUE GALLERY
8523 Germantown Ave.
Philadelphia, PA 19118
(215) 248-1700
antiquegal.com
You could spend hours exploring Gerald Schultz's collections of American, Asian, and European pottery and porcelain; English, French, and American sterling silver and silver plate from 18th century to present; French and Austrian art glass and . . . well, you have to visit and see it all.

PHILADELPHIA PRINT SHOP
8441 Germantown Ave.
Philadelphia, PA 19118
(215) 242-4750
philaprintshop.com
Geography and history—whether or not these were your favorite subjects in school, this shop, with its seemingly endless inventory of rare prints and maps from the 15th through early 20th centuries, will make this combination compelling.

BRANDYWINE VALLEY

Beautiful countryside, ample antiquing—if that's not a perfect day trip, I don't know what is. These antiques shops and multi-dealer markets offer merchandise that spans just about every genre and every time period.

Chadds Ford

BRANDYWINE RIVER ANTIQUES MARKET
The White Barn, 878 Baltimore Pike (Rt. 1)
Chadds Ford, PA 19317
(610) 388-2000
brandywineriverantiques.com
More than 40 dealers in a 19th-century bank barn. Make sure you go up to the 3rd-floor hayloft to check out the furniture, stained glass, and architectural items. Open Wed through Sun.

BRANDYWINE VIEW ANTIQUES
1301 Brintons Bridge Rd. & Baltimore Pike (Rt 1)
Chadds Ford, PA 19317
(610) 388-6060
brandywineview.typepad.com
The inventory in this shop is so extensive it fills 3 full floors. Open Wed through Mon.

PENNSBURY CHADDS FORD ANTIQUE MALL
640 E. Baltimore Pike
Chadds Ford, PA 19317
Upper Level: (610) 388-1620
Lower Level: (610) 388-6546
pennsburyantiquemall.com
This 2-story building houses over 100 dealers and 180 booths and display cases. Upper level open Thurs through Mon, lower level Sat and Sun.

West Chester

BALDWIN'S BOOK BARN
865 Lenape Rd.
West Chester, PA 19382
(610) 696-0816
bookbarn.com
More than 300,000 used and rare books, manuscripts, maps, and estate antiques fill this addictively "browsable" 5-story 1822 stone barn.

i The entire downtown area of West Chester is listed on the National Register of Historic Places. The Greek Revival architecture along High Street gave West Chester the nickname "Athens of the West," and within the borough limits there are over 3,000 structures dating back to the colonial period.

MONROE COLDREN & SON
723 E. Virginia Ave.
West Chester, PA 19380
(610) 692-5651
monroecoldren.com
Over 2,000 architectural elements including mantels, hearth equipment, furniture, and hardware from 1720 to 1890. Repair, restoration, and reproduction, too.

ATTRACTIONS

I could go on and on about the must-visit historical sites in Philadelphia. But then I would take up space that should be dedicated to detailing them for you. I do, however, think I should emphasize that Philly is as much—probably even more—about the present and the future as it is about the past. So make sure that in addition to your magical history tour you make time to experience the city's scientific side, its scholarly side, its whimsical side, even its silly side (there really is a museum dedicated to The Three Stooges). For this chapter, I have categorized the major attractions under the headings "Welcome Centers," "Historical Sites & Museums," "Historic Homes & Gardens," and "Science and Art Museums." All offer tours of their own properties, but for more comprehensive, multi-destination outings, there is a separate chapter on "Tours."

Price Code

You'll find many free or "donation requested" attractions within the city. For those that charge specific admission prices, the price of one adult ticket is indicated with a price code.

$..................... **Less than $10**
$$ .... **$10 to $15**
$$$ .... **$15 to $20**
$$$$ .... **$20 to $25**
$$$$$ .... **$25 and over**

DISCOUNT PACKAGES

The following sightseeing package programs provide substantial discounts on visits to many major Philly and 'burb historical, educational, and entertainment attractions. Each is easy to carry in pocket or purse.

CITY PASS PHILADELPHIA
citypass.com/philadelphia
Six attractions for 47 percent of regular ticket prices. Adults $59, kids $39. Purchase booklet in advance online or at any of the participating attractions.

PHILADELPHIA PASS
buyphiladelphiatours.com
Admission to more than 20 major tours and attractions available for 1 to 5 days. Also special discounts on theater tickets and shopping. One-day adult credit card–size pass is $60. Visit the website for purchase details.

WELCOME CENTERS

CITY HALL VISITOR CENTER
Broad & Market Streets, Room 121
Philadelphia, PA 19107
(215) 686-2840
Philly's City Hall, topped by a statue of founder William Penn, is a fine example of Second Empire architecture and well worth some tour time. The open-to-the-public observation deck offers a gorgeous panoramic view of the city. While you're at the

center, ask one of the friendly concierges for maps, brochures, or any other information you might need. You can also purchase tickets for bus tours here. Open Mon through Sun 9 a.m. to 5 p.m.

FAIRMOUNT PARK WELCOME CENTER
16th Street and JFK Boulevard at Love Park
(1599 JFK Blvd. for GPS)
Philadelphia, PA 19102
(215) 683-0247

LOVE marks the spot for this visitor center; that is, *LOVE* as in the famous giant red sculpture created by artist Robert Indiana for the US Bicentennial celebration. The center has a concierge staff that will help you get where you want to go. Open from 10 a.m. to 5 p.m. Mon through Sat and 10 a.m. to 4 p.m. Sun.

INDEPENDENCE VISITOR CENTER
6th and Market Streets
(525 Market St. for GPS)
Philadelphia, PA 19106
(215) 965-7676, (800) 537-7676
independencevisitorcenter.com

Even if you don't need any brochures, make this your first stop for up-to-the-minute information about all things Philly and the 'burbs, including current special events. Skip the lines at the city's major attractions and get your tickets here, make your hotel and dinner reservations, watch orientation films, and set up free guided tours with National Park Service rangers. The staff is multilingual to make the city easily accessible for all. The center also offers free wireless Internet. The center is open every day except for Thanksgiving and Christmas Day, 8:30 a.m. to 7 p.m. from Memorial Day to Labor Day; Apr, May, and Sept until 6 p.m.; until 5 p.m. in winter.

Leave your car at The Autopark at Independence Mall (entrances at 5th and 6th Streets between Market and Arch Streets) or the National Constitution Center at 5th and Arch Streets.

> **i** If you want to get a "firsthand" account of Colonial Philadelphia, bring the family to the Independence Visitor Center for a Saturday morning "Breakfast with Ben"—that's Benjamin Franklin, of course ($25 for adults, $15 for children 3 to 10).

PARKWAY CENTRAL TOURIST INFORMATION CENTER
19th and Vine Streets (lobby of Philadelphia Free Library)
(1901 Vine St. for GPS)
Philadelphia, PA 19103
(800) 537-7676

The concierge staff will help you get around. Also be sure to tour the library's rare book collection with volumes that date back as far as the early 15th century. Open Mon through Thurs 9 a.m. to 9 p.m.; Fri 9 a.m. to 6 p.m.; Sat 9 a.m. to 5 p.m.; and Sun 1 to 5 p.m.

SISTER CITIES PARK CAFE & VISITORS CENTER
200 N. 18th St.
Philadelphia, PA 19103
(800) 537-7676

Located in the heart of the Parkway Museum District, this is a good place to strategize your approach to the city's vast cultural offerings as you grab a bite to eat and collect any brochures, maps, and tickets for sites you want to see. Open Mon through Fri 9:30 a.m. to 5:30 p.m., Sat and Sun 9:30 a.m. to 5 p.m.

HISTORIC SITES & MUSEUMS

If a guided tour of any particular site is not available, ask about a self-guided audio tour. Audio tours allow you to enjoy the sites at your own pace and learn many "insider" details and personal observations that you won't get during an unguided walk-through.

CARPENTERS' HALL   FREE
320 Chestnut St.
Philadelphia, PA 19106
(215) 925-0167
carpentershall.org

Usually overshadowed by its neighbor, Independence Hall, this Georgian-style building, named after the Carpenters' Company, the oldest trade guild in America, also played an important role in American history. The First Continental Congress met here in 1774. To make sure that books, then so expensive that each one could cost as much as 2 months' wages, would be available to the public, Benjamin Franklin began a free lending library here. After the Revolution, Carpenters' Hall became the headquarters for the US Department of War; in 1794 it became the site of the First Bank of the US and, from 1816 to 1821, the Second Bank of the US. The Bank of Pennsylvania opened here in 1798. That same year, the bank became the site of the nation's very first bank robbery, resulting in a loss of $162,821.61. Today, visitors will see a replica of the Gilbert Stuart portrait of George Washington that hangs in the Library of Congress in Washington, DC, as well as a setup of the room as it may have looked when the First Continental Congress met there in 1774. Two banners—one that was carried in a parade in 1788 to celebrate the ratification of the Constitution, the other in

an 1832 parade celebrating the 100th anniversary of George Washington's birth—are also on display. Be sure to take a close look at the model of Carpenters' Hall that shows in great detail the building methods and equipment of the 18th century. Carpenters' Hall is open daily, except Mon (and Tues in Jan and Feb), from 10 a.m. to 4 p.m.

CITY HALL $–$$
Broad and Market Streets
Philadelphia, PA 19107
(215) 686-2840 (for Visitor Center)
philadelphiacityhallwillpennshomepage
.org

It took 30 years (1871 to 1901) to build—no wonder, because this ornate, 510-foot French Second-Empire-style structure was designed to be the largest and tallest masonry building in the US (larger than the US Capitol) and most expensive to build. Symbolically, it is situated on the original Center Square (now known as Penn Square) that was one of the 5 squares specified in William Penn's city plan. Join the guided tour (available each day at 12:30 p.m.) and take in the more than 250 sculptures, marble carvings of animals, human figures, and symbols; columns; and other ornate architectural features throughout the building. Most magnificent are the Mayor's Reception Room, City Council Chamber, and Conversation Room. Try to figure out how the "floating stairs" in the Northeast Stair Tower were constructed. Located on the 2nd, 4th, and 5th floors outside of the Mayor and City Council Chambers, works from the "Art in City Hall" program are on display. Since the program began in 1984, more than 1,600 emerging professional artists selected through juried exhibitions have been featured. Artwork by students and other nonprofessionals are also displayed.

For information, call (215) 686-9912 or check the website at phila.gov/artincityhall.

HISTORIC CHRIST CHURCH $
**2nd Street above Market
(The Burial Ground
Arch Street between 4th & 5th Streets)
Philadelphia, PA 19106
(215) 922-1695
christchurchphila.org**

George Washington and John Adams were busy guys when they were in Philadelphia. But both found the time to attend services at Christ Church. Benjamin Franklin and his wife, Deborah, were regular parishioners as was Betsy Ross. Founded in 1695, this parish was the first of the Church of England (Anglican) in Pennsylvania and the birthplace of the American Episcopal Church. The current building was constructed in 1744. Visitors are welcome to visit the church any day and worship with the congregation on Sunday. In the adjacent 2-acre burial ground lie Benjamin Franklin and four other signers of the Declaration of Independence along with other dignitaries and church members from colonial to modern times. The church is open year-round, the burial ground Mar through Dec. Guided tours of both are offered. Suggested donations for visits are $2 for adults, $1 for students.

*INDEPENDENCE HALL FREE
**Independence Mall
Chestnut Street between 5th and 6th Streets
(520 Chestnut St. for GPS)
Philadelphia, PA 19106
(215) 965-2305
nps.gov/inde**

Constructed between 1732 and 1756 as Pennsylvania's State House, this Georgian-style building was the meeting place for the Second Continental Congress from 1775 to 1783 (except for the winter of 1777–78 when Philadelphia was occupied by the British Army). In the Assembly Room, George Washington was appointed commander-in-chief of the Continental Army in 1775; the Declaration of Independence was adopted on July 4, 1776; the design of the American flag was agreed upon in 1777; the Articles of Confederation were adopted in 1781; and the US Constitution was drafted in 1787. Most of the furnishings are period pieces except for the original "rising sun" chair that was used by George Washington as he presided over the Constitutional Convention. You will need a free timed and dated ticket to tour—you can only get in with a tour—Independence Hall from March 1 through December (no tickets are required July 4, Thanksgiving, and Christmas Day). You can pick up your ticket beginning at 8:30 a.m. at the Independence Visitor Center—the first tour begins at 9 a.m., so it's a good idea to get there by 10:30 a.m., especially during peak summer season.

i From March through the end of October, families will find extra fun at Franklin Square (200 N. 6th St.; 215-629-4026; historicphiladelphia .org/day/franklin-square), one of Philadelphia's 5 original squares. There's the Liberty Carousel ($), an 18-hole Philly-themed miniature golf course ($), and 2 free playgrounds. The park also has a circa-1838 fountain and Living Flame Memorial sculpture dedicated to the city's fallen police officers and firefighters.

INDEPENDENCE NATIONAL
HISTORIC PARK   FREE

The National Park Service (NPS) preserves and oversees more than 55 acres spanning 20 city blocks within the city of Philadelphia that make up Independence National Historical Park. Included within the parameters of the park are such historically significant sites as:

*LIBERTY BELL   FREE
Entrance on Market between 5th and 6th Streets
(526 Market St. for GPS)
Independence National Historical Park, Philadelphia, PA 19106
(215) 965-2305

The bell itself is housed in a specially designed glass chamber with Independence Hall in the background. There is also a video presentation and exhibits about the Liberty Bell. Open daily 9 a.m. to 5 p.m.

> **i** You can see surviving copies of the Declaration of Independence, the Articles of Confederation, and the Constitution of the US in the "Great Essentials Exhibit" located in the West Wing of Independence Hall. Also on display is the silver inkstand that is believed to have been used during the signing of the Declaration and Constitution. Open daily 9 a.m. to 5 p.m.

*NATIONAL CONSTITUTION
CENTER $$
525 Arch St.
Philadelphia, PA 19106
(215) 409-6600
constitutioncenter.org

Here, history's so real you can feel it and live it as you take the Presidential Oath of Office

or a seat on the Supreme Court. Much more than just a dusty document assigned to the annals of history, the Constitution has remained a central part of our government and daily lives, the extent of which visitors of all ages will become aware through more than 100 multimedia, hands-on exhibits and interactive programs. Each day, the National Constitution Center hosts activities to make the learning process even more fun for younger visitors. An example might be a relay race involving state flags and their symbols, another a junior detective assignment to find the "secret signer" of the Constitution. Check the program sheet at the center for the day's activities schedule. Open Mon through Fri 9:30 a.m. to 5 p.m., Sat until 6 p.m., and Sun noon to 5 p.m. Parking is available at a paid lot on Race Street between 5th and 6th Streets, and the Independence Visitor Center.

NATIONAL MUSEUM OF AMERICAN
JEWISH HISTORY $$
101 S. Independence Mall East
Philadelphia, PA 19106
(215) 923-3811
nmajh.org

Opened in 2010, this 10,000-square-foot, 5-story structure features rare artifacts, interactive displays, and changing exhibitions chronicling the trials and achievements of Jewish people in America. Call for admission prices.

PRESIDENT'S HOUSE
COMMEMORATIVE SITE   FREE
6th & Market Streets
Philadelphia, PA 19104
(215) 597-0060
phila.gov/presidentshouse

🔍 Close-up

Billy Penn: Founder and Fashion Addict

Sitting atop City Hall since 1894 is a 37-foot-tall, 27-plus-ton bronze statue of Philadelphia founder William Penn sculpted by internationally renowned Alexander Milne Calder. Visitors can go up to the observation deck (located at about level with William Penn's shoes) to get one of the best and all-encompassing views of the city and beyond. Cost to visit the deck is $5, and a timed ticket is necessary.

For many years, there was a "gentlemen's agreement" that no building should be higher than the statue of William Penn. However, since the 1980s, there are 5 in the city that have surpassed that height.

Over the years, Billy Penn has sported some pretty spiffy duds. He wore a giant helmet to promote Fire Prevention Week, a Phillies helmet in 1993 during their drive to the World Series, a baseball helmet when Philadelphia hosted Baseball's All-Star game in 1996, and a Flyers jersey during their drive to the Stanley Cup.

If you want to get a close look at the details of the Billy Penn statue, there's a copy at Welcome Park on the east side of 2nd Street between Chestnut and Walnut Streets.

Just opened in fall 2010, this open-around-the-clock site reveals the underground remains of the home where Presidents Washington and Adams lived during their terms. Most important, through interpretive panels and videos, it recognizes the 9 enslaved people who worked for Washington here as he, ironically, led the nation in its struggle for freedom and equality.

UNITED STATES MINT   **FREE**
151 N. Independence Mall East
Philadelphia, PA 19106
(800) USA-MINT or 872-6468
usmint.gov

Although the building for America's first mint is 2 blocks away, here's where all the action is today. During your self-guided tour, you'll watch the actual coining operations from 40 feet above the factory floor. (Today this mint can produce 1 million coins in 30 minutes.) For a close-up view of the various operations, there are video/audio stations located throughout. You can also see the first coining press, used to press the nation's first coins in 1792. Take note of the 7 5-foot glass mosaics created in 1901 by Tiffany & Co. of New York. Call for seasonal hours.

HISTORIC HOMES & GARDENS

BARTRAM'S GARDEN   **FREE**
54th Street and Lindbergh Boulevard
Philadelphia, PA 19143
(215) 729-5281
bartramsgarden.org

No matter what the season, Mother Nature never disappoints at this surprising 45-acre urban oasis, America's oldest living botanical garden, preserved in all of its 18th-century glory. Only 15 minutes from Center City on the banks of the Schuylkill River, its cultivated gardens, wildflower meadows, and bird-attracting wetlands still make it a favorite retreat for Philadelphians. You can roam around on your own, but to make the most of the experience, I would suggest taking one of the guided tours ($$) of the historic gardens and/or the 18th-century handcrafted home of John Bartram.

BETSY ROSS HOUSE $
239 Arch St.
Philadelphia, PA 19106
(215) 686-1252
betsyrosshouse.org

Betsy Ross's family said she made the first flag in 1777 at the request of George Washington and company. Historians aren't so sure, but it certainly makes a heck of a story. Either way, the 2-story, over-250-year-old, 8-room brick row house where Betsy lived is one of Philly's top attractions. You can take a self-guided tour of 7 of the restored house's rooms, including an interpretation of her upholstery shop, all of which are furnished with period antiques, reproductions, and Betsy's own possessions. Open 10 a.m. to 5 p.m. daily.

EDGAR ALLAN POE NATIONAL
HISTORIC SITE FREE
532 N. 7th St. (near 7th and Spring
Garden Streets)
Philadelphia, PA 19123
(215) 597-8780
nps.gov/edal

Poe resided here for only 6 years, but during that time he penned many of his most famous works including "Murders in the Rue Morgue," "The Fall of the House of Usher," "The Pit and the Pendulum," and "The Purloined Letter." You can learn about the tragedies that inspired his macabre works on film and from Park Ranger Service guides. It's unfurnished and suitably spooky, but there's a

raven at the door and a mural on the outside wall. Open Wed to Sun 9 a.m. to 5 p.m.

i While this is a fascinating and worthwhile historical site, the Edgar Allan Poe National Historic Site is in a neighborhood that I cannot recommend as safe. If you want to visit, I would advise you to take a cab, not your car.

FAIRMOUNT PARK HOUSES $
Philadelphia, PA
(215) 763-8100
fairmountpark.org/HistoricHouses.asp

In the 18th and early 19th centuries, Philadelphia's lush Fairmount Park was an area where the affluent lived amid sprawling farms, orchards, and gardens. Two of these houses are preserved and maintained by the Philadelphia Museum of Art, 8 additional ones (plus other historic properties) by various private and civic organizations. Some of the standouts include elaborate Italianate Glen Foerd, with its stained-glass skylit art gallery; the curved rooms of Lemon Hill; the doll and toy collection at Strawberry Mansion; and the antique-filled Woodford. For a map of Fairmount Park, call (215) 988-9334.

i Travel via trolley for visits to a selection of these magnificent former residences complete with decked-out halls during December's Holiday Tours of the Historic Fairmount Park Houses ($$$, self-driven tours cost $5 per house), a major fund-raiser for house maintenance. For information and tickets call (215) 235-SHOW (7469).

PHYSICK HOUSE $
321 S. 4th St.
Philadelphia, PA 19106
(215) 925-7866
philalandmarks.org/phys.aspx

Although it was built by a Madeira wine importer in 1786, this 32-room, Federal-style building in Society Hill was home to Dr. Philip Syng Physick, known as the "Father of American Surgery," from 1815 to 1837. Renowned for his tenacious treatment of victims of Philadelphia's 1739 yellow fever epidemic and attempts to develop public preventive measures, Dr. Physick performed the first successful blood transfusion and pioneered the use of instruments including the stomach pump and operative techniques including cataract surgery. Among his famous patients were President Andrew Jackson, First Lady Dolley Madison, and Chief Justice John Marshall. Today the house is an opulent example of how the other half lived, and on the 2nd floor is Dr. Physick's collection of medical instruments. Guided tours are offered Thurs through Sat noon to 4 p.m., Sun 1 to 4 p.m.

*SHOFUSO JAPANESE HOUSE AND GARDEN $
Lansdowne and Horticultural Drives,
West Fairmount Park
Philadelphia, PA 19131
(215) 878-5097
shofuso.com

Designed in the style of a 17th-century Shoin mansion, this graceful building, presented to America by the Japanese people, was built in 1953 and moved to Philadelphia 5 years later. Inside are 20 magnificent murals; adjacent is a teahouse; and surrounding the house are tranquil gardens. Open Apr and Oct weekends 11 a.m. to 5 p.m.; May through Sept Wed through Fri 10 a.m. to 4 p.m., Sat and Sun 11 a.m. to 5 p.m.

THADDEUS KOSCIUSZKO NATIONAL MEMORIAL   FREE
3rd & Pine Streets
Philadelphia, PA
(215) 597-7130
nps.gov/thko

Learn about the life and courageous accomplishments of this Polish-born engineer-turned-freedom fighter for America and his native country through exhibits of rare artifacts and audiovisual programs in his Philadelphia home. Open Wed through Sun noon to 4 p.m.

> **i** A few blocks north on 3rd Street is the Polish American Cultural Center (308 Walnut St.; 215-922-1700; polishamericancenter.org), where you'll find a wealth of exhibits on more than 1,000 years of Polish history, customs and traditions, culture and art. Free. Open 10 a.m. to 4 p.m. Mon to Fri Jan through Apr; Mon to Sat May through Dec.

Germantown Historic Homes

The neighborhood in Germantown, located in the northwest part of the city near Chestnut Hill, has a number of former private homes of historic significance. The following are open for public tours:

CLIVEDEN OF THE NATIONAL TRUST $$
6401 Germantown Ave.
Philadelphia, PA 19144
(215) 848–1777
cliveden.org

This 6-acre estate, home of suspected British loyalist Benjamin Chew, was the site of Philadelphia's only Revolutionary War confrontation, the Battle of Germantown, between the British and the Continental Army led by George Washington. Guided tours of the house and grounds are available Apr through Dec Thurs through Sun 12:00 p.m. to 4:00 p.m.

DESHLER-MORRIS HOUSE   FREE
5442 Germantown Ave.
Philadelphia, PA 19144
(215) 596–1748
nps.gov/ner/demo

The National Park Service describes this home as the "oldest official presidential residence" and the "Germantown White House" because George Washington came to find refuge from the city's yellow fever epidemic in 1793 and held his cabinet meetings there. He came again the next summer for a family vacation. Today you'll see interactive exhibits featuring Washington, his family, and his household. Open Sunday noon to 4 p.m.

JOHNSON HOUSE $
6306 Germantown Ave.
Philadelphia, PA 19144
(215) 438–1768
johnsonhouse.org

Three generations of Quaker abolitionists lived in this home, now the city's only accessible and intact Underground Railroad stop. On exhibit are artifacts of slavery and other educational materials. Check the website for special events throughout the year. Open Thurs and Fri, 10 a.m. to 4 p.m., Sat 1 to 4 p.m.

Bucks County

*PENNSBURY MANOR $
400 Pennsbury Memorial Rd.
Morrisville, PA 19067
(215) 946-0400
pennsburymanor.org

William Penn was able to live in his dream home, a 3-story brick manor home he had built on 40 acres on the Delaware River 26 miles north of Philadelphia, for 2 years between 1699 and 1701. His wife, Hannah, gave birth to their only American child here. After Penn's death, the house fell into ruin, but between 1933 and 1942 it was reconstructed on its original foundations. Today, you can tour the home, authentically furnished with 17th-century antiques, Penn's herb garden, and several outbuildings including a woodworking shop and bake and brew house where open-hearth cooking demonstrations are held. The resident horses, oxen, sheep, peacocks, and other animals complete the idyllic ambience of Penn's "country" retreat.

Chester County

WILLIAM BRINTON 1704 HOUSE $
21 Oakland Rd.
West Chester, PA 19382
(610) 399-0913
brintonfamily.org

This stone, medieval English-style home, built by a Quaker (an ancestor of President Richard Nixon), has many interesting features including original flooring, leaded casement windows, indoor bake oven, and a colonial herb garden. Open Sat and Sun May through Oct. 1 to 5 p.m.

HISTORIC SITES

FORT MIFFLIN ON THE DELAWARE $
Fort Mifflin and Hog Island Roads
Philadelphia, PA
(215) 685-4167
fortmifflin.us

Originally built by the British in 1771, Fort Mifflin earned a number of distinctions over

🔍 Close-up

Boathouse Row

Every night looks like Christmas when you're riding on Kelly Drive past the 12 architecturally distinctive houses that make up Philadelphia's Boathouse Row. That's because the buildings, located just northwest of the Philadelphia Museum of Art, are outlined year-round in lights (usually white, but able to change color to suit a season or a sports team's win), and their glow as they reflect on the Schuylkill River is one of the most famous of the city's sights. Actually, 10 of these 100- to 150-year-old National Register of Historic Places–listed buildings belong to rowing club members of the Schuylkill Navy. Formed in 1858, it's the oldest amateur athletic governing body in America.

All but one of the boathouses are private except for Lloyd Hall, #1, which is used as a community recreation center. In a shed right next to Lloyd Hall, you can rent bicycles on weekends. Kelly Drive is a super-popular place for biking, walking, jogging, and inline skating. You might also catch some of the local college rowing teams practicing on the river. In May, the Dad Vail Regatta, the largest collegiate event of its kind in the nation, draws rowers from more than 100 educational institutions throughout the US and Canada.

For a gorgeous view of the river and the Row (and of the sunset), consider having a meal at the Water Works Restaurant and Lounge (640 Water Works Dr.; 215-236-9000; thewaterworksrestaurant.com), housed in the magnificent early-19th-century site of one of America's first municipal water delivery systems. Lunches and dinners are pricey, but it is a dining site with exceptional ambience and historic value. Information: Between Kelly Drive and the Schuylkill River; boathouserow.org

its more than 180 years of active service. In 1777 it was the site of an unrelenting 5-week battle, the largest bombardment North America has ever seen, earning it the titles "Valiant Defender of the Delaware" and the "Fort That Saved America." Today you'll see 14 structures from 1778 to 1875. Events throughout the year include battle reenactments from the Revolution through World War II. A wildly popular event is called "Sleep with the Ghosts," with lectures and hunts for haunters. Open Wed through Sun Apr to mid-Dec 10 a.m. to 4 p.m. Costumed guides are available most weekends.

MASONIC TEMPLE $
1 N. Broad St.
Philadelphia, PA 19107
(215) 988-1917
pagrandlodge.org

This circa-1868 headquarters of the Fraternal Order of Freemasons, of which George Washington and Ben Franklin were members, is a must-see for students of historic architectural styles. Guided tours take visitors through 7 grand, elaborately furnished halls, each representing a different style: Corinthian, Ionic, Italian Renaissance, Norman, Gothic, Oriental, and Egyptian. Tours are offered Tues through Sat, but call first because they are suspended if a Masonic function is scheduled.

ℹ️ At Penn's Landing (Columbus Boulevard at Market Street; 215-238-0280; gazela.org) you can see the 1883 wooden *Barkentine Gazela* (née *Gazela Primeiro*) and the lighter *Barge Poplar,* both owned by the Philadelphia Ship Preservation Guild. Also docked there is the 1902 iron tugboat *Jupiter.*

PHILADELPHIA HOLOCAUST MEMORIAL   FREE
17th and Benjamin Franklin Parkway
Philadelphia, PA 19103
Erected in 1964, this moving memorial to the victims of Hitler's Holocaust was built by architect Nathan Rapoport, who also designed the Memorial to the Warsaw Ghetto Uprising in Poland and one at Yad VaShem in Jerusalem.

PHILADELPHIA VIETNAM VETERANS MEMORIAL   FREE
Front and Spruce Streets
Philadelphia, PA 19147
pvvm.org
Dedicated in 1987, this granite memorial featuring 2 walls—one inscribed with the names of the 646 Philadelphians who gave their lives during the Vietnam War, the other scenes from the war itself—is a place for families of veterans and the general public to remember and pay tribute.

SPECIALTY MUSEUMS

AFRICAN AMERICAN MUSEUM IN PHILADELPHIA $$
701 Arch St.
Philadelphia, PA 19106
(215) 574-0380
aampmuseum.org
Opened in 1976, this museum features 4 galleries filled with exhibits exploring the history, politics, culture, and achievements of African Americans in and beyond Philadelphia through everything from personal possessions to personal journals, photographs to paintings and sculptures. Open Wed to Sat 10 a.m. to 5 p.m., Sun noon to 5 p.m. Open on Martin Luther King Day with related programs.

EASTERN STATE PENITENTIARY $$
22nd Street and Fairmount Avenue
Philadelphia, PA 19130
(215) 236-3300
easternstate.org
It's creepy, not quite kooky, mysterious, and spooky . . . very spooky. Mob boss Al Capone slept here for 8 months, bank robber "Slick Willie" Sutton for 11 years. Now this National Historic Landmark, which housed bad guys for 142 years, is a crumbling chamber of horrors that offers tours year-round, but particularly during Halloween when it becomes, according to AOL, "the #1 Haunted House in America." On Bastille Day, a local restaurateur dressed as Marie Antoinette stands on the walls and tosses Tastykakes (Philly's fave packaged cakes) to the masses below. Open every day 10 a.m. to 5 p.m.

Elfreth's Alley, America's First Street

Between 1728 and 1836, a block-long row of Georgian and Federal-style houses were built in a cobblestone-paved alleyway in Old City Philadelphia. Today, 32 of those houses remain, and you can take guided or self-guided tours along Elfreth's Alley, the nation's oldest residential street and one of the last intact early American streetscapes. Once home to an ethnically diverse population of artisans and craftsmen, the majority of the buildings are still the private homes of families who have lived there for more than 3 centuries. Only the gift shop in house number 124 and the restored and furnished residence that serves as the street's museum in number 126 are open to the public except on special event days such as the "June Fete Day" and December "Deck the Alley" celebrations, when some of the residents welcome touring visitors. Be sure to pick up one of the free cell phone tours for a full historical perspective of this unique community. Information: 2nd Street between Race and Arch Streets; (215) 574-0560; elfrethsalley.org.

INDEPENDENCE SEAPORT MUSEUM $$
Penn's Landing
211 S. Columbus Blvd. and Walnut Street
Philadelphia, PA 19106
(215) 925-5439
phillyseaport.org
If you (or your child) have ever wondered how a boat floats, the hands-on exhibits here will help you learn the answer. You'll also have the chance to unload cargo with a miniature crane, experience the cramped conditions immigrants in steerage had to endure to get to America, watch wooden ships being built and restored in the boat shop, and tour 2 historic ships—the *Olympia*, Admiral Dewey's Spanish-American War flagship and the nation's oldest floating (1892) steel warship as well as the World War II submarine *Becuna*—birthed in the adjacent marina. Every Sunday, instead of the regular admission price you may "Pay What You Wish."

MUMMERS MUSEUM $
1100 S. 2nd St.
(2nd Street and Washington Avenue)
Philadelphia, PA 19147
(215) 336-3050
mummersmuseum.com
If you can't be here on New Year's Day to see the fancily feathered string bands do their annual march through the downtown city streets, as they have since the turn of the 20th century, be sure to visit this homage to ostentation and celebration of the strut. Open Oct through Apr Wed to Sat 9:30 a.m. to 4:30 p.m.; May through Sept Wed to Sat 9:30 a.m. to 4:30 p.m. But if you can, visit on a Thurs evening at 8 p.m. from May through Sept for a free outdoor string band concert and Mummers Strut dance lesson.

✳MÜTTER MUSEUM $$
19 S. 22nd St.
Philadelphia, PA 19103
(215) 563-3737
You're going to be either riveted or revolted by the more than 20,000 anatomical anomalies

that include a jaw tumor from President Grover Cleveland, the largest colon on record, the tallest skeleton in North America, and the connected livers from conjoined twins Chang and Eng. This museum was founded to educate future doctors about anatomy and human medical anomalies—so don't say I didn't warn you. Open daily 10 a.m. to 5 p.m.

NATIONAL LIBERTY MUSEUM $
321 Chestnut St.
Philadelphia, PA 19106
(215) 925-2800
libertymuseum.org

In addition to tributes to more than 2,000 heroes past and present from every walk of life, this museum depicts the "beauty and fragility of freedom" with one of the world's largest collections of contemporary glass sculptures including the 21-foot-high *Flame of Liberty* by Dale Chihuly. Open Tue to Sat 10 a.m. to 5 p.m., Sun noon to 6 p.m.

PENN MUSEUM $$
University of Pennsylvania Museum of Archaeology and Anthropology
3260 South St.
Philadelphia, PA 19104
(215) 898-4000
penn.museum

The history of humans is explored through 3 floors filled with nearly 1 million objects and artifacts from ancient Egypt, Mesopotamia, the Bible Lands, Mesoamerica, Asia, the Mediterranean world, the Americas, Africa, and Polynesia. This museum is a true gem. Open Tues 10 a.m. to 5 p.m., Wed 10 a.m. to 8 p.m., and Thurs through Sun 10 a.m. to 5 p.m.

PHILADELPHIA DOLL MUSEUM $
2253 N. Broad St.
Philadelphia, PA 19132
(215) 787-0220
philadollmuseum.com

The only known museum in the US that presents black dolls (more than 300 of them) as a reflection of life, culture, and perception throughout history. Open Thurs to Sat 10 a.m. to 4 p.m., Sun noon to 4 p.m.

PHILADELPHIA FOLKLORE PROJECT   FREE
735 S. 50th St.
Philadelphia, PA 19143
(215) 726-1106
folkloreproject.org

Over the past 20 years, PFP has been dedicated to researching the histories, experiences, and traditions of "ordinary" local people and sharing them with the community at large through exhibitions, concerts, and workshops at its galleries as well as on the road. Open Tues and Thurs 10 a.m. to 6 p.m. Sept through June.

Bucks County

MERCER MUSEUM AND FONTHILL MUSEUM $$
84 S. Pine St.
Doylestown, PA 18901
(215) 345-0210
mercermuseum.org

When you see the magnificent concrete castle, you'll know you've come to the right place to visit 2 museums, each with its own distinctive character and collections. During his lifetime, Henry Mercer collected somewhere around 40,000 tools, furnishings, and decorative and functional decor items representing pre–Industrial Revolution professional and domestic life. Wander the 55 exhibit rooms of the Mercer Museum and you can really immerse yourself in 18th- and 19th-century America. Open Mon to Sat 10 a.m. to 5 p.m., Sunday noon to 5 p.m. Whatever you do, don't miss Fonthill Museum with its 44 rooms featuring 18 fireplaces and wall-to-wall, floor-to-ceiling decorative tiles handcrafted in Mercer's own studio. Mon to Sat 10 a.m. to 5 p.m., Sun noon to 5 p.m.

i If you love the tiles at Fonthill (and who wouldn't?), you can purchase handmade reissues of many of them for your kitchen, fireplace, floors, and walls at the Moravian Pottery & Tile Works ($), a National Historic Landmark described as a "working history" museum. If you're shopping, entry is free; if you just want to take a self-guided tour of the studio, it's a small fee. Call for hours. 130 Swamp Rd., Doylestown; (215) 345-6722. Open daily 10 a.m. to 4:45 p.m.

Chester County

AMERICAN HELICOPTER MUSEUM $$
1220 American Blvd.
West Chester, PA 19380
(610) 436-9600
helicoptermuseum.org
You can feel like a copter captain when you take the controls of one of the 35 civilian and military helicopters or experimental aircraft on display at this one-of-a-kind museum. Trace the evolution of rotary wing aircraft from the earliest to the V-22 Osprey through films and exhibits. Junior pilots are also included in the hands-on fun. Open Wed through Sat 10 a.m. to 5 p.m., opens at noon

on Sun, and by appointment only Mon and Tues.

✳LONGWOOD GARDENS $$$
Route 1
Kennett Square, PA 19348
(610) 388-1000
longwoodgardens.org
One thousand fifty acres covered with 11,000 plants in 20 indoor and 20 outdoor gardens as well as woodlands and meadows. And don't forget the dancing fountains, the more than 80-year-old 62-bell carillon, 1929 organ, or large and architecturally astounding tree houses at this oasis that was owned by DuPont chemical company heir Pierre S. du Pont from 1907 to 1954. Kids will love playing in a garden designed just for them, and the gardens host many special events throughout the year. Opening and closing times vary by season.

Delaware County

MUSEUM OF MOURNING ART FREE
2900 State Rd.
Drexel Hill, PA 19026
(610) 259-5800
arlingtoncemetery.us/museum.asp
Enter the stone gates of suburban Philly's Arlington Cemetery, walk through the graveyard, and enter the funeral home, a full-scale replica of George Washington's Mount Vernon. Inside, you'll find 200 artifacts, mostly from the 17th and 18th centuries, including a horse-drawn hearse, 70 pieces of mourning jewelry (one ring was made with Washington's hair), a 400-year-old instruction manual for getting into heaven, and the pièce de résistance, an early trip-wired gun to foil grave robbers. Open by appointment only.

🔍 Close-up

Once Upon a Nation

Head for the Historic District during the summer (Memorial Day through Labor Day) and you'll see the past come to life as Philly "residents" and other famous folk from the 18th and 19th centuries stroll the streets, inhabit historic buildings, and interact with visitors. Kids can be "recruited" to drill, march, and learn to use muskets as part of the Continental Army. Some of the specific sites are the Independence Visitor Center, Free Quaker Meeting House, Betsy Ross House, and Franklin Court.

Scattered around the Historic District in the summer are also 13 "Storytelling Benches" (each is clearly marked with a "Once Upon a Nation" sign) where historians relate tales of America's past. Each story lasts a few minutes and benches are all within an easy stroll of one another.

All of these activities are free and are also scheduled for additional times during the year. Call or check the website for details and specific locations.

Also offered are daytime "Adventure Tours" available from late May through early Sept, including a "Colonial Kids' Quest" ($$$) to find a missing copy of the Declaration of Independence; and "Turmoil & Treason: The Path to Independence" ($$$), during which "Loyalist" and "Patriot" "townspeople" debate their points of view on the independence issue. Nighttime tours include "Independence After Hours" ($$$$$), a walking tour of Historic District landmarks populated with colonial characters, an exclusive after-hours visit to Independence Hall (complete with Founding Fathers), and a 3-course dinner at Historic City Tavern. A particularly spirited excursion is the "Tippler's Tour" ($$$$$), a colonial-style pub crawl (4 historic and modern-day stops for drinks and snacks) led by a guide who will share traditional stories, drinking songs, and toasts. Nighttime tours are offered from mid-Apr through late Oct.

"Lights of Liberty" ($) is a multimedia light-and-sound show and tour that begins at the PECO Energy Liberty Center (6th and Chestnut Streets; 877-GO 2-1776) with a 12-minute, 360-degree, 3D film. Afterward, you'll take a tour with a costumed guide to see hand-painted images, some up to 5 stories high, projected onto Independence Hall and other historic buildings while you listen to stirring music and celebrity-narrated stories of America's patriots through supplied headphones. The soundtrack is available in 5 languages.

Information: (215) 629-4026; historicphiladelphia.org

Montgomery County

THE STOOGEUM   **FREE**
904 Sheble Ln., just off Bethlehem Pike
Ambler, PA 19002
(267) 468-0810
stoogeum.com

Larry Fine was a Philly-born boy, so what better place to pay homage to The Three Stooges' hilarious brand of slapstick humor with the first and only museum dedicated to this timeless trio. More than 100,000 artifacts filling 3 floors include personal effects, props and costumes, rare photos and movie posters, arcade games, and every kind of toy and novelty item imaginable—even Stooges toilet paper. No buying, just enjoy the memories. It's only open once a month, so call before you come.

SCIENCE MUSEUMS

ACADEMY OF NATURAL SCIENCES $$
1900 Benjamin Franklin Pkwy.
Philadelphia, PA 19103
(215) 299-1000
acnatsci.org

Don't let the scary teeth and claws fool you; the 42-foot-long, 7.5-ton *Tyrannosaurus rex* (one of the largest predators to ever walk the earth) stationed right inside the front door is there to welcome you to the Western Hemisphere's oldest natural sciences institution. Founded in 1812 and opened to the public 16 years later, the Academy astounds with its collection of more than 30 species of dinosaurs and other Mesozoic creatures and other related items (there's even a "Big Dig" where visitors can hunt for dino bones). You can surround yourself with live butterflies ($2 extra), observe the daily routines of over 100 live, rescued wild animals, and kids can explore the wonders of the great outdoors indoors. Open Mon to Fri 10 a.m. to 4:30 p.m., weekends and holidays 10 a.m. to 5 p.m. Consider a "Safari Overnight" sleepover with the family ($40 per person) offered at various times throughout the year.

*FRANKLIN INSTITUTE SCIENCE MUSEUM $$
222 N. 20th St.
Philadelphia, PA 19103
(215) 448-1200
fi.edu

Okay, I'm going to say it—you can't come to Philadelphia without coming to the Franklin Institute. Come on, where else can you walk through a beating heart 15,000 times bigger than the one in your body or let your kids crawl through an 8-foot-long artery? You can also explore the universe from a space research station replica and in the state-of-the-art Fels planetarium, attend a simulated air show, unravel the mystery of electricity, and learn firsthand the science behind your favorite sports. Open daily 9:30 a.m. to 5 p.m. There are also 3D and IMAX theaters (additional cost).

ANIMAL ATTRACTIONS

*ADVENTURE AQUARIUM $$$$
1 Riverside Dr.
Camden, NJ 08103
(856) 365-3300
adventureaquarium.com

You have to cross the Delaware River for this one, but this place is way too cool to let a little extra water stop you. Waiting on the other side are 200,000 square feet of sharks, hippos, penguins, seals, free-flying birds, and sea life from around the world living in their own lagoons, rain forests, and saltwater seas. You can even touch a shark. Open daily 10 a.m. to 5 p.m. For some pretty hefty fees—but a lifetime of bragging rights—you can swim with the sharks ($165), frolic with the seals ($145), or make friends with some black-footed penguins ($125). Getting there can be part of the fun if, instead of driving, you take the Riverlink Ferry from Penn's Landing (215-925-LINK; riverlinkferry.org; $7 round-trip) to the aquarium or other Camden waterfront attractions.

*PHILADELPHIA ZOO $$$
3400 W. Girard Ave.
Philadelphia, PA 19104
(215) 243-1100
philadelphiazoo.org

Whether you prefer your friends to be furry or feathered, scaly or slimy, you'll see your favorites (and make some neat new animal acquaintances) in habitats as natural as possible on the 42-acre campus at America's First Zoo. Open since 1874, this longtime landmark is home to more than 1,300 animals, many of them rare and endangered. My favorite part is the lorikeet exhibit, where you can feed the birds as they perch on your arms and shoulders. For an extra $6, you can ride a camel, pony, or swan boat, and for $15 you can take in the view 400 feet above it all in a helium balloon. Check the website for animal feeding and program times. The zoo is open daily 9:30 a.m. to 5 p.m. Mar 1 through Oct 31; 9:30 a.m. to 4 p.m. Nov 1 to Feb 28. Purchase and print out your zoo admission and parking tickets online and walk right in without waiting at the ticket booth.

TOURS

This section is devoted to those tours that are not of single sites; here we present tours of neighborhoods, clusters of attractions, and "theme" city tours. Whether you want to see the city and beyond on your own two feet, on two or four wheels, or even by Segway, there's a tour designed just for you. You will also find more tours of the Historic District under the previous chapter heading "Historic Sites & Museums." Ask about extremely economical audio and cell phone self-guided tours.

WALKING TOURS

AUDIOWALK & TOUR OF HISTORIC PHILADELPHIA
6th and Market Streets
Philadelphia, PA
(215) 965-7676
ushistory.org/audiowalk

Travel Holiday magazine called this 72-minute CD tour "the best way to see historic Philadelphia." Rental of the CD, lightweight player with earphone, and Historic District map costs $10 for one person, $14 for two. Available at Independence Visitor Center and Lights of Liberty.

GHOSTS OF PHILADELPHIA
5th and Chestnut Streets
Philadelphia, PA 19106
Candlelight Stroll and Ghost Hunting
Tour: (215) 413-1997
Haunted Trolley: (215) 413-7000
ghosttour.com

When Philly native son M. Night Shyamalan wrote the line, "I see dead people" in his famous film *The Sixth Sense*, could he have just come home from taking one of these spooky sojourns? Maybe you'll see dead people, too (or at the very least you'll hear about them) during one of these after-dark 90-minute candlelight strolls ($17), haunted trolley rides ($30), or graveyard and haunted house tours ($22)—they'll even equip you with an EMF (electromagnetic field meter) so you can successfully stalk any resident spirits.

i You can save $2 off any Ghosts of Philadelphia tour ticket price if you order your tickets online or by phone.

PRESERVATION ALLIANCE FOR GREATER PHILADELPHIA
1616 Walnut St., Ste. 1620
Philadelphia, PA 19103
(215) 546-1146
preservationalliance.com

Almost 70 different 1.5-hour walking tours ($10 adults; $8 students) are categorized by city and suburban neighborhoods, genres such as art deco and "Athens of America," historic periods, and more. Available May through Oct.

RIDING TOURS

BIG BUS TOURS
5th & Market Streets
Philadelphia, PA 19146
(215) 788-6001
bigbustours.com

Hop on and off this London-style double-decker at any of 20 different stops. Live guides provide narration.

i A partnership between Big Bus Tours and Trolley Tours allows you to use your tickets for one or the other interchangeably. Tickets for both are good for 24 hours. You can arrange a complimentary pickup at your Center City, Airport, or City Line Avenue hotel by calling (215) 389-TOUR (8687).

I GLIDE TOURS AND RENTALS
Segway Tour of Philadelphia
Philadelphia, PA 19101
(877) GLIDE-81
iglidetours.com

Once you get the hang of it (even I did and I'm a klutz), you'll want to ditch your car and glide everywhere. Your 2.5- to 3-hour daytime ($69) or 1.5-hour nighttime ($49) glide includes 30 minutes of training. As you cruise, you'll see past historic buildings, gorgeous gardens, Fairmount Park, and Boathouse Row. Tours run from Mar through Nov. You must weigh between 100 and 250 pounds to ride.

MURAL ARTS PROGRAM (MAP) TOUR
Philadelphia, PA 19130
(215) 685-0750
muralarts.org

Even as a born-and-bred Philadelphian, I was totally surprised to learn that there are more than 3,000 murals throughout the city, the largest collection of public murals in the country.

The majority of them are the result of the Mural Arts Program (MAP), which began in 1984 as an anti-graffiti initiative encouraging young, at-risk kids to redirect their energy into being creative rather than destructive. The program now involves more than 1,500 young people. You can download maps from the website if you want to take a self-guided sampling tour of the murals (particularly the "Mural Mile," which walks you past 17 in Center City), but unless you have an intimate knowledge of the city, I would suggest that you take one of the train- or trolley-transported guided tours offered by MAP. All tours begin at the LOVE Park Visitor Center at 16th Street and JFK Boulevard.

✳PHILADELPHIA TROLLEY WORKS
5th & Market Streets
Philadelphia, PA 19146
(215) 925-TOUR (8687)
phillytour.com

Hop on and off this open-air trolley at any of 21 different stops. Live guides provide narration.

76 CARRIAGE COMPANY
5th and Chestnut Streets
(215) 923-8516
Philadelphia, PA 19146
phillytour.com

Ride like royalty in a private horse-drawn carriage for a short (15 to 20 minutes, $30), medium (30 to 35 minutes, $40), or deluxe (1 hour, $80) guide-narrated tour. Free courtesy shuttle available from Center City locations.

Chester County

WEST CHESTER RAILROAD
Market Street Station
West Chester, PA 19382
(610) 430-2233
westchesterrr.net

"Museum Without Walls"

As you travel through Philly, you can't miss Robert Indiana's lipstick-red *LOVE* sculpture, Claes Oldenburg's weirdly whimsical *Clothespin* (frankly, I still don't get it), A. Thomas Schomberg's long-debated ("Is it art or is it just a movie prop?") yet iconic Rocky statue, and Auguste Rodin's incomparable *The Thinker*. But, as the old vaudevillians used to say, "You ain't seen nothin' yet!" According to the Smithsonian Institution, Philly has more outdoor sculptures than any other city in the country.

To help you find more of them, the Fairmount Park Association offers a Museum Without Walls audio program (215-546-7550; museumwithoutwallsaudio.org), an interactive experience available for free by cell phone, audio download, or on the web.

One of the wonderful things about this program is that, instead of using one overall narrator, each sculpture is described and discussed by an individual who is somehow connected with or particularly knowledgeable about it.

Take a relaxing 90-minute round-trip ride through scenic countryside and historic stations along the Chester Creek Valley from West Chester to the lovely village of Glen Mills. It's a great way to enjoy the drama of the fall foliage. Prices are usually $12.50 for adults, $10.50 for children (December's Santa Express is $20/$12.50).

MISCELLANEOUS TOURS

Chester County

HERR'S SNACK FACTORY TOUR
Route 272 and Herr Drive
Nottingham, PA 19362
(800) 637-6225
herrs.com

The recipe is simple: Watch them make potato chips, pretzels, and cheese curls; eat potato chips, pretzels, and cheese curls. What else do you need to know? One-hour tours are offered Mon through Thurs, 9 to 11 a.m. and 1 to 3 p.m.; tours are sometimes offered Fri, but there's no guarantee that production will be running. Call for reservations.

QVC STUDIO PARK
1200 Wilson Dr.
West Chester, PA 19380
(484) 701-6789
qvctours.com

Okay, armchair shopoholics, this one's for you. Take a tour of the 58,000-square-foot broadcasting facility where products are scrutinized, sampled, sold, and shipped to millions of customers across the country. You may even be able to watch a program in progress (or, if you check their website for opportunities, take a seat in the audience). Tours are available every day. And you'll certainly want to get a firsthand look at "Today's Special Value" at the on-site QVC Studio Store. Tours are available daily at 10:30 a.m., noon, 1 p.m., 2:30 p.m., and 4 p.m.

KIDSTUFF

Few cities are as overall kid-friendly as Philly—both inside and out. The majority of the attractions in this book pertain to and, in fact, welcome your young'uns. But there are some places that can only be described as kid magnets. Those are the ones listed in this chapter. You'll also find more in the State Parks, Recreational Areas & Sports chapter.

The price code pertains to the cost of 1 adult admission. Children's tickets are generally less expensive and some attractions offer family package discounts.

Price Code

$	Under $10
$$	$10 to $15
$$$	$15 to $20
$$$$	$20 to $25
$$$$$	More than $25

AMUSEMENT PARKS & PLAYGROUNDS

Bucks County

GIGGLEBERRY FAIR $$
Routes 202 and 263
Doylestown, PA 18902
(215) 794-4000
peddlersvillage.com

Give the kids a break from shopping at Peddler's Village and let them expend some of their excess energy taking on the challenges of the 3-story, 6-level Giggleberry Mountain, the region's largest indoor obstacle course. Take a spin on the antique Grand Carousel. Toddlers have their own safe play area with age-appropriate themed stations to stimulate their imaginations and learning skills. Open Sun to Thurs 10 a.m. to 6 p.m., Fri and Sat 10 a.m. to 9 p.m.

KIDS CASTLE FREE
425 Wells Rd.
Doylestown, PA 18901
(215) 348-9915
doylestownpa.org

Located in Doylestown's Central Park, right next door to the Township Building is this 8-story-high wooden play castle that was designed and named by the township's children. And you can tell by all of the fun features they included such as a huge twisty slide, friendly dragon, tree house, barnyard, rocket ship, toddler area, swings, and a children's amphitheater. Your kids will never guess that it's free.

SESAME PLACE $$$$$
100 Sesame Rd.
Langhorne, PA 19047
(215) 752-7070
sesameplace.com

All of the beloved characters are there from Elmo to Ernie, Bert to Big Bird, and Cookie Monster to the Count, and they're all integrated into the dry and wet rides, parades, and shows that make this 14-acre preschoolers' paradise a major Philadelphia area (it's 30 miles north of the city) attraction. There is plenty of fun for parents and older siblings, too, especially in the water park where you'll find the 6-story-high "Sky Splash" with its 8-foot-high Rubber Duckie and the multilevel, interactive "Count's Splash Castle."

i Every year in early spring, the Philadelphia International Children's Festival brings dancers, musicians, storytellers, jugglers, artisans, and foods from all over the world to the Annenberg Center at the University of Pennsylvania, 3680 Walnut St.; (215) 898-3900; pennpresents.org/tickets/childfest.php.

KIDS' MUSEUMS

PHILADELPHIA INSECTARIUM $
8046 Frankford Ave.
Philadelphia, PA 19136
(215) 335-9500
myinsectarium.com
Scientists estimate that for every 1 person on earth, there are at least 200 million insects. Well, here the human-to-bug ratio is a lot less unsettling, but there are plenty of crawlies—thousands of them, some alive and some mounted—on display to creep you out at the largest insect museum in the nation (the brainchild of an exterminator, of course) located less than 20 minutes northeast of Center City. The giant bugs crawling

up the outside wall welcome you to their world where hundreds of cockroaches rule the roost in a kitchen setting, bees and butterflies go about their business, and a "petting zoo" of pests show their warm and fuzzy side. You can even snack on a chocolate-covered cricket or mealworm. Yum! Open Mon through Sat 10:00 a.m. to 4 p.m.

PLEASE TOUCH MUSEUM $$
Memorial Hall, Fairmount Park
4231 Avenue of the Republic
Philadelphia, PA 19131
(215) 581-3181
pleasetouchmuseum.org
I wish I could devote an entire chapter to the wonders of this fabulous 38,000-square-foot "imaginarium," the nation's first museum dedicated to children 7 years and younger, and one of Philadelphia's true treasures. Here, kids can do anything such as plan and build a city, pilot a flying machine, play on clouds, build their own fantasy car, race a sailboat, explore a river and rain forest, slide down a rabbit hole into Wonderland, and too much more to mention. In short, if you have young children, don't miss it. Open Oct through Mar Mon to Sat 9 a.m. to 4 p.m., Sun 11 a.m. to 4 p.m.; Apr through Sept Mon to Sat 9 a.m. to 5 p.m.; Sun 11 a.m. to 5 p.m.

i Rainy days and morning hours (except on Monday) are the most crowded times at the Please Touch Museum, so if possible, try to plan your visit for a sunny afternoon.

ARTS

A rt aficionados of all kinds will find plenty to love in the Philadelphia area. From small galleries to major museums, grand theaters to intimate concert venues, the entire area in and around the city is a stage for the visual, performing, and design arts. Within 1 square mile in Old City alone, you'll find more than 40 venues (for a full listing, visit the Old City Arts Association (800-555-5191; oldcityarts.org). A great time to get the real flavor of the range and extent of Philly's art community is on "First Fridays" of each month, when galleries hold open houses, and "First Saturdays," when artists, curators, and gallery owners are available for one-on-one conversation. Both events are free.

Regular admission prices for each venue can vary widely according to performance, day, and time, so call or visit their websites for details.

PERFORMANCE VENUES

ACADEMY OF MUSIC
240 S. Broad St.
Philadelphia, PA 19102
(215) 893-1999 (tickets), (215) 790-5800 (tours)
academyofmusic.org

Don't let the humble facade fool you; "the Grand Old Lady of Locust Street" is quite the stunner inside. When built in 1857, the budget was limited, so most of it was poured into the opulent interior with its 50-foot-round, 5,000-pound crystal chandelier, elaborately carved and gilded wood sculptural accents, and murals on the ceiling. Today the 2,900-seat Academy is home to the Opera Company of Philadelphia and Pennsylvania Ballet (well, it's actually one of two homes to the ballet; the other is the Merriam Theater at the University of the Arts) and presents a wide range of other music, dance, and classical and Broadway theater productions

throughout the year. If you're here during the holiday season, don't miss *The Nutcracker*! Ticket prices vary widely.

i Still one of the shining stars of Philly's Avenue of the Arts, the Academy has hosted some of history's most illustrious performers including Marian Anderson, Anna Pavlova, Luciano Pavarotti, Sergei Rachmaninoff, and Pyotr Ilyich Tchaikovsky.

ANNENBERG CENTER FOR THE PERFORMING ARTS
3680 Walnut St.
Philadelphia, PA 19104
(215) 898-3900
pennpresents.org

Located on the campus of the University of Pennsylvania, the "center" is actually a group of 3 venues, the Harold Prince Theatre,

Zellerbach Theatre, and Irvine Auditorium, all of which are dedicated to presenting cross-cultural and cutting-edge performers, films, and speakers. Ticket prices vary widely. On Halloween, the original silent movie, *The Phantom of the Opera*, is shown in the Irvine, complete with accompaniment from its more than 85-year-old pipe organ.

ARDEN THEATRE COMPANY
40 N. 2nd St.
Philadelphia, PA 19106
(215) 922-1122
ardentheatre.org

If you found it challenging to stay awake while reading the required works of classic literature in school, you'll see them in a whole new light when they are performed on the Arden stage. The resident professional children's theater troupe is also world-class. Ticket prices vary widely.

i At Arden Theatre, intimate family- and adult-oriented "salons" offer opportunities for extensive behind-the-scenes experiences, including conversations with the performers. $25 per person.

KIMMEL CENTER FOR THE PERFORMING ARTS
260 S. Broad St.
Philadelphia, PA 19102
(215) 893-1999
kimmelcenter.org

In 2001 a star was born when this 2-venue dazzler became home to the Philadelphia Orchestra, Philadelphia Chamber Music Society, Chamber Orchestra of Philadelphia, Peter Nero and The Philly Pops, and PHILADANCO on its 2,500-seat Verizon Hall and 650-seat Perelman Theater stages. Ticket prices vary.

MANN CENTER FOR THE PERFORMING ARTS
5201 Parkside Ave.
Philadelphia, PA 19131
(215) 893-1999
manncenter.org

There's nothing like enjoying a great concert outdoors on a beautiful summer night. And this city-owned venue in Fairmount Park, which combines covered, outdoor, and lawn seating, has been the premier place to do it since 1935. To say that its annual roster features all musical genres and classical and contemporary dance is an understatement. Think the American Ballet Theatre with Mikhail Baryshnikov, Sarah Brightman, Riverdance, Yo-Yo Ma, James Taylor, CeCe Winans, Lyle Lovett, and k.d. lang. Ticket prices vary.

MERRIAM THEATER AT THE UNIVERSITY OF THE ARTS
250 S. Broad St.
Philadelphia, PA 19102
(215) 732-5446
merriam-theater.com

In addition to being one of the two principal residences of the Pennsylvania Ballet, this 1,870-seat theater has been hosting entertainment legends past, present, and future since 1918. John Barrymore played Hamlet here, Al Jolson and Sammy Davis Jr. sang, and Helen Hayes, Katharine Hepburn, and Sir Laurence Olivier owned the stage. It's also a popular stop for Broadway and comedy shows on the road.

THEATER OF THE LIVING ARTS
334 South St.
Philadelphia, PA 19147
livenation.com

Affectionately known as the TLA, this converted, single-screen movie house is a standing-room-only (capacity a little over 800) South Street staple that is frequented by the rap, heavy metal, rock, and grunge crowd. Edgy comedy acts also appear here. Prices are generally between $25 and $30.

i The TLA's big brother (2,500 to 3,000 capacity), but still standing-room-only spot, is the Electric Factory at 421 N. 7th St. between Callowhill and Spring Garden Streets; (215) 627-1332; electricfactory.info. Tickets tend to range from around $20 to $35.

Bucks County

SELLERSVILLE THEATER 1894
24 W. Temple Ave.
Sellersville, PA 18960
(215) 257-5808
st94.com
This little taste of acoustic heaven is hidden away in a tiny town in Bucks County. The decor of its bar and seating area are ornate, but the feeling is far from ostentatious. Look for a truly eclectic mix of musicians from classic rockers to up-and-comers. If I lived there, I would go every week. (The "1894" comes from a date found on a cornerstone from the days when the building was a livery stable.) Make it an entire evening and have a before-the-show dinner or after-the-show drink next door at the historic Washington House Restaurant (136 N. Main St.; 215-257-3000; washingtonhouse.net; $$).

Chester County

THE PEOPLE'S LIGHT AND THEATRE COMPANY
39 Conestoga Rd.
Malvern, PA 19355
(610) 644-3500
peopleslight.org

Resident pros present up to 9 plays per year (including 3 excellent children's productions) ranging from world premieres to contemporary topics to new twists on the classics on its Main Stage, housed in a restored 18th-century barn, or more intimate Steinbright Stage. Ticket prices vary.

Delaware County

TOWER THEATRE
69th & Ludlow
Near the 69th Street Terminal
Upper Darby, PA 19082
(215) 627-1332
philadelphia-theater.com
Built in 1927, this former Delaware County vaudeville house and movie theater has long been one of the best acoustic venues in the area. The Tower is the place where David Bowie (he later recorded one of his biggest-selling albums here) and Genesis with Peter Gabriel made their American debuts. And it hasn't missed a beat ever since.

Camden, NJ

SUSQUEHANNA BANK CENTER
1 Harbour Blvd.
Camden, NJ 08103
(856) 635-1445 or (800) 663-4643
livenation.com
It has changed names several times since its opening in 1995, but this indoor 7,000-seat concert venue/25,000-seat outdoor amphitheater located directly across the Delaware from Penn's Landing and just south of Adventure Aquarium consistently delivers the headliners you want to see and hear whether your preference is Jimmy Buffett or Black Eyed Peas, Michael Buble or Justin Bieber.

ACTING COMPANIES

BUSHFIRE THEATRE OF PERFORMING ARTS
224 S. 52nd St.
Philadelphia, PA 19139
(215) 747-9230
bushfiretheatre.org

For more than 30 years, Bushfire has been featuring the works of established and emerging African-American playwrights, actors, and directors in a small historic (circa-1909) theater. Check out the Walk of Fame in front that honors such luminaries as August Wilson, Glynn Turman, Ruby Dee, and Esther Rolle.

FREEDOM REPERTORY THEATRE
1346 N. Broad St.
Philadelphia, PA 19121
(215) 765-2793
freedomtheatre.org

Founded in 1966, Pennsylvania's oldest African-American theater has evolved from a small community theater to a nationally recognized award-winning regional (but, with fewer than 300 seats, still intimate) venue that promotes 4 productions each year ranging from classic to contemporary dramas, comedies, and musicals. Tickets generally cost between $20 and $35.

PAINTED BRIDE ART CENTER
230 Vine St.
Philadelphia, PA 19106
(215) 925-9914
paintedbride.org

For more than 40 years "the Bride" has been a place for emerging local to international artists of all kinds, particularly traditionally underrepresented populations such as women, people of color, gay and lesbian, and disabled, to find their own voices and communicate original (and often controversial) ideas. Themes span the spectrum of cultures and points of view, genres from theater to music to dance and visual art exhibits. Tickets are around $25.

SOCIETY HILL PLAYHOUSE
507 S. 8th St.
Philadelphia, PA 19147
(215) 923-0210
societyhillplayhouse.org

The building is Victorian, complete with pressed-tin walls and ceilings, but the performances are as far from stuffy as you can get. This is the place to come for new comedies, East Coast premieres, or standards such as *Nunsense*, which was originally booked for a 6-week run and ended up playing for 10 years. The very intimate downstairs Red Room is comedy cabaret at its best. Main stage tickets run from $40 to $45, Red Room from $28 to $30.

THE WILMA THEATER
265 S. Broad St.
Philadelphia, PA 19107
(215) 546-7824
wilmatheater.org

The Wilma was founded to foster conversation and controversy with productions that range from international classics to new American plays to original adaptations of classic novels. Tickets generally start at $45.

DANCE COMPANIES

PENNSYLVANIA BALLET
Academy of Music/Merriam Theater
Philadelphia, PA 19102
Tickets: (215) 893-1999
paballet.org

The resident company of 40 dancers presents 6 productions per season (including the must-see *Nutcracker*) peppering its mostly classic (a la George Balanchine) repertoire with more contemporary works choreographed by contemporary greats such as Twyla Tharp, Jerome Robbins, and Agnes de Mille. Tickets range from $30 to more than $100. Every year, the Pennsylvania Ballet performs *Shut Up and Dance* to benefit MANNA, a local organization that delivers nutritious meals to families living with AIDS, cancer, or another devastating illness.

PHILADANCO!
Kimmel Center's Perelman Theater
9 N. Preston St.
Philadelphia, PA 19104
(215) 893-1999
philadanco.org

The name of this nonprofit organization is an acronym for the Philadelphia Dance Company, and its mission is to utilize this art form to preserve and share predominantly African-American traditions. Try to catch the annual holiday performance of the signature *Xmas Philes* with its spirited twists on traditional (and some new) tunes.

Montgomery County

VOLOSHKY UKRAINIAN DANCE ENSEMBLE
700 Cedar Rd.
Jenkintown, PA 19046
(215) 663-0294
voloshky.com

Combine traditional athletic Ukrainian folk dance with the grace of ballet and you have some idea of the style this unique ensemble brings to a variety of stages, festivals, and churches around the Philadelphia area.

MUSIC

BOYER COLLEGE OF MUSIC AND DANCE
Temple University
1715 N. Broad St.
Philadelphia, PA 19102
(215) 204-7600
temple.edu/music

In addition to ticketed (around $28) performances by the Temple University Orchestra, Jazz Band, Wind Ensemble, and Sinfonia as well as headliner guest artists in the newly renovated, 1,200-seat auditorium at the Baptist Temple, the college offers free jazz monthly at the Howard Gittis Student Center.

CONCERT OPERETTA THEATER
The Academy of Vocal Arts
1920 Spruce St.
Philadelphia, PA 19103
(215) 389-0648
concertoperetta.com

Who would have thought that "the only Viennese concert operetta in the USA" would make its home in Philly? Well, Jeanette MacDonald was born here. Tickets are $25.

CURTIS INSTITUTE OF MUSIC
1726 Locust St.
Philadelphia, PA 19103
(215) 893-7902
curtis.edu

When Curtis was founded in 1924, world-famous conductor Leopold Stokowski predicted that it "will become the most important musical institution of our country, perhaps of the world." He was right. You'll find alumni from this super-selective, tuition-free school playing in and conducting many of the world's leading orchestras and singing on its most prestigious stages. (Leonard

Bernstein was one of its illustrious alumni.) From Oct through May, the Curtis Student Recital Series offers free performances Mon, Wed, and Fri night. Opera and Alumni Recital Series tickets range from $28 to $40. Twice a year, the Curtis Institute performs "Family Concerts," which introduce children between the ages of 5 and 12 to the contribution of each instrument to the overall musical experience. Adult tickets are $5, children are free.

PHILADELPHIA CHAMBER MUSIC SOCIETY

Various venues
Philadelphia, PA 19103
(215) 569-8080
philadelphiachambermusic.org

Created to make internationally acclaimed chamber music and recital artist performances affordable to a wide audience (tickets are $23 or less), this organization presents more than 60 concerts, recitals, and special programs each year.

PHILADELPHIA ORCHESTRA

Kimmel Center (Verizon Hall)
Broad and Spruce Streets
Philadelphia, PA 19102
(215) 893-1999
philorch.org

Since 1900, some of the greatest music directors in the world have led the Philadelphia Orchestra to widespread acclaim and international fame. Among those who have passed the baton over the years have been Leopold Stokowski, Eugene Ormandy, and Riccardo Muti, and the orchestra sounds better than ever in the "cello-shaped" Verizon Hall at the Kimmel Center that was designed specifically to make its music soar.

SPOKEN HAND PERCUSSION ORCHESTRA

Various venues
(215) 990-7277
spokenhand.org

If you think that drums are only good for keeping a background beat, you haven't heard the richly textured music that can be produced when percussion takes center stage to communicate and crisscross cultures with and without choral accompaniment. This is true world music.

ART MUSEUMS/GALLERIES

*BARNES FOUNDATION

2025 Benjamin Franklin Pkwy.
Philadelphia, PA 19130
(215) 278-7000
barnesfoundation.org

After 90 years on display in a Main Line mansion, the Barnes packed up its Picassos (as well as its Manets, Monets, and Van Goghs) and now makes its home on the Benjamin Franklin Parkway at 20th Street to take its place alongside Center City's other cultural treasures. Not to be upstaged by its new neighbors, the Barnes brings a vast collection of Post-Impressionist masterpieces along with an eclectic collection that includes African, ancient Egyptian, Greek art, medieval manuscripts, and sculptures. Docent-led and audio tours are available. Open Mon, Wed, Thurs, Sat, and Sun 9:30 a.m. to 6 p.m., Fri 9:30 a.m. to 10 p.m.

INSTITUTE OF CONTEMPORARY ART

118 S. 36th St.
Philadelphia, PA 19104
(215) 898-7108
icaphila.org

Andy Warhol and Robert Indiana are among the cutting-edge, controversial artists that have had their first museum shows at this dynamic showcase for contemporary art. Open Wed 11 a.m. to 8 p.m., Thurs and Fri 11 a.m. to 6 p.m., and Sat and Sun 11 a.m. to 5 p.m.

Bucks County

✳JAMES A. MICHENER ART MUSEUM
138 S. Pine St.
Doylestown, PA 18901
(215) 340-9800
michenerartmuseum.org
The focus here is on Bucks County and the artists who created the genre that became known as "Pennsylvania Impressionism" to capture the beauty and soul of their surroundings. A separate space is devoted to the distinctive furniture of another Bucks County artist, woodworking master George Nakashima. An outdoor sculpture garden also celebrates the bucolic side of Bucks County. Open Tues through Fri, 10 a.m. to 4:30 p.m., Sat 10 a.m. to 5 p.m., and Sun from noon to 5 p.m.

i If you're a Maxfield Parrish fan, step into the lobby of the Curtis Center (601 Walnut St.) and feast your eyes on "The Dream Garden," a 15-by-49-foot mosaic of mountains and waterfalls inspired by a Parrish painting and assembled from 100,000 pieces of favrile (iridescent art glass) by Louis Comfort Tiffany in 1916.

PENNSYLVANIA ACADEMY OF THE FINE ARTS
118–128 N. Broad St.
Philadelphia, PA 19102
(215) 972-7600
pafa.org

Think of a famous name in American art and odds are that he or she has some connection with PAFA, the oldest art museum and school in the nation. Painter Charles Willson Peale and sculptor William Rush founded the institution in 1805. In 1876 it moved into the Historic Landmark Building, a dramatic example of Victorian Gothic architecture designed by Frank Furness and George W. Hewitt. Among the alumni and faculty represented in the collection, which ranges from colonial to contemporary, are Mary Cassatt and Maxfield Parrish. Other featured artists include Winslow Homer, John Singer Sargent, Edward Hopper, and the Wyeths, and among its star attractions is a portrait of George Washington by Gilbert Stuart. The two galleries, in the Historic Landmark and Samuel M. V. Hamilton Building, are open Tues through Sat from 10 a.m. to 5 p.m., Sun from 11 a.m to 5 p.m.

✳PHILADELPHIA MUSEUM OF ART
Benjamin Franklin Parkway and
26th Street
Philadelphia, PA 19130
(215) 763-8100
philamuseum.org
With its dramatic Greek-inspired columns and friezes and majestic presence, this all-eyes-on-me structure is often referred to as the "Parthenon on the Parkway." Sprint up the steps if you must, but save plenty of energy to enjoy one of the nation's largest art museums, featuring a collection of more than 225,000 works representing in more than 200 galleries the epitome of creativity spanning geography, time, and genres. PMA was the first institution of its time to utilize a "walk through time" format by grouping paintings, sculptures, architectural elements, and other objects from specific historic periods

in authentic settings such as a Chinese palace hall and a stone temple from India. To expand the available exhibition space, the museum recently opened the art deco–style Perelman Building nearby—admission to the Main Building ($16) includes both museum sites, or you can visit the Perelman Building alone ($8). On the first Sunday of the month, you may "Pay As You Wish." A free shuttle connects the two buildings. Main museum is open Tues through Sun 10 a.m. to 5 p.m., Fri. 10 a.m. to 8:45 p.m.; Perelman Building is open Tues through Sun 10 a.m. to 5 p.m.

i On Friday evenings, stick around for the museum's "Art After 5" programs of jazz in the Great Stair Hall in the Main Building. The event is free with regular museum admission, and guided tours of select galleries are offered throughout the evening.

RODIN MUSEUM
Benjamin Franklin Parkway at 22nd Street
Philadelphia, PA 19130
(215) 568-6026
rodinmuseum.org

This is the largest public collection of the works by late-19th-century sculptor Auguste Rodin outside of Paris. Yes, a bronze cast of Rodin's iconic *The Thinker* is outside, marking the spot (it has recently been restored after being buffeted by the elements) where this 1929 structure stands. A beautiful formal garden courtyard with reflecting pool provides a serene spot for contemplation or relaxation. Open Wed through Mon 10 a.m. to 5 p.m. An $8 donation is suggested.

i For $20, you can get a two-day pass for admission to the Philadelphia Museum of Art main building, Perelman Building, Rodin Museum, and Historic House Mount Pleasant. Free for kids 12 and under.

TALLER PUERTORRIQUEÑO
2721 N. 5th St.
Philadelphia, PA 19133
(215) 426-3311
tallerpr.org

Affectionately known as "el Corazón Cultural del Barrio," the cultural heart of Latino Philadelphia, this organization operates the region's only gallery dedicated to Latin American and Caribbean paintings, sculptures, and culture. Located in North Kensington, a neighborhood that's less than a 10-minute drive from Old City, the gallery exhibits centuries-old artifacts as well as the works of contemporary artists. Open Mon through Fri 10 a.m. to 5 p.m., Sat 11 a.m. to 5 p.m.

WOODMERE ART MUSEUM
9201 Germantown Ave.
Philadelphia, PA 19118
(215) 247-0476
woodmereartmuseum.org

Thousands of works by Philadelphia artists throughout the city's history have been the focus at this museum housed in a restored 19th-century stone Victorian mansion in Chestnut Hill for more than 70 years. Admission is free except for special exhibitions.

ANNUAL EVENTS

No matter what time of year you're here, Philly is Party Central. Whether the theme is ethnic, cultural, culinary, athletic, patriotic, or just plain fun, there's always some sort of celebration going on. I only have space to list a small sampling of the annual events, but to get the year-round, up-to-the-minute scoop, check the Greater Philadelphia Tourism Marketing Corporation's (GTMC) website (visitphilly.com), Philly's blog (uwishunu.com), call (215-599-0776), or listen to the city's online radio station (visitphilly.com/hear-philly). If there is no specific phone number listed for an event, contact the GTMC. Some events offer discounts on tickets purchased in advance and/or online. Check the specific event websites for details.

JANUARY

MUMMERS PARADE
Along Broad Street
Philadelphia, PA 19148
(215) 683-3622
mummers.com
You have to see it to believe it, and you'll only see it in Philly. Every year, more than 10,000 marchers don their most ostentatious outfits (sequins, beads, and other dazzlers as well as feathers are de rigueur) and strut through the city streets to the string band sounds of "O Dem Golden Slippers." Ask about tickets for bleacher seats and for special pre- and post-parade shows (all of these require paid tickets).

JANUARY/FEBRUARY

CHINESE NEW YEAR
Corner of 10th and Race Streets
Philadelphia, PA 19107
uwishunu.com

Gung Hay Fat Choy—Happy New Year! Chinatown is the only place to be when lions and dragons take to the street, fireworks light the skies, and a 10-course authentic banquet at the Chinese Cultural Center will fill you up enough to last the rest of the year.

PHILADELPHIA INTERNATIONAL AUTO SHOW
Pennsylvania Convention Center
12th and Arch Streets
Philadelphia, PA 19107
(610) 279-5229
phillyautoshow.com
All show, no sell, so you can take your time feasting your eyes on (and even sitting inside of) hundreds of the automotive industry's latest and future concepts and creations. One dollar of every ticket sold is donated to The Children's Hospital of Philadelphia.

FEBRUARY

MANAYUNK ON ICE
Main Street
Philadelphia, PA 19127
(215) 482-9565
manayunk.com

This National Ice Carving Association–sanctioned 3-day event features more than 15 top competitive ice carvers from around the country creating themed sculptures of all sizes.

MARCH

PHILADELPHIA FLOWER SHOW
Pennsylvania Convention Center
12th and Arch Streets
Philadelphia, PA 19107
(215) 988-8899
theflowershow.com

Founded in 1827, the Pennsylvania Horticultural Society (PHS) was the first organization of its kind in the nation, ditto for its flower show, which began 2 years later and blossomed into the largest indoor flower show in the world. Professionals vie for "Best of Show" with imaginative full-scale gardens. Individuals and garden clubs from around the world compete for coveted ribbons and awards. Experts will also lead 150 free gardening presentations. Tickets are $26 weekdays, $28 weekends. All proceeds, including tickets and sponsorship contributions, support PHS and its urban greening program, Philadelphia Green.

MARCH/APRIL

SAKURA MATSURI—THE CHERRY BLOSSOM FESTIVAL
Various locations throughout the city
(215) 790-3810
subarucherryblossom.org

This 6-week festival is as much a celebration of the friendship between two countries and cultures as it is the annual *o-hanami,* viewing of the cherry blossoms (*sakura*) that open on the more than 2,000 trees gifted to the city by Japan and the Japan Society of Greater Philadelphia. (Download a map for the best sighting spots from the website.) Major events during the festival include showcases of Japanese crafts; musical, dance, and martial arts performances; stories; food (an amateur sushi-making contest); and a 5K run. Most of the events are free except for the Sukura Sunday picnic ($5).

APRIL

PENN RELAYS
University of Pennsylvania Franklin Field
235 S. 33rd St.
Philadelphia, PA 19104
(215) 898-6145
thepennrelays.com

Begun in 1895, this largest amateur track meet in America attracts more than 22,000 high school and college track stars from around the nation. Over this 2-day event, these athletes will run more than 425 races, at least 2 dozen of which will be distance races.

PHILADELPHIA ANTIQUES SHOW
The Pennsylvania Convention Center
1101 Arch St.
(610) 902-2109
philaantiques.com

The half-century-old show is one of the longest-running in the nation, showcasing 50 leading antiques dealers and fine arts galleries. It costs $18 per ticket. Proceeds benefit Penn Medicine.

PHILADELPHIA BOOK FESTIVAL
Free Library of Philadelphia
Author Events Office
1901 Vine St.
Philadelphia, PA 19103
(215) 567-4341
libfreelibrary.org/bookfestival

It's a street fair filled with free programming for all ages including talks by best-selling authors, musical performances, and interactive children's programs.

PHILADELPHIA INVITATIONAL FURNITURE SHOW
Pennsylvania Convention Center
Cruise Ship Terminal
in the Philadelphia Navy Yard
5100 S. Broad St.
Philadelphia, PA 19107
(215) 387-8590
philaifs.com

Don't come here expecting to find the latest style of chest of drawers by Broyhill. This event is a showcase for a carefully selected group of the nation's artisans, whose works run from major focus-of-the-room furniture to wall and tabletop accessories. You can also order custom-made pieces. Price ranges go from "hey, I can afford that" to "put it on my Gold Card." Tickets are $12.

MAY

BLUE CROSS BROAD STREET RUN
Central High School Athletic Field
Broad Street and Somerville Avenue
Philadelphia, PA 19141
(215) 683-3594
broadstreetrun.com

Ten miles is a long way to run, but nearly 18,000 people, some pros, some not, come out every year hoping to break records (or just finish alive) on this USATF-certified course, rated one of the fastest in the county by *Runner's World* magazine. Donations and pledges benefit the American Cancer Society. There are also 1-mile runs and diaper dashes for fleet-of-foot—or knee—fledglings.

CHEROKEE FESTIVAL
Temple University–Ambler Campus
580 Meetinghouse Rd.
Philadelphia, PA 19122
(215) 549-4191
secherokee-confederacypa.org

Sponsored by the Southeastern Cherokee Confederacy of Pennsylvania and held over Memorial Day weekend, this 3-day festival features traditional music, dancing, foods, jewelry, clothing and craft sales, and activities for children, all to increase awareness and appreciation of Native American culture. Proceeds go to the Native American College Scholarship Fund. Call for admission prices.

DAD VAIL REGATTA
Kelly Drive and Strawberry Mansion Drive
Philadelphia, PA 19121
(215) 542-1443
dadvail.org

Two days, 3,500 athletes from more than 100 colleges and universities in the US and Canada, and 1 river (the Schuylkill). This more-than-70-year-old rowing race is the largest collegiate regatta in the nation.

MAY/JUNE

DEVON HORSE SHOW AND COUNTRY FAIR

23 Dorset Rd.
Devon, PA 19333
(610) 688-2554
thedevonhorseshow.org

From a 1-day show in 1896 to a 10-day extravaganza, this is the nation's oldest and largest outdoor multi-breed competition and the pride and joy of the Main Line. In 2010, Devon, which attracts elite equestrians from around the world, was just the fourth American show to receive a United States Equestrian Federation (USEF) Heritage Competition designation and was named Horse Show of the Year by the National Show Hunter Hall of Fame for multiple years. Call for ticket prices.

JUNE

BLOOMSDAY

Rosenbach Museum and Library
2008–2010 DeLancey Place
Philadelphia, PA 19103
(215) 732-1600
rosenbach.org

Celebrate the genius of James Joyce and the odyssey through Dublin on June 16 of Leopold Bloom, the protagonist of his masterpiece, *Ulysses*. Come in and see the special Joyce exhibition and gather outside for readings from the novel by famous Philadelphians. (In its collection, the Rosenbach has a complete 800-page draft of the book handwritten by Joyce.)

ODUNDE AFRICAN AMERICAN STREET FESTIVAL

23rd Street and South Street
Philadelphia, PA 19146
(215) 732-8510
odundeinc.org

Held the 2nd Sunday in June, this 3-day event, which is in its 4th decade and one of the oldest African-American street festivals in the country, is a celebration of history, culture, and family.

PHILLY BEER WEEK

Various venues throughout the city and the 'burbs
phillybeerweek.org

The Philadelphia area is home to more than 30 breweries and brewpubs, prompting *Maxim* magazine to dub it "the best beer city in America" in 2010. This 10-day festival features hundreds of events, including tours, pub crawls, tastings, meet-the-brewer nights, and just about everything to do with brews. Some events are free; others are pay as you go.

TD BANK PHILADELPHIA INTERNATIONAL CYCLING CHAMPIONSHIP

20th and Vine Streets
(Spectator areas line the entire course, stretching from Manayunk to Logan Square)
Philadelphia, PA 19130
(610) 676-0390
procyclingtour.com

At this, the nation's largest international cycling classic, hundreds of world-class cyclists put mettle to the pedal, speeding through the scenic streets of Philly including the Benjamin Franklin Parkway, Kelly Drive, and the ultra-arduous Manayunk "Wall," a

17 percent grade hill off the banks of the Schuylkill, as more than 300,000 spectators cheer them on. For suggestions on the best viewing places for the race, go to visitphilly .com.

JULY

ANNUAL HISPANIC FIESTA
Penn's Landing/Waterfront
Columbus Boulevard and Chestnut
Street
Philadelphia, PA 19106
(215) 922-2FUN
visitphilly.com

For more than 3 decades, this celebration of Hispanic heritage has featured authentic music and dance, artisan crafts, and foods from Latin America and the islands.

WAWA WELCOME AMERICA! FESTIVAL
Various locations throughout the city
(215) 683-2200
welcomeamerica.com

In Philly, the July 4th celebration of freedom isn't just 1 day—it's 10. Sample the best of Philly's top chefs at "Taste of Philadelphia," share hot dogs with historic heroes at a city-sponsored picnic, have a piece of a hoagie that's more than a mile long and all the ice cream you can eat, enjoy great films al fresco at LOVE Park, special programs at the Franklin Institute, Philadelphia Museum of Art, a block party in Chinatown, music, music, music, and fireworks galore. And that's all before the big day! On Independence Day, Philly will host a gigantic parade, the largest free concert in America with international headliners representing all musical genres, and, of course, more fireworks. Some events are free; some are not.

AUGUST

PHILADELPHIA FOLK FESTIVAL
Old Pool Farm
1323 Salford Station Rd.
Schwenksville, PA 19473
(800) 556-FOLK, (215) 247-1300
folkfest.org

You never know who you're going to see (there have been Bob Dylan and Bonnie Raitt sightings) and hear (Arlo Guthrie, Pete Seeger, and Richie Havens to name a few) at this 3-day festival that has been bringing fabulous folkies from headliners to rising stars to thousands of fans in Philly for upward of 50 years. Make yourself comfortable for 75 hours of music on 5 stages in this pastoral setting. Better yet, camp out so you don't have to miss a minute of the music. Call for ticket prices.

SEPTEMBER

PHILADELPHIA LIVELY ARTS FRINGE FESTIVAL
Venues across Philadelphia
(215) 413-9006
pafringe.com

This event is actually 2 concurrent 16-day festivals showcasing some of the finest contemporary new and established performing artists in the world, about half of whom are based in Philly, demonstrating the wealth of talent you'll find right here. There's no selection or filtering process for the theatrical, dance, music, and other performances, so expect the unexpected. If you're an aspiring artist, be sure to take in some of the workshops. Call for ticket information.

OCTOBER

PHILADELPHIA OUTFEST
252 S. 12th St., #1
Philadelphia, PA 19107
(215) 875-9288
phillypride.org
More than 20,000 people gather in Philly every year for this great big block party, the largest National Coming Out Day event in the nation. Outfest features live music, lots of food, and an abundance of community spirit.

USARTISTS: AMERICAN FINE ART SHOW & SALE
Pennsylvania Academy of the Fine Arts, Samuel M.V. Hamilton Building
128 N. Broad St.
Philadelphia, PA 19102
(215) 972-7600
usartists.org
Since 1992, the world's largest show and sale of American art, featuring 18th- through 21st-century works from galleries and dealers across the country, is a major annual fund-raiser for the Academy. Tickets are $15 per person.

NOVEMBER

PHILADELPHIA MARATHON
4231 N. Concourse Dr.
Philadelphia, PA 19131
(215) 685-0054
philadelphiamarathon.com
If you can maintain a 16-minute-per-mile pace on this USA Track & Field–sanctioned course through scenic Philadelphia, you're eligible for the big 26-mile sneaker-smoker. Novices might want to test out their fleet feet in the 13-mile half marathon or the 8K race. Kids have their own noncompetitive Fun Run, too. Because of the field size, there is a limit of 23,000 marathon runners, so if you intend to enter, do it early. Call for entry fee information. Or you can just come out and cheer the competitors on.

PHILADELPHIA MUSEUM OF ART CRAFT SHOW
Pennsylvania Convention Center
12th and Arch Streets
Philadelphia, PA 19107
(215) 684-7930
pmacraftshow.org
Less than 200 out of more than 1,400 applicants qualify to exhibit at this more-than-30-year-old prestigious show and sale of contemporary crafts. Tickets are $15 for 1 day, $20 for 2, and benefit the Philadelphia Museum of Art.

NOVEMBER/DECEMBER

ANNUAL PEACE AROUND THE WORLD: PASSPORT TO CULTURES
Penn Museum
3260 South St.
Philadelphia, PA 19104
(215) 898-4000
penn.museum
You'll get a "Passport to Cultures" that will lead you to various galleries within the museum where you'll learn about global holiday traditions through music, stories, arts, crafts, games, and other family-oriented activities. Free with regular museum admission donation.

PHILADELPHIA CHRISTMAS VILLAGE
Dilworth Plaza (west side of City Hall)
Philadelphia, PA 19102
philachristmas.com

From Thanksgiving until Christmas Eve, Dilworth Plaza becomes a European-style market bedecked with thousands of lights and other decorations. More than 50 booths and a large tent make up the "village" where you can shop for global holiday gifts while enjoying old-world foods and sweets. Free admission.

DECEMBER

ARMY/NAVY GAME
Lincoln Financial Field
1020 Pattison Ave.
Philadelphia, PA 19148
(215) 463-2500
phillylovesarmynavy.com
The more-than-a-century-old legendary college football rivalry between West Point and Annapolis continues. Games will be held in Philly in 2013, 2015, and 2017.

**LATKEPALOOZA AND JEWISH
  BAKEOFF GERSHMAN Y**
401 S. Broad St.
Philadelphia, PA 19147
(215) 545-4400
gershmany.org
You don't have to be Jewish to scarf down gourmet latkes, a traditional Hanukkah treat, cooked up by some of the city's top restaurants. And if you think your babka is better than bubby's, enter the Jewish Baking Contest if you dare. Bring the whole family for a festival of music and other fun stuff. Tickets are $15 for adults, $5 for kids.

SPECTATOR SPORTS

In Philadelphia, sports are no walk in the park—or on the field or court. Not for the teams and certainly not for the fans. Philly fans have spirit (okay, so maybe some people would call it being somewhat rowdy). They don't hesitate to express their opinions, whether positive or negative. In this town, fans are as enthusiastic about local high school and college teams as they are about their high-profile pros.

ARENA FOOTBALL

PHILADELPHIA SOUL
Wells Fargo Center
3601 S. Broad St.
Philadelphia, PA 19148
(800) 298-4200
philadelphiasoul.com
The city's indoor football team is back to keep fans passionate about pigskin pageantry happy from April through July. Call for ticket prices.

BASEBALL

PHILADELPHIA PHILLIES
Citizens Bank Park
One Citizens Bank Way
Philadelphia, PA 19148
(215) 463-1000
philadelphia.phillies.mlb.com
Who deserves a great, big (more than 43,000 seats) state-of-the-art stadium more than the multiple–World Series and many times National League Championship–winning Phils? The grass is as real as the passion of the players and Philly fans. The season is April through October. Single-game tickets range

from $20 for bleachers to $60 for the best field-level seats. Parking is pricey.

i Over the right-field bleachers at the Phillies' stadium, 100 feet above street level, hangs a 50-foot-high, 35-foot-wide neon outline of the Liberty Bell that "swings" and "rings" to celebrate every home run.

BASKETBALL

PHILADELPHIA 76ERS
Wells Fargo Center
3601 S. Broad St.
Philadelphia, PA 1914
Box office: (800) 298-4200
nba.com/sixers
Over a more than 70-year history, the Sixers, a National Basketball Association team, has counted among its illustrious alumni some of the nation's greatest kings of the court, including Wilt Chamberlain, "Dr. J" Julius Erving, Moses Malone, and Charles Barkley. The season runs from October through early May; depending on the competing team, tickets can start as low as $15 and soar to over $200 per seat.

FOOTBALL

PHILADELPHIA EAGLES
Lincoln Financial Field
1 Lincoln Financial Field Way
Philadelphia, PA 19130
(215) 463-5500
philadelphiaeagles.com

Twice they came this close to winning the gold ring, but Philadelphians remain hopeful and super-supportive of their beloved Birds. Season-ticket holders fill the majority of the seats, but if there are any available, they will run between $79.55 and $105.20 for regular games. When the Dallas Cowboys or New York Giants come to town, you'll be lucky to get standing-room-only tickets—and even they'll cost you $63.20.

HOCKEY

PHILADELPHIA FLYERS
Wells Fargo Center
3601 S. Broad St.
Philadelphia, PA 19148
(800) 298-4200
flyers.nhl.com

Having had a double-dose of Stanley Cup glory in the '70s, the team—and its faithful Philly fans—are determined to go all the way again. In recent years the Flyers have once again become strong contenders for the Cup, and everybody wants to be there to see it. The season runs from October through April. Expect to pay anywhere between $46 and $180, depending on the opposing team (among their biggest archrivals are the Montreal Canadiens, New York Rangers, and Pittsburgh Penguins).

HORSE RACING

Bucks County

PARX RACING
3001 Street Rd.
Bensalem, PA 19020
(215) 639-9000
philadelphiapark.com

Formerly named Philadelphia Park, this National Thoroughbred Racing Association Grade II has live thoroughbred racing 4 to 5 days a week for most of the year. In 2003, a colt named Smarty Jones made his debut here; the next year he won the Kentucky Derby and Preakness Stakes. Admission is free, and you're welcome to bring a picnic. Also available is the phonebet self-wagering system (voicebet: 800-bet-race; phonebet .com). Parx also has 5 racing turf clubs showing racing from around the world on video walls featuring 280 to 400 digital monitors. Their locations are Brandywine (1021 Baltimore Pike; 610-361-9000); Center City (7 Penn Center, 1635 Market St.; 215-246-1556); Northeast Philly (Roosevelt Mall, Cottman and Bustleton Avenues; 215-338-1887); South Philly (700 Packer Ave.; 215-551-8270); and Valley Forge (600 Cresson Ave., Oaks Corporate Center, Oaks; 610-650-0100).

i The biggest race of the year is the annual 9-furlong Pennsylvania Derby for 3-year-olds, held the last Saturday in September.

Chester County

HARRAH'S CHESTER CASINO & RACETRACK
777 Harrah's Blvd.
Chester, PA 19013
(800) 480-8020
harrahschester.com
Live harness racing season runs from the end of April through mid-December. Simulcast races from the nation's greatest tracks are televised every day.

LACROSSE

PHILADELPHIA WINGS
Wells Fargo Center
3601 S. Broad St.
Philadelphia, PA 19148
(215) 389-WINGS
wingslax.com
This team has given its Philly fans a reason to sing "We Are the Champions" 6 times, making it the "winning-est" team in the National Lacrosse League. The season runs from January through mid-April; single tickets are $18 to $62.

SOCCER

PHILADELPHIA KIXX
Wells Fargo Center
3601 S. Broad St.
Philadelphia, PA 19148
(215) 336-3600
kixxonline.com
One of the founding franchises of the 7-team Major Indoor Soccer League (formerly the National Indoor Soccer League) in 2008, the KIXX had already established a record of championship wins and are strong up-and-comers in the hearts of Philly fans. The season runs from November to March; tickets range from $19 to $60.

TENNIS

PHILADELPHIA FREEDOMS
The Pavilion at Villanova University
800 E. Lancaster Ave.
Radnor Township, PA 19085
(866) WTT-TIXS
philadelphiafreedoms.com
After Wimbledon, July's World TeamTennis pro matches are the most anticipated and exciting in the sport. Founded by Billie Jean King, home team for 5 years to Venus Williams and currently to number 8 world-ranked player Andy Roddick, the Freedoms play world-class coed singles, doubles, and mixed doubles against such top competitors as Venus and Serena Williams, Anna Kournikova, and Martina Hingis. Call for ticket prices.

STATE PARKS, RECREATIONAL AREAS & SPORTS

Philadelphia's state parks offer a wide range of recreational opportunities. All, unless specified, have scenic hiking and biking trails and allow picnicking. Fishing and hunting both require state licenses. Check with the Pennsylvania State Game Commission for regulations, seasons, and limits.

PARKS

Permits Needed

Boating—usually your own motorboats; but some also have motorboat, canoe, kayak, and other small craft rentals.

Ice Fishing—sites are generally unmonitored so be sure the ice is at least 4 feet thick and take any necessary safety equipment out with you.

Ice Skating—sites are generally unmonitored so be sure the ice is at least 4 feet thick.

Fishing—State license is required (Pennsylvania Game Commission, 717-787-2084; pgc.state.pa.us).

Hunting—usually restricted to deer, pheasant, rabbit, and turkey, unless otherwise specified. State license is required (Pennsylvania Game Commission, 717-787-2084; pgc.state.pa.us).

ℹ️ While Pennsylvania residents can use Fairmount Park's recreational trails for free, out-of-staters must purchase a permit—valid for 1 week—for $20.

Philadelphia

FAIRMOUNT PARK
Philadelphia, PA
(215) 988-9334 for maps, (215) 683-0200 for general park information
fairmountpark.org

If you think New York City's Central Park is big, multiply that by more than 10 and you have the size of Philly's Fairmount Park. This green goliath encompasses 63 regional and neighborhood parks, one of which is located within walking distance for every city resident. The park features over 200 miles of scenic hiking and biking trails suitable for all ages and physical ability levels. There are also 368 athletic fields for baseball, softball, soccer, football, rugby, and cricket along with basketball, tennis, and bocce courts, 6 public golf courses, and a disc golf course. Thirty-four miles of waterways make for some great fishing (a license is necessary). For skateboarding, roll on over to FDR Skate Park at Broad Street and Pattison Avenue (215-683-0200).

JOHN HEINZ NATIONAL WILDLIFE REFUGE
8601 Lindbergh Blvd.
Philadelphia, PA 19153
(215) 365-3118
heinz.fws.gov

This is a true birder's paradise—more than 300 species have been recorded, even a bald eagle family, at this rest stop along the Atlantic Flyway. Ten miles of trails, some wooded, some boardwalk, make it easy to find prime spots to keep an eye out for bills and beaks. Ask about guided bird and flower walks.

Camping

Many of the Philadelphia area's state parks and other recreational areas offer camping sites that range from bare-bones basic to yurts to modern amenity-filled cabins. Some cabins require multiple-night stays (some as long as a week during peak summer season).

Camping cabins range widely in price depending on size and time of year. For specifics and prices for cabins and other camping facilities go to dcnr.state.pa.us/stateparks/staythenight/camping/index.htm or call toll-free (888) 727-2757. Add a 6 percent hotel tax to cabin rates unless otherwise specified.

Bucks County

DELAWARE CANAL STATE PARK
11 Lodi Hill Rd.
Upper Black Eddy, PA 18972
(610) 982-5560

You can take a mule-drawn boat ride on this only remaining continuously intact early- to mid-19th-century canal. Walk, bike, or cross-country ski along the 60-mile towpath, a National Recreation Trail, that leads you through farmlands and historic towns and offers viewing of wildlife, migrating raptors, waterfowl, and songbirds. Fish in the Delaware River (shad migration starts in early spring) and Delaware Canal (warm-water game fish). Canoeing is permitted. Environmental educational and interpretive programs are available.

NESHAMINY STATE PARK
3401 State Rd.
Bensalem, PA 19020
(215) 639-4538
dcnr.state.pa.us/stateparks/findapark/neshaminy/index.htm

Four miles of hiking trails include the scenic River Walk in this 330-acre park. You'll find many species of warm-water fish, including bass, in part of the Delaware River and Neshaminy Creek.

NOCKAMIXON STATE PARK
1542 Mountain View Dr.
Quakertown, PA 18951
(215) 529-7300
dcnr.state.pa.us/stateparks/findapark/nockamixon/index.htm

If you want to windsurf, you can do it here. The 1,450-acre Lake Nockamixon is a popular destination for boating and warm-water fishing. In season, about 3,500 acres are open to hunting and trapping. There are 35 miles of walking trails through forests, fields, and lakeside plus a curvy, non-loop, paved biking trail with a waterfall; this trail is used for cross-country skiing in winter. Ice skating and ice fishing are permitted on the lake. Sledding and tobogganing are permitted in the area above the marina. Modern camping cabins are available for weekly rental in summer, minimum 2 nights rest of the year.

PEACE VALLEY PARK
170 Chapman Rd.
Doylestown, PA 18901
(215) 345-7860
peacevalleynaturecenter.org

Fourteen miles of nature trails ranging from groomed footpaths to remote hiking trails alongside beautiful Lake Galena. The blacktop trail around the lake is also perfect for biking. More than 250 species of birds have been sighted here, and there's a blind near the Solar Building. The Special Wildlife Area is off-limits, but you can enjoy the view from the Chapman Road Bridge or the duck blind. Guided programs include Sunday afternoon and summer evening nature walks, moonlight hikes, and star watches.

RALPH STOVER STATE PARK
5998 State Park Rd.
Pipersville, PA 18947
(610) 982-5560

Neither the rock climbing (200-foot sheer rock face with safety rail) nor the Class III and IV whitewater course for closed deck canoes and kayaks are for beginners—or even intermediates, but the 1-mile walking trail is easy. There is plenty of warm-water species fishing in trout-stocked Tohickon Creek.

i Although there is no camping in Ralph Stover, you will find 22 family or individual campsites as well as cabins plus a swimming pool in adjacent Tohickon Valley Park (Cafferty Road, Point Pleasant; 215-297-0754; bucks county.org/government/departments/ ParksandRec).

RINGING ROCKS PARK
Ringing Rocks Road
Upper Black Eddy
Bridgeton, PA 18972
(215) 348-6114

You might think that an 8-acre boulder field wouldn't have anything to offer, but just strike one lightly with a hammer and the vibration might make it ring like a bell. Only about one-third of the rocks ring, so you'll probably have to tap a few before you get a song.

TYLER STATE PARK
101 Swamp Rd.
Newtown, PA 18940
(215) 968-2021

This park features 1,711 acres in Bucks County. Fish along the banks of Neshaminy Creek or from a canoe for warm-water species including sunfish, black crappie, carp, and smallmouth bass. Ice skating and fishing are permitted on Neshaminy Creek. Sledding and tobogganing slopes are available. Hiking and biking trails are unplowed in winter for cross-country skiing—nearly all of the trails on the west side of the creek are hilly.

WASHINGTON CROSSING STATE PARK
1112 River Rd.
Washington Crossing, PA 18977
(215) 493-4076

Take a guided tour ($5–9) of the park where George Washington and his troops crossed the Delaware River on Christmas Eve 1776 for a surprise attack on the Hessians in New Jersey. Among the historic structures included on the tour are a boathouse with replicas of George Washington's watercraft and a former private home that served as a medical center for the soldiers. Don't miss climbing to the top of the 125-foot-high

Bowman's Hill Tower for some of the best views around.

i The annual reenactment of George Washington and his troops' 1776 crossing of the Delaware River is held at 1 p.m. on Christmas Day (free) at Washington Crossing State Park. But you can see a full dress rehearsal ($8)—along with period life and work demonstrations—earlier in December. Unless you're a history purist, there is a lot more to do on rehearsal day.

Chester County

FRENCH CREEK STATE PARK
843 Park Rd.
Elverson, PA 19520
(610) 582-9680
dcnr.state.pa.us/stateparks/findapark/
frenchcreek/index.htm

Designated by the National Audubon Society as an Important Bird and Mammal Area, this 7,730-acre park's forests, lakes, wetlands, and fields are home to many species of flora and fauna that are rare in Pennsylvania. Cold-water Scotts Run Lake offers great trout fishing, while Hopewell Lake hosts warm-water species including big bass. You can rent boats daily from Memorial Day to Labor Day and on weekends during May and September. The park features 35 miles of hiking (naturalist hikes are available in spring, summer, and fall) and 20 miles of mountain biking trails. Two major courses have earned French Creek the nickname "Orienteering Capital of America." Over 60,000 acres are open to hunting and trapping deer, turkey, rabbit, pheasant, and squirrel. About 3 miles southeast are also 1,800 acres of state game land. Camping is available year-round at 200 wooded, modern sites (over 60 have electric hookups) that have access to shower and flush toilet facilities. Pet-friendly sites are available.

MARSH CREEK STATE PARK
675 Park Rd.
Downingtown, PA 19335
(610) 458-5119

Sailboaters flock to 535-acre Marsh Creek Lake. If you don't have one, you can rent all kinds of boats throughout the summer and on weekends during spring and autumn (610-458-5040; marshcreeklake.com). About 900 acres are open to hunting and trapping rabbit, squirrel, pheasant, waterfowl, and deer. Marsh Creek Lake is excellent for warm-water fishing, particularly for bass. Ice skating, iceboating, and ice fishing are permitted. Seven acres of slopes provide great sledding and tobogganing terrain.

WHITE CLAY CREEK PRESERVE
Landenberg
London Britain Township, PA 19350
(610) 274-2900
dcnr.state.pa.us/stateparks/findapark/
whiteclaycreek/index.htm

Click on the website for directions to this 2,072-acre preserve, considered to be one of the best trout streams around. Hiking, biking, and cross-country skiing trails explore the various park habitats. About 1,800 acres are open to deer hunting only.

Delaware County

RIDLEY CREEK STATE PARK
351 Gradyville Rd.
Newtown Square, PA 19073
(610) 892-3900
dcnr.state.pa.us/stateparks/findapark/
ridleycreek/index.htm

Bisected by Ridley Creek, which is stocked with trout, this 2,600-plus-acre woodland and meadow park offers 12 miles of hiking trails and 5 miles of paved trails for biking and cross-country skiing. A large slope by the park office is a local favorite for sledding and tobogganing.

i Inside Ridley State Park, you can visit the Colonial Pennsylvania Plantation, a 3-century-old working farm restored to a late-18th-century appearance with authentically clothed historical interpreters and animals typical to the period. On weekends from April to November, you can watch a "family" cook over an open hearth, preserve foods, create textiles, and tend crops (610-566-1725; colonialplantation.org); adult plantation admission fee for non-event days is $6, $8 for event days.

Montgomery County

EVANSBURG STATE PARK
851 Mayhall Rd.
Collegeville, PA 19426
(610) 409-1150
dcnr.state.pa.us/stateparks/findapark/evansburg/index.htm

Skippack Creek is stocked with brown and rainbow trout. Six miles of easy-to-moderate hiking and 5 miles of specified biking trails are available. Most trails are open for cross-country skiing. Over 1,000 acres are open to hunting and trapping. The 18-hole, par 71 Skippack Golf Course (610-584-4226; skippackgolfclub.com) is open to the public.

i The Friedt Visitor Center, a circa-1700 farmhouse and gardens in Evansburg State Park, interprets the lifestyles of the German Mennonite families who owned the home for 190 years.

FORT WASHINGTON STATE PARK
500 S. Bethlehem Pike
Fort Washington, PA 19034
(215) 591-5250
dcnr.state.pa.us/stateparks/findapark/fortwashington/index.htm

Nothing remains of the temporary fort where General Washington's army camped for a little more than a month prior to moving on to Valley Forge, but this almost 500-acre recreation destination has a long history of making area outdoors lovers happy. Hike, bike, or cross-country ski the 2.5-mile Green Ribbon Trail, fish for trout in the Wissahickon Creek, climb to the top of Hawk Watch Observation Deck to search for raptors (16 species) and butterflies, and sled or toboggan down a 400-foot slope. A 1.7-mile loop trail offers cross-country skiing for beginners to experts.

GREEN LANE PARK
2144 Snyder Rd.
Routes 29 and 63
Green Lane, PA 18054
(610) 278-3555
parks.montcopa.org

In this 3,400-acre park, there are several miles of nature trails for hiking, mountain biking, and horseback riding as well as 3 bodies of water. The Montgomery County Environmental Education Center located here offers year-round programs for all ages. Electric boats and rowboats are available for rental. Fishing, ice skating, cross-country skiing, sledding, and ice fishing are permitted. In September, Green Lane Park hosts one of the largest Scottish-Irish festivals in Eastern Pennsylvania. This 3-day event features highland games, sheep dog demos, dancing, bagpiping, and children's activities.

NORRISTOWN FARM PARK
2500 Upper Farm Rd.
East Norristown, PA 19403
(610) 270-0215
dcnr.state.pa.us/stateparks/findapark/
norristown/index.htm

This 690-acre park is home to a working farm in continuous use since colonial times, 15 historic buildings, a trout farm, and loads of wildlife. There's an interpretive nature trail that takes you through The Millennium Grove, one of two Pennsylvania sites selected by the American Forest Foundation and the White House Millennium Council to promote the planting of historic tree groves. Paved roads are open to bikers and in-line skaters. Fishing is permitted at the Farm Pond or either of two trout-stocked streams. More than 170 species of birds have been recorded, and there's a viewing blind for close-up observation. During winter, any part of the park may be used for sledding and downhill or cross-country skiing.

VALLEY FORGE NATIONAL
   HISTORICAL PARK
1400 N. Outer Line Dr.
King of Prussia, PA 19406
(610) 783-1077
nps.gov/vafo/index.htm

For 6 months in 1777–78, George Washington's Continental Army braved brutal weather conditions and meager supplies to continue their fight for American freedom. You can still visit George Washington's headquarters here and see a fascinating film on how the soldiers survived. When you visit the park today, the hardships of that historic winter seem far way. Year-round beautiful Valley Forge National Park is one of the Philadelphia area's most-visited outdoor places for education and recreation. You can hike, bike, or horseback ride along 28 acres of trails. Bike rentals are available at the Welcome Center. Visitors can also rent a hybrid bike and explore the park on their own. Bike rentals are available from the lower Welcome Center (610-783-4593; valleyforgebikes.com) from June through Labor Day for $10 per hour, $20 per day. Audio tour CDs and maps are available at the Welcome Center. Or you can take an audio tour via your own cell phone by calling (484) 396-1018 for English, (484) 396-1015 for Spanish. The tour is free, but you will have to use your own cell phone and minutes. Every day during the summer and on spring and fall weekends, guided tours are available, including free ranger-led walking excursions and fee-based 90-minute trolley tours (610-783-1074). Also, check the online schedule for Saturday "Join the Continental Army" events during which kids ages 6 to 12 will be enlisted into service, learn to stand and march like a soldier, and carry, "load, and fire" a wooden musket. Specific activities vary per event.

ARBORETUMS

Philadelphia

MORRIS ARBORETUM
100 E. Northwestern Ave.
Philadelphia, PA 19118
(215) 247-5777
upenn.edu/arboretum

This is the place to come to chill out on a beautiful day in any season. There's always something new to see as you stroll the arboretum's 92 acres of gorgeous global gardens that feature 13,000 plants, trees, and flowers (over 2,500 types) labeled for easy identification. Make sure you take in the view from the 450-foot-long "Out on a Limb" canopy walk, 50 feet up in the treetops. Check the website for classes on a variety of subjects, such as sustainable gardening, landscaping, and fun for kids and families. Print out a self-guided tour from the website or choose one of the guided tours each weekend.

Open every day except for certain holidays. Bring your frail or fading flora to the free plant clinic, 1 to 3 p.m. Mon through Fri (except for Thurs); (215) 247-5777, ext. 141.

Delaware County

TYLER ARBORETUM
515 Painter Rd.
Media, PA 19063
(610) 566-9134
tylerarboretum.org

Even Type A personalities will want to slow down and admire the ancient trees and multihued wildflowers along the more than 20 miles of hiking trails that will take you through 450 acres (the total acreage of the arboretum is 650) of uncultivated woodlands and past ruins of centuries-old buildings. Meander through the 4-ringed Meadow Maze where there is something new to learn at Discovery Stations at every turn and visit a 1,400-square-foot house where native butterflies flutter free. Ask about nature programs for adults and kids as well as year-round special events. Open year-round except for selected holidays (the Butterfly House is open from June through early Sept).

OUTDOOR RECREATION

Bicycling

You don't have to be a member to ride with these clubs in the Philadelphia area. Just make sure you check in advance for any rules, regulations, and/or age restrictions.

BICYCLE CLUB OF PHILADELPHIA
640 Waterworks Dr.
Philadelphia, PA 19130
phillybikeclub.org

DELAWARE VALLEY BICYCLE CLUB
dvbc.org

Horseback Riding

GATEWAY STABLES
949 Merrybell Ln.
Kennett Square, PA 19348
(610) 444-1255
gatewaystables.com

From ponies for the little ones to draft horses for adults of all sizes, this is a great place to bring the family for a guided scenic trail ride. The price is $40 for a 1-hour regular trail ride or 45-minute hand-led ride for children, or $25 for a 0.5-hour pony ride. Lessons and horse boarding are also available. A portion of all proceeds goes to the Juvenile Diabetes Research Foundation.

HAYCOCK STABLES
1035 Old Bethlehem Rd.
Perkasie, PA 18944
(215) 257-6271
haycockstables.com

Rides for all ages on trails located by Lake Nockamixon for $30 per hour. Cash or checks only. Lessons are also available.

HIDDEN VALLEY FARMS
Ridley Creek State Park
351 Gradyville Rd.
Newtown Square, PA 19073
(610) 892-7260

One-hour scenic trail rides are $45 (must be at least 8 years old). Pony rides cost $1 for once around a big ring. Lessons, horse boarding, and pony rentals for parties are also available.

HOPE SPRINGS FARM
Marsh Creek State Park
800 N. Reeds Rd.
Downingtown, PA 19335
(610) 321-1960
hopespringshorsefarm.com
One-hour-long trail rides are $40 (cash only). Must be at least 18 years old. Lessons and horse boarding are available.

RED BUFFALO RANCH
1106 Anders Rd.
Collegeville, PA 19426
(610) 489-9707
redbuffaloranch.com
One- to 4-hour trail rides through Evansburg Park, $35 to $140. Cash or checks only. Lessons are available.

Orchards

LINVILLA ORCHARDS
137 W. Knowlton Rd.
Media, PA 19015
(610) 876-7116
linvilla.com
Almost a century old and still operated by members of the founding family, this 300-acre working farm has been a Philadelphia landmark. You can purchase anything from apples to apricots, peaches to pumpkins, and strawberries to sweet corn at the on-site market or, better yet, go out in the fields and orchards and pick your own. You can fish (no license required) in the well-stocked Orchard Pond ($9 for adults, $5 for children, additional per caught fish fees). Open year-round.

WILLOW CREEK ORCHARDS
3215 Stump Hall Rd.
Collegeville, PA 19426
(610) 584-8202
The first and only USDA Certified Organic produce farm in Montgomery County, Willow Creek grows strawberries that you can pick or purchase at the on-premises market. They also grow and sell pasture-raised, 100 percent organic-fed chicken, beef, and lamb.

Water Sports

BUCKS COUNTY RIVER COUNTRY
2 Walters Ln.
Point Pleasant, PA 18950
(215) 297-5000
rivercountry.net
Ride the gentle currents of the Delaware River any way you like—floating on a tube (single or double "snuggle" kind) or raft or paddling a canoe or kayak. For an extra $3, you can add a burger, chips, and soda meal to any activity. Check the website for special discounts on all activities.

NORTHBROOK CANOE COMPANY
1810 Beagle Rd.
West Chester, PA 19382
(610) 793-2279
northbrookcanoe.com
Canoe, kayak, or tube on the easygoing Brandywine River. Check the website for prices and special deals.

PHILADELPHIA RECREATION CENTERS
Philadelphia, PA
(215) 683-3600
phila.gov/recreation
Many of Philly's 100-plus municipal rec centers have pools that are open to visitors. For the address of a public pool near you, call the

Recreation Department or go to phila.gov/recreation/sports/Pool_Opening_Sched.html.

i For kids (and adults) on boards and skates, more than 20 skate parks operate in the Greater Philadelphia area. For a listing with addresses and phone numbers, go to phila.gov/skateparks.

Ice Skating

BLUE CROSS RIVERRINK
201 S. Columbus Blvd.
Philadelphia, PA 19147
(215) 925-RINK
riverrink.com
Philadelphia's only outdoor ice rink, this Olympic-size facility is open every day, including holidays, in winter. For kids who are physically or developmentally challenged, RiverRink provides "sled skates"—skate-blade-equipped sleds with special poles for riders who want to propel themselves or handlebars that skaters can push. Rental skates and skating and sled skating lessons are available. Admission is under $10.

INDOOR RECREATION

Gyms/Health Clubs/Tennis

AQUATIC AND FITNESS CENTER, PHILADELPHIA
3600 Grant Ave.
Philadelphia, PA 19114
(215) 677-0400
afcfitness.com
Classes, personal training, state-of-the-art equipment—you'll find everything you

could possibly want in a fitness facility from Ashtanga Yoga to Zumba. AFC also has locations in Bala Cynwyd and Jenkintown, both in Montgomery County.

JOLTIN' JABS
4303 Main St.
Philadelphia, PA 19127
(215) 482 4802
joltinjabs.com
Don't expect any coddling from former professional boxer "Joltin'" Joey Malavez (he was a trainer for former 76ers basketball star Charles Barkley, too), but you can expect some dramatic results in how fit you look and feel. You can pay as you go, purchase a package, or arrange for private lessons. Call for prices.

YMCA
Philadelphia, PA
(800) 872-9622
ymca.net
Most communities in the city and each of the 'burbs has a YMCA branch in it or nearby. Check the main website and enter "Philadelphia" or the particular city or town you want.

Montgomery County
AQUATIC AND FITNESS CENTER, BALA CYNWYD
601 Righters Ferry Rd.
Bala Cynwyd, PA 19004
(610) 664-6464
afcfitness.com
In addition to other activities listed for all Aquatic and Fitness Centers, this location also offers tennis and baseball instruction.

AQUATIC AND FITNESS CENTER, JENKINTOWN
921 Old York Rd.
Noble Town Center
Jenkintown, PA 19001
(215) 887-8787
afcfitness.com

State-of-the-art-equipped facilities featuring group fitness classes including cardio, Pilates, weight training, and yoga; personal training; tennis; swimming; nutritional counseling; and a form of land/water physical therapy called "aquarehab." Membership agreements are on a month-by-month basis. Call for prices.

Bowling

While the object of the game hasn't changed, the atmosphere has completely morphed into family-oriented by day, adults-only (ages 21 and up) entertainment complexes serving much more sophisticated fare than the traditional pizza and hot dogs after 9 p.m. Most have bars and some even offer bottle service. They're great places for a first date. Prices are not marked because they vary by day and time of day.

BRUNSWICK ZONE XL
100 E. Street Rd.
(215) 322-7755
bowlbrunswick.com

This recreation center offers 48 lanes, 6 billiard tables, laser tag, and a bar and grill.

CENTER BOWLING LANES
7550 City Ave.
Philadelphia, PA 19151
(215) 878-5050
center-lanes.com/location.asp

No frills, just bowling for the whole family.

LUCKY STRIKE BOWLING LANES
1336 Chestnut St.
Philadelphia, PA 19107
(215) 545-2471
bowlluckystrike.com

Twenty-four alleys and 6 billiard tables. Bottle service is also available.

NORTH BOWL LOUNGE AND LANES
909 N. 2nd St.
Philadelphia, PA 19123
(215) 238-BOWL
northbowlphilly.com

A winning combination of retro and cool from the lanes to the bar.

STRIKES BOWLING LOUNGE
4040 Locust St.
Philadelphia, PA 19104
(215) 387-BOWL
strikesbowlinglounge.com

Bowling, billiards, table tennis, and foosball. Drink specials every night.

THUNDERBIRD LANES
5830 Castor Ave.
Philadelphia, PA 19149
(215) 743-2521
tbirdlanes.com

Sixteen lanes, bumper bowling for kids.

WYNNEWOOD LANES AND LOUNGE
2228 Haverford Rd., Ste. 1
Ardmore, PA 19003
(610) 642-7512
wynnewoodlanes.com

Rock 'n' Bowl features music, state-of-the-art lighting, DJ, karaoke, and prizes. Check the schedule on the website.

Casinos

The Philadelphia area has had slot machines for a few years but only recently introduced table gaming. Casinos are open 24 hours, 7 days a week.

HARRAH'S CHESTER CASINO & RACETRACK
777 Harrah's Blvd.
Chester, PA 19013
(800) 480-8020
harrahschester.com

You'll find 2,900 slots plus electronic and live game tables including poker, blackjack, craps, roulette, and baccarat. There's also full-card simulcast horseracing every day and live harness racing in season. Dining options include the upscale, fixed-price Cove at Riverview to more economical options including Mien Noodles, End Zone Sports Bar, and Temptations Buffet.

PARX CASINO
2999 Street Rd.
Bensalem, PA 19020
(888) 588-7279
parxcasino.com

More than 3,500 slots as well as live and e-table games including blackjack, ultimate Texas hold 'em, craps, midi-baccarat, and single-zero roulette. The 360 Lounge features live music and bottle service. If you're new to Philly, make sure you eat at the new on-site Chickie & Pete's Crab House. If you're a local, you already know that.

SUGARHOUSE CASINO
1001 N. Delaware Ave.
Philadelphia, PA 19125
(877) 477-3715
sugarhousecasino.com

Just opened in September 2010, this is Philadelphia's first (and as of the writing of this book) only casino authorized to operate slots (1,600) and table games (40 including poker, blackjack, roulette, craps, and mini baccarat). Live entertainment is available Wed through Sat. Watch the Big Game on Sunday during football season on the big screen or right on your slot machine. Three on-site restaurants offer easygoing food and drink.

GOLF

Greater Philadelphia's golf courses accommodate every skill level, from world-class pro to beginning duffer. Some of the greatest names in golf have played here, including Sam Snead, Babe Didrikson Zaharias, Gary Player, and Arnold Palmer. You'll also have the opportunity to play on courses designed by the likes of Robert Trent Jones, Rees Jones, Alex Findlay, Arnold Palmer, Donald Ross, and Dick Wilson. Here are profiles of some of the area's premier courses. I have kept them as brief as possible to be able to include as many as possible. I have also kept the private course listings to a minimum because you must be a guest of a member to play them . . . but how could I omit Aronimink? Unless otherwise noted, greens fees quoted are top in-season rates; taxes are extra. Cart fees are also extra unless specified otherwise.

Private Courses

ARONIMINK GOLF CLUB
3600 Saint Davids Rd.
Newtown Square, PA 19073
(610) 356-8000
aronimink.org

Two decades after famed course designer Donald Ross laid out this par-70 championship course, which opened in 1928, he remarked, "I intended to make this my masterpiece but not until today did I realize I built better than I knew." *Golf Digest* magazine agrees, having recently named Aronimink among the top 100 courses in the country. In 2010, it was the site of the AT&T Championship. $95 to $125.

BUCKS COUNTY COUNTRY CLUB
2600 York Rd.
Jamison, PA 18929
(215) 343-0350
golfbucks.com

Patterned after the environment-inspired courses of the 1920s, Bucks County was designed by celebrated course architect William Gordon in the early '60s. Today, his original front 9 remain the same, while the back 9 have gotten a more contemporary makeover. It's not a long course, but don't sell its difficulty short. $30 weekdays, $40 weekends.

HERSHEY'S MILL GOLF CLUB
401 Chandler Dr.
West Chester, PA 19380
(610) 431-1600
hersheysmillgolfclub.com

This 770-acre, par-72 course, suited to golfers of all skill levels, wanders through the immaculately kept grounds of a gated residential community. Guest with member, $50 to $60.

Semiprivate

BLUE BELL COUNTRY CLUB
1800 Tournament Dr.
Blue Bell, PA 19422
(215) 616-8100
bluebellcc.com

Wide fairways and large greens make this 18-hole, par-72 Arnold Palmer Signature course a pleasure to play. $95 to $100.

BROAD RUN GOLFER'S CLUB
1520 Tattersall Way
West Chester, PA 19380
(610) 738-4410
broadrungc.com

Keep your eye on the ball when you take on this Rees Jones–designed, 18-hole, par-72 course that locals long knew as Tattersall Golf Club. You don't want to have to wade into one of the swamps to retrieve it. Greens fees (including cart) are $54 to $74.

DOWNINGTOWN GOLF CLUB
93 Country Club Dr.
Downingtown, PA 19335
(610) 269-2000
golfdowningtown.com

This par-72 was designed in 1967 by a Fazio—not Tom, but his uncle George, who was a championship player in the '50s and an outstanding architect himself. And Downingtown does the name proud with its gently rolling fairways and prominent bunkers that allow confident golfers to test their skills and up-and-comers to hone theirs. Fees begin at $49 weekdays, $53 weekends.

HICKORY VALLEY GOLF CLUB
1921 Ludwig Rd.
Gilbertsville, PA 19525
(610) 754-7733
hickoryvalley.com

Golf Digest awarded this 36-hole club 4.5 stars, and *Zagat Golf* named it number 2 in Pennsylvania. The 18-hole, par-71 Ambassador course is the shorter of the two but weaves through 70-foot trees. Green fees are $34 to $42. Large ponds and bunkers bring some drama to the the par-72, links-style front 9 of The Presidential while the fairways get tighter and the greens smaller on the back 9. Greens fees are $14 to

$36 at the Ambassador, $22 to $33 at the Presidential.

WYNCOTE GOLF CLUB
50 Wyncote Dr.
Oxford, PA 19363
(610) 932-8900
wyncote.com

Brian Ault designed this *Golf Digest* 4-star-rated, par-72 course in the traditional Scottish links style, following the natural terrain and incorporating wetlands. Greens fees with cart are $49 to $69.

Public Courses

Golf Philly (866-785-2635; golfphilly.org) is a group of four 18-hole public courses at 3 municipal facilities, all managed by Billy Casper Golf. Substantial recent updates of these decades-old facilities have made them among the city's popular go-to courses. The only major complaints I've heard about the courses are about their club-unfriendly hard tee-boxes. The outdoor **City Line Sports Center,** part of the Golf Philly group, offers a driving range ($15 for all-you-can hit golf balls weekdays, $20 weekends), minigolf ($5 to $6), and batting cages ($2 for 20 pitches).

i Ask about the super-money-saving Golf Philly Annual Pass that gives you unlimited play on one course of your choice and discounts on the other two during specified times.

BELLA VISTA GOLF COURSE
2901 Fagleysville Rd.
Gilbertsville, PA 19525
(601) 705-1855
bellavistagc.com

As the name suggests, the view is definitely beautiful as you play this par-70 course that

received a 4-star rating (for excellence in course playability, conditions, and experience) from *Golf Digest* magazine. Rates are $35 to $40.

COBB'S CREEK GOLF CLUB
7400 Lansdowne Ave.
Philadelphia, PA 19151
(215) 877-8707
golfphilly.org

Site of the first public golf course in 1916, Cobb's Creek now features two 18-hole layouts—"The Olde Course" and "The Karakung Course." The Olde Course: Designed by Hugh Wilson in the 1930s, this tree-lined course was the site of several PGA Tour events and hosts numerous tournaments. The creek that gives the club its name wanders through the first 6 holes, and the back 9 are no picnic either, particularly hole 14. $43 weekdays/$48 weekends with cart. The Karakung Course: Choose your clubs carefully to conquer the elevation changes on this par-71, 1929 course. $33 weekdays and weekends with cart.

FDR GOLF CLUB
1954 Pattison Ave.
20th and Pattison Avenues
Philadelphia, PA 19145
(215) 462-8997
golfphilly.org

This par-69 course, established in 1940 as one of namesake Franklin Roosevelt's public works projects, is the closest to and provides the best views of Center City. The generous-size fairways and greens make it perfect for all skill levels, but the canal that runs through it can present some interesting challenges. $38 weekdays, $43 weekends with cart.

THE GOLF COURSE AT GLEN MILLS
221 Glen Mills Rd.
Glen Mills, PA 19342
(610) 558-2142
glenmillsgolf.com

Don't let the nonintimidating first hole fool you; this par-71, Bobby Weed–designed course, which has been celebrated by *Golf Digest*, *Golf* magazine, and *Golfweek*, isn't for beginners. Be prepared for a whole new adventure at every hole. Greens fees with cart are $79 to $95.

i Net proceeds from the Glen Mills Golf Course provide funding for student programs at the Glen Mills School, the nation's oldest residential school for troubled youths. Students also work on the course to gain skills and experience that they can use for the rest of their lives.

JOHN F. BYRNE GOLF CLUB
9500 Leon St.
Philadelphia, PA 19114
(215) 632-8666
golfphilly.org

The Torresdale Creek meanders through and adds an extra element of challenge to the first 10 holes of this par-67 course designed more than 70 years ago by Alex Findlay. It has hosted a number of tournaments including the Philadelphia Publinks Senior Open Amateur Championship. $38 weekdays, $43 weekends with cart.

WALNUT LANE GOLF CLUB
800 Walnut Ln.
Philadelphia, PA 19128
(215) 482-3370
walnutlanegolf.com

Alex Findlay, the acknowledged "Father of American Golf," designed this par-62 course in Wissahickon Valley Park (northern Fairmount Park) in 1940. His thoughtful use of the natural topography gives you all kinds of gullies, uphill shots, and holes away in hills and valleys, making this one of the area's most respected courses. Greens fees (with cart) are $32 to $38.

LIVING IN PHILADELPHIA

RELOCATION

In Greater Philadelphia, there is no shortage of resources to help you relocate, and one of your first calls will be to find a real estate agent to help you search for a new home.

AGENTS

Greater Philadelphia

ASSOCIATION OF REALTORS
1341 N. Delaware Ave., Ste. 200
Philadelphia, PA 19106
(215) 423-9381
gpar.org

Montgomery County

ASSOCIATION OF REALTORS
Blue Bell Executive Campus
470 Norristown Rd., Ste. 300
Blue Bell, PA 19422
(610) 260-9931
mcarealtors.org

SUBURBAN WEST REALTORS ASSOCIATION
Malvern Executive Center
100 Deerfield Ln., Ste. 240
Malvern, PA 19355
(610) 560-4800
delvalrealtors.com

CITY/COUNTY SERVICES

Philadelphia

If you have any question pertaining to Philadelphia regulations and services, just dial 311. Tell the operator what your question or concern is and you will be connected to the appropriate city department. The City of Philadelphia's website (phila.gov) also offers a wealth of easily accessible information on and resources for finding just about everything from after-school programs to zip codes and including tax forms, a library card application, tenant/landlord guidelines, public transportation (SEPTA) accessible services, and paying a parking ticket. This is also the best place to find services for senior citizens.

Outside the City of Philadelphia

Bucks County: (888) 942-8257, (215) 348-6000; buckscounty.org
Chester County: (800) 692-1100, (610) 344-6000; dsf.chesco.org
Delaware County: (610) 891-4000; co.delaware.pa.us
Montgomery County: (610) 278-3000; montcopa.org

i To help you navigate the often confusing collection of federal, state, and local government social services programs such as Medicare, county assistance, Social Security, disability, job training, and drug counseling in the 5-county Greater Philadelphia area, just go to connect211.org or call (215) 831-0130.

🔍 Close-up

EMERGENCIES

For Philadelphia and the suburbs, the general phone number for health and safety emergencies is 911.

The city also offers the following contacts for specific departments and services.

Nonemergency police: (215) 686-3010

Accidental poisoning: (215) 386-2100

Fire and rescue: (215) 922-6000

Ambulance: Network Ambulance Service (215) 482-8560 or SEPTA Paratransit (215) 580-7800

Pet emergencies: University of Pennsylvania Veterinary Hospital (215) 898-4685; will make referrals

To reach a doctor quickly, call the Philadelphia County Medical Society (215-563-5343). All hospitals in Philadelphia have emergency rooms.

For a dental emergency, contact the Philadelphia County Dental Society (215-925-6050).

ActionAIDS: Philadelphia's largest AIDS service organization, (215) 981-0088

Al-Anon/Alateen: for families and loved ones of alcoholics, (215) 222-5244

Alcoholics Anonymous: (215) 923-7900

Animal Bites (Department of Public Health, Division of Disease Control), 24-hour hotline: (215) 685-6748

Narcotics Anonymous: (215) NAWORKS (629-6757)

Planned Parenthood: (800) 230-PLAN, (215) 351-5500

Poison Control Emergency 24-hour Hotline: (800) 222-1222

Suicide and Crisis Intervention, 24-hour emergency hotline, referrals:

Philadelphia County: (888) 855-5525

Lower Bucks County: (215) 355-6000, (215) 547-1889

Central Bucks County: (215) 536-0911

Upper Bucks: (610) 649-5250

Main Line and Delaware County: (215) 686-4420

Women Organized Against Rape, individual and group counseling: (215) 985-3333

ℹ The Edwin A. Fleisher Collection of Orchestral Music at the Free Library of Philadelphia is the world's largest lending library of orchestral performance material with more than 21,000 titles.

LIBRARIES

CENTRAL LIBRARY
1901 Vine St.
Philadelphia, PA 19103
(215) 686-5322
freelibrary.org
Philadelphia's first free library opened in 1895 and moved into its current beautiful Beaux Arts Building location on Logan Square on the Benjamin Franklin Parkway in 1927. Today this wide-ranging resource houses more than 6 million items, ranging from books and magazines to art, music, films, and other media. Also available are adult education (e.g., GED high school equivalency) and English as a Second Language classes, programs for visually impaired/physically handicapped individuals, author events, career services and workshops, children and teen programs, and senior services. There are also 54 library branches throughout the 5-county area. You can find the one closest to you on publiclibraries.com/pennsylvania.htm.

ℹ Kids can get help with difficult assignments, have their written papers reviewed, and find guidance on term papers from expert tutors on the Free Library of Philadelphia's Homework Help Online, brainfuse.com. They can also take practice SAT, ACT, and other tests on brainfuse.com.

TAXES

PHILADELPHIA CITY TAXES
Dial 311
phila.gov/revenue
Income tax: gross earned income of Philadelphia residents is taxed at 3.93 percent, regardless of whether the income was earned in Philadelphia or in a surrounding city.
Real estate tax: $8.264 per $100 of assessed value. Surrounding cities all have their own income and property tax structures; you can call their municipal offices for information, or call the State of Pennsylvania's Fact and Information Line at (888) PA-TAXES or visit revenue.state.pa.us.
Philadelphia sales tax: 8 percent is applied to items sold in Pennsylvania. Exceptions to the sales tax include food, clothing, drugs, and textbooks.

STATE INCOME AND SALES TAX
Pennsylvania State Taxes
(888) PA-TAXES
revenue.state.pa.us
State income tax: 3.07 percent of gross income.
State sales tax: 6 percent state tax is applied to items sold in Pennsylvania. Exceptions to the sales tax include food, clothing, drugs, and textbooks.

UTILITIES

Natural gas and electricity now are deregulated in Pennsylvania, so consumers can choose their own energy providers and packages. Wading through the options and deciding which is best for you can be a daunting task, but if you would like some guidance, contact the **Pennsylvania Public**

Utility Commission (PUC), (800) 692-7380 (general information); papowerswitch.com.

ℹ️ For complaints or issues you cannot resolve with your specific utility provider, you may call the Pennsylvania Public Utility Customer Hotline at (800) 692-7380 or visit puc.state.pa.us.

Natural Gas

PHILADELPHIA GAS WORKS (PGW)
800 W. Montgomery Ave.
Philadelphia, PA 19122
(215) 235-1000
pgworks.com
If you smell gas or have an unsafe condition, call (215) 235-1212 immediately.

Telephone

In Pennsylvania, you may choose your own telephone local service provider (LSP) that will provide the basics—dial tone, 911 emergency access, directory assistance, etc. Each LSP may offer optional services and calling plans in addition to basic service. For more information, go to puc.state.pa.us, and for a list of LSPs, call the Pennsylvania Public Utility Commission (PUC) at (888) PUC-FACT or go the PUC website, puc.state.pa.us, to find the providers for your particular county.

Water

PHILADELPHIA WATER DEPARTMENT
(215) 685-6300
phila.gov

VOTER INFORMATION

Information about how and where to register is available from the **Pennsylvania Department of State** at (877) VOTESPA (877-868-3772); votespa.com.

DRIVER'S LICENSES

In Pennsylvania, new residents must obtain a local driver's license within 60 days of establishing their permanent residence. All new residents are required to make an application for Pennsylvania title and registration of their vehicle(s) within 20 days of establishing residency in Pennsylvania. In-state: (800) 932-4600; out-of-state: (717) 412-5300; dmv.state.pa.us.

RESOURCES FOR SENIORS

For Philadelphia: Dial 311; phila.gov
For Bucks County: (215) 348-0510; buckscounty.org
For Chester County: (610) 344-6350; dsf.chesco.org
For Delaware County: (800) 416-4504, (610) 490-1300; co.delaware.pa.us
For Montgomery County: (610) 278-3601; montcopa.org

EDUCATION

They grow 'em smart in Philadelphia. With more than 860 public elementary, middle, and high schools in more than 60 public school districts in the 5-county Greater Philadelphia area—not to mention hundreds more charter, parochial, and private schools—educating kids is a top priority.

Higher education in Philly started before the country itself was formed, with Benjamin Franklin's founding of the University of Pennsylvania in 1740. Today more than 80 colleges and degree-granting institutions are located here—27 of them within Philadelphia's city limits—graduating 50,000-plus students each year. Future leaders come to Philly's 6 post-graduate business schools, 5 law schools, and 5 medical schools from all over the world.

But it's in the early years that education helps shape the mind. With so many hundreds of public schools, it would be impossible to profile individual schools, or even the area's 80 school districts, in a guidebook—but don't be overwhelmed, because there are easy resources for researching education in Greater Philadelphia. If your child will be joining the close to 150,000 students already attending Philly's city schools, your first stop should be the website of the school district of Philadelphia, phila.k12 .pa.us. There you will find the policies and programs guiding the system's 242 public schools, including 163 elementary, 23 middle, and 56 high schools. There are also 84 charter schools.

PHILADELPHIA

SCHOOL DISTRICT OF PHILADELPHIA
440 N. Broad St.
Philadelphia, PA 19130
(215) 400-4000
phila.k12.pa.us

The School District of Philadelphia is the 8th largest in the nation with an enrollment of close to 150,000 students grades K through 12. Of these students, almost 55 percent are African American, close to 19 percent are Hispanic, and a little over 14 percent are Caucasian. Many schools offer free or reduced-price breakfast and/or lunch programs.

Kindergarten students must be 5 years old by September 1 of the upcoming school year in order to register. To register your child in the city school system, you must bring some proof of the child's age, such as a birth certificate, baptismal certificate or other religious document, passport, or immigration documentation. You also should bring proof of a current address such as parent's driver's license, nondriver's ID, recent utility bill, or voter registration. That document must display the parent's name and address.

If your child is entering Philadelphia public schools for the first time, you also should bring proof that the child's immunizations are current (you may use a health passport or immunization summary sheet issued by a licensed health care provider or facility).

A recent report card and/or other document, and, if applicable, a copy of the child's Individualized Education Plan (IED), are required to ensure that the child is placed in the correct grade.

School closings due to weather or other emergencies are posted on the website at phila.k12.pa.us as well as announced on KYW 1060AM. This posting usually occurs by 5 a.m. of the day in question.

Breakdown of Schools by Type

Elementary: 163
Middle: 23
High School: 56
Charter Schools: 84

In-depth Information for Individual Public, Private, and Parochial Schools in the Philadelphia Area

NATIONAL CENTER FOR EDUCATION STATISTICS (NCES)
US Department of Education
1990 K St., NW
Washington, DC 20006
(202) 502-7300
nces.ed.gov
Includes enrollment by grade, race/ethnicity, gender, and availability of free and/or reduced-price meal programs.

At the Pennsylvania Department of Education website (portal.state.pa.us, choose the tab on the left-hand side of the page that says "Data and Statistics"), you can find the following information for individual public schools in the Philadelphia area: SAT scores and high school graduation and post-secondary education rates.

i Parents or guardians can access their child's school data including report card grades, attendance, test scores, and instructional resources at Family Net (phila.schoolnet.com).

ENROLLING IN PHILADELPHIA AREA SCHOOLS

Each of the 5 counties has its own "Intermediate Unit" that will provide information about curriculum, enrollment, and other school-related topics.

BUCKS COUNTY INTERMEDIATE UNIT
705 N. Shady Retreat Rd.
Doylestown, PA 18901
(800) 770-4822, (215) 348-2940
bucksiu.org

CHESTER COUNTY INTERMEDIATE UNIT
455 W. Boot Rd.
Downingtown, PA 19320
(484) 237-5000
cciu.org

DELAWARE COUNTY INTERMEDIATE UNIT
200 Yale Ave.
Morton, PA 19070
(610) 938-9000
dciu.org

MONTGOMERY COUNTY INTERMEDIATE

1605 W. Main St.
Norristown, PA 19403
(610) 539-8550
mciu.org

PENNSYLVANIA COALITION OF PUBLIC CHARTER SCHOOLS (PCPCS)

999 West Chester Pike, Ste. B-6
West Chester, PA 19382
(484) 356-0191
pacharters.org

You can find a list of charter schools through-out the state at this website.

PHILADELPHIA CHARTER SCHOOLS

440 N. Broad St.
Portal A–3rd Floor
Philadelphia, PA 19147
(215) 400-4090
webgui.phila.k12.pa.us

Philadelphia has 84 independently operated, nonprofit, nonsectarian charter schools, established to provide families with additional alternatives for their children's education. They are funded with federal, state, and local tax dollars and are approved by the local Board of Education. Charter schools hire their own teachers, design their own academic program, select textbooks and other instructional materials, determine the length of the school day and of the school year, decide on the number and kind of extracurricular activities, and make all other decisions. You will find a list of Philadelphia charter schools on this website.

PHILADELPHIA COUNTY INTERMEDIATE UNIT

7012 Rising Sun Ave.
Philadelphia, PA 19111
(see School District of Philadelphia)

Catholic Schools

ARCHDIOCESE OF PHILADELPHIA'S OFFICE OF CATHOLIC EDUCATION

222 N. 17th St.
Philadelphia, PA 19103
(215) 965-1740
catholicschools-phl.org

The Archdiocese of Philadelphia has 156 elementary schools, 17 high schools, and 4 schools of special education throughout the 5-county Greater Philadelphia area. On this website, you will find listings for and all other information about all of them.

Jewish Schools

PHILADELPHIA JEWISH DIRECTORY

jewishinphiladelphia.com
jewishphilly.org (The Jewish Community Website of Greater Philadelphia)

These websites include a listing of Jewish schools in the 5-county Greater Philadelphia area plus synagogues and seniors, singles, and community activities.

Private Schools

ASSOCIATION OF DELAWARE VALLEY INDEPENDENT SCHOOLS

701 W. Montgomery Ave.
Bryn Mawr, PA 19010
(610) 527-0130
advis.org

More than 130 private schools—including the best of the best—in the Delaware Valley (which includes eastern Pennsylvania, northern Delaware, and central and southern New Jersey) are described in detail on this site. On these listings you will find day and boarding schools, coed and boys or girls only, and with and without religious affiliations. Most are college preparatory.

Colleges & Universities

THE GREATER PHILADELPHIA ALLIANCE OF COLLEGES AND UNIVERSITIES

phillycolleges.org

With more than 90 colleges and universities located within the 5-county area, Philadelphia is one of the largest college towns in the US. Among the crown jewels are the University of Pennsylvania, which is consistently ranked among the top undergraduate, medical, research, law, engineering, and business schools in the country. In 2010, *Forbes* magazine included three suburban Philadelphia schools, Swarthmore, Haverford, and Bryn Mawr, among its "America's Best Colleges." Swarthmore also had the distinction of being named one of the nation's institutions by *Kiplinger* magazine.

In addition to the University of Pennsylvania, Philadelphia is also home to three other top medical schools at Temple University, Thomas Jefferson University, and Drexel University, which has the largest medical student enrollment of any private medical school in the nation.

Tuition prices quoted generally cover only tuition and board. Additional fees may be incurred for labs, first-year orientation, student activities, and/or other items.

Community Colleges

BUCKS COUNTY COMMUNITY COLLEGE
275 Swamp Rd.
Newtown, PA 18940
(215) 968-8100
bucks.edu

COMMUNITY COLLEGE OF PHILADELPHIA
1700 Spring Garden St.
Philadelphia, PA 19130
(215) 751-8010
ccp.edu

DELAWARE COUNTY COMMUNITY COLLEGE
901 S. Media Line Rd.
Media, PA 19063
(610) 359-5050
dccc.edu

Delaware County Community College also has 4 campuses in Chester County—in Downingtown, Exton, Jennersville, and West Chester.

MONTGOMERY COUNTY COMMUNITY COLLEGE
340 DeKalb Pike
Blue Bell, PA 19422
(215) 641-6551
mc3.edu

Philadelphia

ARCADIA UNIVERSITY
450 S. Easton Rd.
Glenside, PA 19038
(877) ARCADIA (272-2342)
(215) 572-2900
arcadia.edu

Founded in 1853, this coed school offers students a chance to study abroad for a semester in England or Scotland or during spring break in London, Ireland, Italy, Mexico, Scotland, or Spain.

DREXEL UNIVERSITY
3141 Chestnut St.
Philadelphia, PA 19104
(215) 895-2000
drexel.edu

Drexel's co-op program, providing under-graduate students with up to 18 months of professional experience before graduation, is the only mandatory one of its kind in Pennsylvania and one of only 3 in the US. With 9 colleges and 5 schools, the institution offers 73 undergraduate plus 82 master's and 32 graduate doctoral programs. Drexel is nationally recognized as one of the top engineering schools in the country and also offers highly regarded medical and law programs.

LASALLE UNIVERSITY
1900 W. Olney Ave.
Philadelphia, PA 19141
(215) 951-1500
lasalle.edu

This private Catholic university offers more than 50 majors in its undergraduate and graduate programs. The most popular majors are nursing, communications, education, accounting, and psychology; for graduate studies they are business administration, clinical counseling, psychology, and nursing. In addition to the Main Campus, the university offers degree programs on campuses in Bucks and Montgomery Counties.

MOORE COLLEGE OF ART AND DESIGN
1916 Race St.
Philadelphia, PA 19103
(215) 965-4000
moore.edu

Founded in 1848, Moore was the first and remains the only visual arts college in the US.

PENNSYLVANIA ACADEMY OF THE FINE ARTS
118 N. Broad St.
Philadelphia, PA 19102
(215) 972-7600
pafa.edu

PAFA was the first and remains the oldest art school (and museum) in the US. The academy's certificate program offers 2 years of classical training, then a term of practical fine arts work in a private studio. Partnerships enable students to earn a BFA degree from the University of Pennsylvania, or a 2-year MFA.

PHILADELPHIA UNIVERSITY
4201 Henry Ave.
Philadelphia, PA 19144
(215) 951-2700
philau.edu

Although its student body is small—around 3,500 including undergrads and grads—Philadelphia University has a big reputation in the disciplines of architecture, design, engineering, business, textiles, health, and sciences.

TEMPLE UNIVERSITY
1801 N. Broad St.
Philadelphia, PA 19122
(215) 204-7000
temple.edu

Temple is a big, big school—the 27th largest in the US—with an almost all-commuter student body of 39,000 enrolled in its 17 schools and colleges. Among its claims to fame are its schools of law, medicine, pharmacy, podiatry, and dentistry. It is also known as a top-notch research institution. I must add here that Temple is known for its journalism program as well—of which I am a graduate. In addition to its Main Campus in North Philadelphia, Temple has 3 other campuses in and around Philadelphia and 1 in Harrisburg.

UNIVERSITY OF PENNSYLVANIA
3451 Walnut St.
Philadelphia, PA 19104
(215) 898-7507
upenn.edu

Benjamin Franklin founded this world-renowned institution, the country's first university. The student body consists of 10,000 students in its undergraduate program plus another 10,000 attending its 12 graduate and professional schools. Penn is probably most well known for its Wharton School of Business, and its schools of law, medicine, veterinary medicine, nursing, and the Annenberg School for Communications are equally strong. Cross-disciplinary programs make it possible to design dual degrees in such areas as management and engineering or management and technology.

UNIVERSITY OF THE ARTS
320 S. Broad St.
Philadelphia, PA 19102
(800) 616-ARTS
uarts.edu

Founded over 130 years ago, University of the Arts was the first and remains the only university in the US dedicated to offering undergraduate and graduate degree programs in the visual, performing, and communication arts.

Chester County
CHEYNEY UNIVERSITY OF PENNSYLVANIA
1837 University Circle
Cheyney, PA 19319
(800) CHEYNEY, (610) 399-2275
cheyney.edu

Founded in 1837 as the Institute for Colored Youth, Cheyney is the oldest of the historically black colleges and universities in America and began as a teachers' college. Today it offers undergraduate degrees in more than 30 disciplines and a master's degree program in education.

LINCOLN UNIVERSITY
1570 Baltimore Pike
Lincoln University, PA 19352
(610) 932-8300
lincoln.edu

Langston Hughes and Thurgood Marshall were among the luminaries who graduated from Lincoln. For the first 100 years after its founding in 1854, this 2,000-student institution graduated approximately 20 percent of the black physicians and more than 10 percent of the black attorneys in the US.

Delaware County
SWARTHMORE COLLEGE
500 College Ave.
Swarthmore, PA 19081
(610) 328-8000
swarthmore.edu

This private school, founded by the Quakers in 1864, offers more than 50 courses of study that allow students to earn a BA degree in liberal arts or a BS in engineering. In recent years close to half of the school's students have spent one or two semesters studying abroad in some very unusual parts of the world such as Asia, New Zealand, and Africa.

ℹ️ Swarthmore, Bryn Mawr, and Haverford Colleges are part of a Tri-College Consortium, an inter-institutional collaboration that allows students to enroll at courses at all 3 schools. They may also cross-register for undergraduate courses at the University of Pennsylvania.

VILLANOVA UNIVERSITY
800 Lancaster Ave.
Villanova, PA 19085
(610) 519-4000
villanova.edu

US News and World Report named Villanova's master's program the best in the northern region. The school is also one of the top US Master's institution producers of Fulbright Scholars. It is composed of 5 colleges: the College of Liberal Arts and Sciences, School of Business, College of Engineering, College of Nursing, and School of Law.

Montgomery County
BRYN MAWR COLLEGE
101 N. Merion Ave.
Bryn Mawr, PA 19010
(610) 526-5000
brynmawr.edu

The *Wall Street Journal* ranked this all-women's institution among the nation's top 10 feeder schools to the nation's top law, medical, and business schools as well as in percentage of graduates going on to earn a Ph.D. Bryn Mawr offers 36 majors; 30 percent of students pursue majors in the natural sciences or mathematics (compared to 7 percent national average). Students have a 75 percent rate of acceptance to medical schools.

HAVERFORD COLLEGE
370 Lancaster Ave.
Haverford, PA 19041
(610) 896-1000
haverford.edu

This undergrad-only coed college, the first founded by the Quakers in 1833, has graduated numerous Fulbright and Rhodes Scholars, Nobel and Pulitzer Prize winners, and a score of other internationally prestigious honors. Seventy-five percent of its undergrads attend graduate school within 5 years.

CHILD CARE

Whether you're traveling or just settling in a new city, child care is always a big question mark. The factors are complicated: Is the agency or center licensed? What are the hours when traveling parents can get child care assistance, and how far is the center from the hotel? Should you get references from other parents—and if you're not from that city, how can you find references?

In most cases the questions are the same as when you're searching for child care at home. You'll want to know about the caregiver/child ratio, the history and safety record of the agency, and staff experience. You should find time to visit the center beforehand, to be sure the premises are cheery and clean, and to see if the center's philosophy and activities are a good match for your child. In these matters, your intuition is always your best guide.

In Philadelphia several online resources can make the research easier for you. One is Child Care Aware (CCA) (800-424-2246; childcareaware.org), an organization partly funded by the US Department of Health and Human Services that is able to offer services to families in 99 percent of all populated zip codes in the US.

CCA also is an excellent resource in learning how to ascertain which child care centers will suit your needs and your child's personality. The site offers articles to help you become a better informed parent, such as information on licensing and accreditation and what they mean, how to choose the best day care, and an "average rates finder" that will tell you what to expect to pay for child care in your zip code.

NATIONAL CHILDCARE CHAINS

BRIGHT HORIZONS
950 Walnut St., Ste. 102
Philadelphia, PA 19107
(215) 955-6556
brighthorizons.com
With more than 600 locations nationwide and in Canada, Ireland, and the United Kingdom, Bright Horizons specializes in worksite child care—but they do take drop-ins for parents on vacation or on a business trip. The Center City facility is open weekdays, 6:30 a.m. to 6:30 p.m., and they work with kids 6 weeks to 12 years old. The fee depends on the number of children, ages, and time they spend with Bright Horizons. Their Early Childhood Program offers a highly regarded curriculum, "The World at their Fingertips," which encourages all kids to be active in their communities. Bright Horizons also has centers in Bensalem and King of Prussia.

THE LEARNING EXPERIENCE
915 Old Fern Hill Rd., Bldg. C
West Chester, PA 19380
(610) 692-5004, (800) 865-7775
thelearningexperience.com

Taking the approach that children develop to their highest potential if they're allowed to learn at their own pace, The Learning Experience operates dozens of day care centers in the Mid-Atlantic states. Features include "Make Believe Boulevard," where kids can "work" at the firehouse, post office, market, or in shops, and a "Fun 'n Fit" program, teaching children that fitness is fun. Kids over 5 can participate in organized after-school sports, computer games, and arts and crafts.

ONLINE RESOURCES

A citywide babysitting subscription service, **Babysitters.com,** serves parents whether they typically need a sitter at the last minute or plan their nights out weeks in advance. They can search the detailed babysitter profiles for someone who suits them or post a job. Parents also will be interested in the "How To" series for both sitters and parents, with step-by-step advice on doing background checks, how much to pay a sitter, how to interview, and tips for working with a new family. Babysitters.com covers sitting for infants to children age 12; a subscription costs $39.95 for the first 3 months and $8.95 per month from then on.

For longer-term help, **4Nanny.com** is a nanny clearinghouse where parents can advertise for a nanny ($25 and up for a 30-day classified), research and compare fees of nanny agencies, and learn from sample work agreements and an "Ask the Experts" forum. FAQs here start with the basics, such as the differences between a nanny and an au pair. Prospective nannies, too, will find the site useful; they can post a resume, and both parties can learn the pros and cons of live-in versus live-out nannies.

Another service, **4sitters.com**, covers the globe, helping parents locate babysitters, nannies, home day care providers, house sitters, and even pet sitters worldwide. Parents will find the sitter "rating system" helpful, along with sitters' posted resumes—which viewers can review free of charge. Once you see that there are suitable nannies in your area, more information on them is available with a membership, $49.99 for the first 3 months, $9.99 per quarter thereafter.

HEALTH CARE

Because of the medical technology and research centers affiliated with Philadelphia's major universities, this city is fortunate to have more than its share of mega-hospital systems, large and small independent hospitals, and a wealth of walk-in and alternative-care facilities.

From state-of-the-art neonatal care to expert diagnostics, Philly has health care covered. With 20 hospital systems—and multiple hospitals within each system—it would be impossible in this guide to provide detailed information on each center in Greater Philadelphia. However, we have given contact information for walk-in centers and hospital systems, with notes on their locations, hospitals, and, in some cases, special details about the care offered.

HEALTH CARE CENTERS

CITY HEALTH CARE CENTERS
(215) 685-6790
phila.gov/health/AmbulatoryHealth
The Philadelphia Department of Public Health operates 8 health centers in neighborhoods across the city. Each center is staffed with doctors, nurses, dentists, and other health care providers that offer a wide range of services including diagnosis and treatment of chronic and acute illnesses; medical checkups and medications; emergency and basic dental care; family planning; prenatal and well baby care; immunizations and health screenings and tests. Some services are available on a walk-in basis, and some locations have bilingual staff. You must be a Philadelphia resident to use the services of these clinics. Call or visit the website to find the center near you and to make sure it provides the type(s) of services you need.

HOSPITAL SYSTEMS

ALBERT EINSTEIN HEALTHCARE NETWORK
(part of Jefferson Health System)
5501 Old York Rd.
Philadelphia, PA 19141
(215) 456-7890
einstein.edu
Albert Einstein Medical Center is a teaching hospital offering a full range of advanced health services including such specialties as behavioral health, geriatric services, heart care, kidney disease and transplantation, liver disease/transplantation, neurosurgery, orthopedics, and women's and children's services. Included are the following 5 facilities:

Einstein Center One (9880 Bustleton Ave.; 215-827-1600) serves Northeast Philadelphia and Lower Bucks and Montgomery Counties with a wide range of primary care and specialty services, including outpatient surgery.

Einstein at Elkins Park (60 Township Line Rd., Elkins Park, Montgomery County; 215-663-6000) is an acute care hospital with a 24-hour emergency department and inpatient and outpatient surgery capabilities.

Germantown Community Health Services (1 Penn Blvd., next to LaSalle University, near the intersection of Chew Street and Olney Avenue; 215-951-8000) provides care to residents of Northwest Philadelphia. Medical emergency services and crisis care response center are available 24 hours a day. Specialties include cardiology, dentistry, and ophthalmology.

Moss Rehab Centers (14 centers located in and beyond the 5-county Philadelphia area, 800-CALL-MOSS; mossrehab .com) have been named one of the top 10 hospitals for rehabilitation.

Einstein Neighborhood Healthcare is a network of primary care physicians including family practice doctors, internists, obstetricians, gynecologists, and pediatricians in Philadelphia, Bucks, and Montgomery Counties. Call (800) EINSTEIN or (215) 456-7800.

Willowcrest (5501 Old York Rd.; 215-456-8710) provides physician-directed, skilled nursing care and rehabilitation to help patients return to independence following hospitalization.

CROZER KEYSTONE HEALTH SYSTEM
(800) CK-HEALTH (254-3258)
crozer.org

This health system is composed of 5 hospitals and numerous other centers that provide prevention, acute care, rehabilitation and restorative care, a physician network of primary care and specialty practices, a Level 2 trauma center, regional burn center, 2 regional cancer centers, fertility center,

sleep-disorders center, and US Olympic Committee designated sports science and technology center. All of Crozier's facilities are located in Delaware County. The 5 major hospitals are Crozer-Chester Medical Center (1 Medical Center Blvd., Upland; 610-447-2000), Delaware County Memorial Hospital (501 N. Lansdowne Ave., Drexel Hill; 610-284-8100), Taylor Hospital (175 E. Chester Pike, Ridley Park; 610-595-6000), Springfield Hospital (190 W. Sproul Rd., Springfield; 610-328-8700), and Community Hospital (2600 W. 9th St., Chester; 610-494-0700).

HAHNEMANN UNIVERSITY HOSPITAL
Broad and Vine Streets
Philadelphia, PA 19102
(215) 762-7000
hahnemannhospital.com

Hahnemann has long been viewed as a model teaching hospital, and that tradition continues with its recent affiliation with Drexel University College of Medicine and St. Christopher's Hospital for Children. *USA Today* has ranked 9 of the hospital's specialties as among the best in the country.

HOLY REDEEMER HEALTH SYSTEM/
HOLY REDEEMER HOSPITAL AND
MEDICAL CENTER
1648 Huntingdon Pike
Meadowbrook, PA 19046
(800) 818-4747, (215) 947-3000
holyredeemer.com

Holy Redeemer provides comprehensive acute care and community-based diagnostics, home health services, and other care services and programs.

JEFFERSON HEALTH SYSTEM
259 N. Radnor-Chester Rd.
Radnor, PA 19087
(610) 225-6200
jeffersonhealth.org

In 2010, *US News & World Report* rated Thomas Jefferson University Hospitals among the nation's top medical centers in 8 specialties. The system consists of numerous hospitals and other health care facilities. The ones that are located in Philadelphia and its suburbs are: Thomas Jefferson University Hospital–Center City Campus (111 S. 11th St.; 215-955-6000), Jefferson Hospital for Neuroscience (900 Walnut St.; 215-503-1000), Methodist Hospital (2301 S. Broad St.; 215-952-9000), and Jefferson at the Navy Yard (3 Crescent Dr.; 800-JEFF-NOW). Also part of the Jefferson Health System are the hospitals and other health care facilities that operate under the **Main Line Health Banner** (866-CALL-MLH; 866-225-5654; mainline health.org). Main Line Health is suburban Philadelphia's most comprehensive health care resource, offering a full range of medical, surgical, obstetric, pediatric, psychiatric, and emergency services. At the core are 4 of the area's top acute care hospitals: Bryn Mawr Hospital (130 S. Bryn Mawr Ave., Bryn Mawr; 484-337-4507), Lankenau Hospital (100 Lancaster Ave., Wynnewood; 484-476-2000), Paoli Hospital (255 W. Lancaster Ave., Paoli; 484-829-6060), and Riddle Hospital (1068 W. Baltimore Pike, Media; 610-891-3178).

ℹ️ For referrals to or appointments with any physician within the Jefferson Health System, call 800-JEFF-NOW (800-533-3669).

MERCY HEALTH SYSTEM
1 W. Elm St.
Conshohocken, PA 19428
(610) 567-6000
mercyhealth.org

This largest Catholic health care system serves the Delaware Valley, including 4 acute care hospitals: Mercy Fitzgerald Hospital (1500 Lansdowne Ave., Darby, Delaware County; 610-237-4000), Mercy Philadelphia Hospital (501 S. 54th St.; 215-748-9000), Mercy Suburban Hospital (2701 DeKalb Pike, East Norriton; 610-278-2000), and Nazareth Hospital (2601 Holme Ave.; 215-335-6000).

TEMPLE UNIVERSITY HEALTH SYSTEM
Temple University Hospital (TUH)
3401 N. Broad St.
Philadelphia, PA 19140
(800) TEMPLE-MED
templehealth.org

One of the nation's most highly regarded academic, research, and medical centers, Temple University Hospital (TUH) provides inpatient and outpatient services to its North Philadelphia community and expert specialty services (for example, it was named one of the nation's top hospitals for pulmonology by *US News & World Report*). Two other Philadelphia locations are part of the Temple University Health System: Jeanes Hospital (7600 Central Ave.; 215-728-2000) and TUH Episcopal Campus (100 E. Lehigh Ave.; 215-707-1200).

UNIVERSITY OF PENNSYLVANIA HEALTH SYSTEM
(Penn Medicine)
(800) 789-PENN
pennmedicine.org

Operating under the Penn Medicine umbrella are the following hospitals:

Hospital of the University of Pennsylvania (3400 Spruce St., Philadelphia; pennmedicine.org/hup): The only thing I can say about Penn without taking up an entire chapter is that if something is seriously wrong with you, this is where you want to be. Period.

Penn Presbyterian Medical Center (51 N. 39th St., Philadelphia; 215-662-8000): Among this hospital's specialty areas are cardiology, cancer, family medicine, internal medicine, ophthalmology, orthopedics, radiology and imaging, and surgery. It is also considered a regional leader in performing minimally-invasive and robotic-assisted surgery.

Pennsylvania Hospital (800 Spruce St., Philadelphia; 215-829-3000): Founded in 1751 by Thomas Jefferson and Dr. Thomas Bond, this hospital now offers an extensive roster of specialties ranging from behavioral health to vascular medicine/surgery and is one of the area's premier teaching and clinical research institutions.

SPECIALTY HOSPITALS/HEALTH CARE FACILITIES

CHILDREN'S HOSPITAL OF PHILADELPHIA (CHOP)
34th Street and Civic Center Boulevard
Philadelphia, PA 19104
(215) 590-1000, (800) 879-2467
(physician referral)
chop.edu

Parents magazine's number one pediatric hospital and one of only 8 on the prestigious *US News & World Report* Honor Roll for 2010, CHOP is truly a groundbreaking facility both in patient care and research. CHOP's Pediatric Advanced Care Team (PACT) is focused specifically on coping with the physical, psychological, social, and spiritual support for terminally ill children and their families.

ℹ️ CHOP's Center for Fetal Diagnosis and Treatment is one of the premier facilities in the world for severely high-risk pregnancies. The team is a leader in fetal surgery and care. The Garbose Family Special Delivery Unit is the world's first birthing unit for expectant parents of babies with a known birth defect.

FOX CHASE CANCER CENTER
333 Cottman Ave.
Philadelphia, PA 19111
(215) 728-6900
fccc.edu

There are only 100 beds in the only hospital in the region devoted entirely to cancer treatment, research, and prevention, and it is one of the most respected in the nation. Comprehensive programs encompass every aspect of care.

PHILADELPHIA SHRINERS HOSPITAL
3551 N. Broad St.
Philadelphia, PA 19140
(215) 430-4000, (800) 281-4050
shrinershq.org/hospitals/philadelphia

One of 22 Shriners Hospitals in North America, Philadelphia Shriners provides complete care for children up to age 18 with orthopedic conditions, burns, spinal cord injuries, and cleft lip and palate in a family-centered environment, regardless of the patients' ability to pay.

ST. CHRISTOPHER'S HOSPITAL FOR CHILDREN
3601 A St.
Philadelphia, PA 19134
(215) 427-5000
stchristophershospital.com

Pediatrics is the specialty here, with 270 experts on staff representing a wide range of specialties. St. Chris has a Level I Pediatric Trauma Center, sleep center, cystic fibrosis center, and pediatric kidney transplant program. Its Burn Center is the only dedicated facility of its kind in the Philadelphia area.

MEDIA

Perhaps it's Philadelphia's prominent role in forging a new nation that initially planted the take-no-prisoners mentality in its publications. Whatever the origins, that same boldness and uncompromising journalistic integrity still drives Philly's publishing community today. Simply put, journalism here has attitude.

As in every city, media outlets here are changing and evolving constantly. What we do know is that all the media in Philadelphia—as in every major city—has faced new challenges in recent years from the Internet. Readers, viewers, and listeners get more information online every day, and no doubt the audiences for print, TV, and radio will pressure even more outlets to reinvent themselves.

NEWSPAPERS

Daily

PHILADELPHIA INQUIRER/DAILY NEWS
400 N. Broad St.
Philadelphia, PA 19130
(215) 854-2000
philly.com

First published in 1829, the *Inquirer* is the third-oldest surviving newspaper in the nation. The 1970s and '80s were the daily paper's heyday when it won 17 Pulitzer Prizes in 15 years. Today, like just about every other major city newspaper in the county, the "Inky" struggles for survival, so far always coming up for a last gasp when it seems that all is lost. Sister publication *The Daily News* is a 3-time Pulitzer-winning tabloid format that is also teetering on the edge, yet managing to remain on its feet, as of the writing of this book. It is particularly prized by Philly sports fans for its in-depth coverage of and commentary on the local teams. Available by subscription and in street boxes at retail,

hospitality, and other outlets, their combined circulation is a little more than 356,000.

Weekly

CATHOLIC STANDARD & TIMES
222 N. 17th St.
Philadelphia, PA 19103
(215) 587-3660
catholicphilly.com

The official newspaper for the Archdiocese of Philadelphia, the *Catholic Standard* presents news, opinions, and features of interest to the Catholic community. Available by subscription, it reports a circulation of about 125,000.

JEWISH EXPONENT
2100 Arch St.
Philadelphia, PA 19103
(215) 832-0700
jewishexponent.com

Founded in 1887, the *Exponent* publishes local and international news, opinion, and features of interest to Philadelphia's Jewish community. Published weekly, the paper has about 50,000 paid subscribers.

PHILADELPHIA BUSINESS JOURNAL
400 Market St., Ste. 1200
Philadelphia, PA 19106
(215) 238-1450
philadelphia.bizjournals.com

The *Business Journal* is part of a chain of 40 newspapers across the country published by American City Business Journals. This weekly paper, which is available by subscription, publishes local and national news pertinent to small and large businesses with in-depth coverage on close to 15 industries including health care, real estate, technology, retail, hospitality, banking, and insurance.

PHILADELPHIA CITY PAPER
123 Chestnut St., 3rd Fl.
Philadelphia, PA 19106
(215) 735-8444
citypaper.net

One of Philly's two rival alternative weeklies, *City Paper* is the town's largest weekly, distributed free every Thursday in more than 2,000 locations including offices, high-traffic retail outlets, restaurants, street boxes, and other public places.

PHILADELPHIA GAY NEWS
505 S. 4th St.
Philadelphia, PA 19147
(215) 625-8501
epgn.com

Founded in 1975, *PGN* is the nation's oldest and the East Coast's largest weekly newspaper serving the gay community with news, entertainment, event listings, and other items of specific interest. Circulation for this free publication is 15,000.

PHILADELPHIA SUNDAY SUN
6661-63 Germantown Ave.
Philadelphia, PA 19119
(215) 848-7864
philasun.com

The *Sun's* target audience is the African-American community, whom it reaches with commentary, health, news, and sports coverage. Published weekly and available by paid subscription, it has a circulation of about 20,000.

PHILADELPHIA WEEKLY
1500 Sansom St., 3rd Fl.
Philadelphia, PA 19102
(215) 563-7400
philadelphiaweekly.com

With a circulation of over 107,000, the *Weekly* is the *City Paper's* biggest competition for the alternative-paper audience.

PERIODICALS

PHILADELPHIA
1818 Market St., 36th Fl.
Philadelphia, PA 19103
(215) 564-7700
phillymag.com

If you can only read one publication in this city, read *Philadelphia* magazine. It will tell what waits around every corner and under every rock. Whether they're doing an investigative report or reviewing restaurants, these writers and editors don't mind controversy. In fact, the style is often snarky. In other words, it has "atty-tude."

PHILADELPHIA STYLE
141 League St.
Philadelphia, PA 19147
(215) 468-6670
phillystylemag.com

Published 6 times a year, *Philadelphia Style* offers stories on beauty, fashion, home decor and style, art, and travel. Profiles of artists and restaurateurs add to the mix.

TELEVISION

Comcast Cable is the cable provider for the city of Philadelphia: 1 Comcast Center; (800) COMCAST (266-2278); comcast.com.

Other locally based television stations:
WKYW-TV 3 (CBS)
WPVI-TV 6 (ABC)
WCAU-TV 10 (NBC)
WHYY-TV 12 (PBS)
WPHL-TV 17
WTXF-TV 29 (FOX)

RADIO

The following is just a partial list of the dozens of radio stations broadcasting from Philadelphia. We've included their specialties as of this writing, but, as in any part of the country, they can change formats virtually overnight.

Alternative

WRFF 104.5 FM

Country

WXTU 92.5 FM

Hip-Hop

WRDW Wired 96.5 FM
WUSL Power 99 98.9 FM
WPHI 103.9 FM

News/Talk

For all things headline, weather (including school closings), and traffic all the time, Philly's go-to station is KYW Newsradio 1060 AM.

WPHT 1210 AM "The Big Talker" (including Rush Limbaugh, Glenn Beck, and Sean Hannity)
WNTP 990 AM

Oldies/Nostalgia

WBUD 1260 AM (News/Oldies)
WRDV 89.3 FM (Big Band/Oldies)
WOGL 98.1 FM
WWDB 96.5 FM (The Point/All '80s)
WHAT 1340 AM

Public Radio

NJN 88.1 FM (National Public Radio)
WRTI 90.1 FM (Temple University/Classical and Jazz)
WHYY 90.9 FM (PBS)
WXPN 88.5 FM (University of Pennsylvania/World Music)

Religious/Gospel Music

WFIL 560 AM
WNAP 1110 AM
WISP 1570 AM

Rock

WMMR 93.3 FM (Classic Rock)
WMGK 102.9 (Classic Rock)

Spanish

Mega 1310 AM

Sports

WIP 610 AM
97.5 FM (The Fanatic)

Top 40

WIOQ 102.1 FM
MY106.1 FM

PENNSYLVANIA DUTCH COUNTRY

Although Philadelphia was my home for most of my life, Pennsylvania Dutch County in south-central Pennsylvania, about 2 hours away from the City of Brotherly Love, is now. The way it happened was simple: I came here as a journalist looking for a story and never left.

Many visitors come to south-central Pennsylvania in search of a place where farms, homes, and businesses are still fueled by wind and water instead of by amps and watts and transportation runs on horsepower of the hay-munching rather than gas-guzzling variety. Lancaster County has the second largest Amish population and the oldest surviving settlement in the world.

But first-timers are often confused by the sight of sprawling big-brand shopping outlets, the razzle-dazzle of theme parks, the bright lights of theaters, and the profusion of fast-food emporia that line the major arteries of Pennsylvania Dutch Country. Where are all the horses and buggies? The windmills? The distinctively named delicacies such as shoofly pie, chowchow, schnitz, and knepp? Above all, where are the Amish?

They're all here, if you know where to look.

Turn off just about any main highway and you'll discover the back roads, country byways that meander for miles, winding their way past fields, farms, and home-based barn and basement businesses advertised by small, hand-lettered signs. You'll see eggs gathered from the henhouse that morning, fresh-pressed cider from homegrown apples, the sweetest corn you'll ever taste, and cakes and pies baked from generations-old family recipes. At stores large and small you'll find quilts stitched into centuries-old patterns that weave together history and artistry, as well as hand-hewn wooden furniture and toys destined to become heirlooms.

The traffic moves slower back there; horses don't have speedometers. If you're not in a hurry, the steady clip-clop pace of the old-fashioned buggies gives you time to get a good glimpse of a very different lifestyle. (Some of those buggies are carrying tourists, but most are filled with resident farmers and their families just going about their daily routines.)

But don't dismiss Pennsylvania Dutch Country as a one-trick pony. It isn't a living history museum, frozen in a time centuries past. It is a living culture, one that has remained stable at its core amid an onslaught of technological, ideological, and theological change. And the influence of the Amish on their surroundings—and vice versa—continues to evolve.

While interest in the Amish is undoubtedly a major reason why more than 11 million visitors travel to Lancaster County every year, it's definitely not the only one.

If it's greener pastures you're after, you can book a stay at a working dairy, produce, or horse farm where the resident rooster can roust the kids at chore time, while you just snuggle in your feather bed. Perhaps the only birdie you want to see is on a score card. For you, there is a galaxy of stellar golf courses and resort-style facilities that make them family-friendly.

Find out how the tiny towns of Intercourse, Blue Ball, and Bird-in-Hand got their colorful names, and discover each one's unique personality and charm. For railroad aficionados, all tracks lead to Strasburg, where you can still take a steam train to Paradise. Or you can take to the sky for a whole new perspective on the countryside from the basket of a hot air balloon.

Then let your sweet tooth lead you to two towns that were built on chocolate—Lititz, home of Wilbur Chocolate, and, of course, Hershey. You can work off those chocolate calories during your shopping spree. Whether you're looking for discounts (Lancaster is home to two humongous, side-by-side outlet centers), priceless antiques (Adamstown, in northeastern Lancaster County, is nicknamed the "Antiques Capital of the US"), or world-class artisan crafts, you'll find opportunities in abundance to give your credit cards a good workout.

Although Lancaster County, the heart of Pennsylvania Dutch Country, covers close to 950 square miles spanning 60 independent municipalities, it is only 46 miles at its widest and 43 at its longest, so you can easily drive to any point within its boundaries in an hour or less. But you couldn't see or do it all if you stayed here for years.

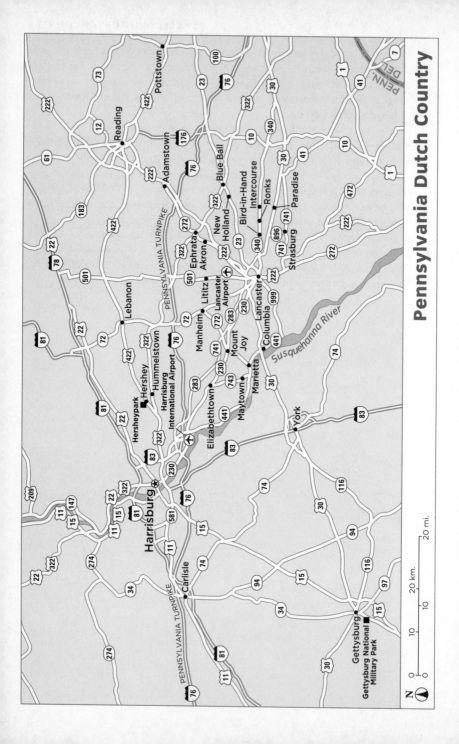

Pennsylvania Dutch Country

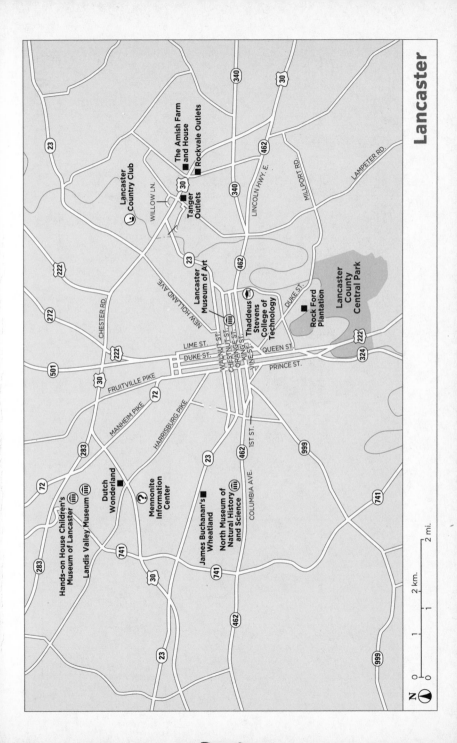

Lancaster

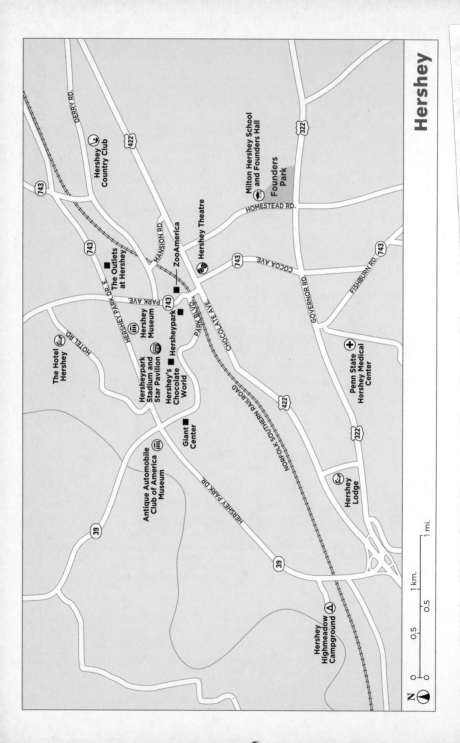

Hershey

AREA OVERVIEW

Although the term "Pennsylvania Dutch Country" is usually associated with the cities, towns, and villages of Lancaster County, the Pennsylvania Tourism Office also includes Hershey in Dauphin County under the same destination umbrella.

LANCASTER COUNTY

Many of the most popular Amish-oriented tours and attractions are located just east of Lancaster City, in the towns and villages of Bird-in-Hand and Intercourse. North of the city are numerous small communities— including Ephrata, Denver, Lititz, and Adamstown—many of which blend the pastoral beauty of rolling farmlands (including more than 66,300 acres of family farmland on 770 family farms under preservation) with quaint main street business districts and a combination of faithfully preserved old and chic new residential areas.

i During the American Revolution, Lancaster City was the capital of the US for one day. On September 27, 1777, the Continental Congress, which had fled Philadelphia just ahead of invading British troops, convened in Lancaster before continuing across the Susquehanna River to the city of York, around 25 miles to the southwest.

Western Lancaster County offers the charming Susquehanna River towns of Columbia, Marietta, and scenic Mount Joy. And a highlight of the southern part of the county is the railroad-centric town of Strasburg and miles of natural areas, recreational parks, and state parks.

Lancaster County's agricultural diversity—and appeal as a year-round tourism destination—is supported by a climate in which each of the four seasons brings its own distinctive weather patterns, beauty, and activity opportunities.

Spring is planting time for farmers and gardening hobbyists, so even though the flowers and fields aren't yet in full bloom, there are plenty of colorful sights to see. As you pass by the farms, keep an eye out for the baby calves, sheep, and foals wobbling as they try out their legs under watchful parental supervision.

For the most part, you can expect the roads to be emptier, the lines to be shorter, and the lodging rates to be lower from March through mid-June. But keep in mind that seasonal festivals, limited openings of certain outdoor attractions, art shows, craft fairs, local auctions, and just the opportunity to ramble along budding country roads often bring out fair numbers of pleasure seekers. Spring temperatures can range from the 50s to the 70s Fahrenheit, so keep an eye on the local forecasts if you plan to visit, and pack a sweater or light jacket, just in case.

i Lancaster was the home of the only Pennsylvania-born (and only bachelor) president of the US, James Buchanan. His mansion, Wheatland, is open for public tours.

Summer is peak season, not just for tourism, but also for sunshine and temperatures that average in the low 80s Fahrenheit, but have often been known to rise into the 90s. Mid-June to early September can be pretty humid here, too, which is great for the crops but may cause you to wilt if you spend too much time out in the heat. You're never too far, though, from a refreshing drink of homemade birch beer (a locally loved, reddish, carbonated root beer–type drink that packs a flavor punch with a finish of wintergreen) or a cone of ice cream from a dairy down the road. Fields and orchards are full to bursting with veggies and fruit ripe and ready for you to pick or buy at the farm stands that spring up everywhere like wildflowers.

Fall in Lancaster County is generally crisp and cool (actually, it can range from the warmth of an Indian summer to an early winter chill), like the apples that come from its orchards. Farms and vineyards are in full harvest mode. Pumpkins proliferate in the fields and at the farm stands for jack-o'-lantern making and pie baking.

In late September and early October, leaf peepers will love the golden and flame-colored foliage. After the harvest, in November and early December, look for the blue dresses of the Amish brides.

Some winters are whiter than others (average snowfall for the season is 26.4 inches), but from mid-December through February, there are mugs of steaming mulled cider, Currier and Ives-type scenery, horse-drawn sleigh rides, and warm, snuggly inns with fireplaces and feather beds to keep you cozy. Shopping is an all-season sport and holiday shopping an all-star event whether you're looking for something homespun or haute couture. Temperatures can plummet (low 30s Fahrenheit and below), so button up and break out the long johns.

i All of the drama wasn't on film when Harrison Ford and company came to Intercourse, Lancaster County, to film scenes for the movie *Witness*. Complaints about the crowds from some Amish customers prompted the owner of W. L. Zimmerman & Sons General Store (3601 Old Philadelphia Pike, Intercourse; 717-768-8291), where some of the filming was done, to take out a letter of apology in the community's newspaper.

HERSHEY

Located about a 40-minute drive from Lancaster City is a place that is known by many names, including "Chocolatetown USA" and "The Sweetest Place on Earth." An interesting tidbit is that the town of Hershey doesn't really exist because it was never officially incorporated. The people who live there are actually citizens of Derry Township—that's where they pay their taxes and send their children to school. But if you mail a letter addressed to Hershey, it will arrive because the post office does bear the name of the famous chocolatier who built the town.

The history of Milton Hershey and the place and company that bear his name are further explored in the Hershey chapter of this book.

For chocoholics, Hershey is not just a vacation destination, it's a pilgrimage that leads you to a town where the major intersection is Chocolate and Cocoa Avenues and the street lamps are shaped like candy Kisses. Located in Dauphin County, Hershey's proximity to the state capital of Harrisburg (12 miles to the west) makes it part of Pennsylvania's "Capital Region." But its proximity to Lancaster (20 miles to the south) and heritage make it very much Pennsylvania Dutch.

Founder Milton Hershey was born in this area, then still known as Derry Township, in 1826. You might be surprised to know that Milton, who only had a fourth-grade education, made several failed attempts at starting candy companies (making caramels) in Lancaster, New York, and Chicago before he finally opened the Hershey Chocolate Company in 1894.

Here are a few more interesting facts:

- Prior to succeeding in the candy business, Milton Hershey, along with his father, went to Denver, Colorado, to seek his fortune in the silver mines.
- When Milton Hershey first started producing chocolate, it was called "sweet" but was actually what we now refer to as "dark." At that time, the lighter and more delicate "milk chocolate," which was made only in Switzerland, was so expensive it could only be afforded by the wealthy. Milton Hershey worked for many years to come up with a combination of milk, sugar, and cocoa that could rival the coveted Swiss recipe.
- To pay debts, Milton Hershey's father, Henry, sold their family farm in Derry Township. In 1896 Milton bought it back and in 1909 made it the first location of his school for orphan boys.
- The Derry Church School, one of the many one-room schoolhouses Milton Hershey attended during his early years, sits next to the entrepreneur's High Point Mansion, which he built after his success in the business world. After he created the now iconic Hershey Bar in 1900, Milton decided to build a much larger factory and a model family-oriented town around it in Derry Township. In 1907 he opened a small picnic park for the residents' use. That community recreational spot eventually grew into today's more than 110-acre Hersheypark.
- In 1907 Milton Hershey invented his eponymous chocolate Kiss candy, which is believed to have been so named for the sound or motion of the chocolate being deposited during the manufacturing process.

GETTING HERE, GETTING AROUND

Whether you're making the trip by car, plane, train, or bus, getting to Lancaster County is pretty much a snap, especially when you consider that early-18th-century traders and travelers from Philadelphia used to slog for 4 days along bumpy, rut-pocked, mired-in-mud "roads." Although that route had the regal name of "King's Highway," it was really nothing more than a glorified dirt trail.

The construction of the nation's first turnpike, which opened in 1795, significantly smoothed the way, allowing stagecoaches to make the journey from Philadelphia in around 12 hours. Sharing the turnpike were Conestoga wagons (which, by the way, were invented in Lancaster County) drawn by horses specially bred to haul hefty loads of produce from Lancaster County farms to Philadelphia markets. Lancaster also became a primary "Gateway to the West" for settlers on their way to the Allegheny Mountains.

GETTING HERE

By Car

Turnpike driving has changed a lot since the 18th century, but it's still the quickest way to get to Lancaster County. The Pennsylvania Turnpike (US Route 76) travels in an east–west direction across the northern part of Lancaster County. Exit 266/Lancaster-Lebanon (old exit 20) will take you into Lancaster via PA Route 72, exit 286/Lancaster-Reading (old exit 21) via US Route 222.

All of Lancaster County's major highways (except the Pennsylvania Turnpike) come together in Lancaster City, so it's a perfect geographical launching point for a grand tour of Pennsylvania Dutch Country, as well as a worthy historic and entertaining destination on its own.

You can take your time and soak in all the scenery because the entire county is only 46 miles wide and 43 miles long. That means you can be anywhere you want to be in an hour or less.

By Air

Lancaster County
LANCASTER AIRPORT
Lancaster Airport (717-569-1221; lancaster airport.com), located at the intersection of Route 501/Lititz Pike and Airport Road in Lititz, 6 miles north of Lancaster City, is serviced by Sun Air. For more information call (877) 849-4998 or visit gosunair.com.

Dauphin County

HARRISBURG INTERNATIONAL AIRPORT (FAA CODE MDT)

Harrisburg International Airport, aka HIA (513 Airport Dr., Middletown, PA 17057; 717-944-8933; flyhia.com), is served by 7 major airlines offering nonstop daily flights to 13 domestic and 1 international destination, along with one-stop service to cities around the world.

AIR CANADA

Reservations: (888) 247-2262

aircanada.ca

All Air Canada flights at this airport are handled by Continental. This includes check-in and baggage.

Nonstop daily to Toronto.

AIR TRAN AIRWAYS

Reservations: (800) 247-8726

airtran.com

Daily nonstop to Orlando and Fort Lauderdale.

AMERICAN EAGLE

Reservations: (800) 433-7300

aa.com

Nonstop daily to Chicago–O'Hare.

CONTINENTAL AIRLINES

Reservations: (800) 525-0280

continental.com

Nonstop daily to Cleveland and Newark.

DELTA AIRLINES

Reservations: (800) 221-1212

delta.com

Nonstop daily to Atlanta, Cincinnati, and Detroit.

UNITED

Reservations: (800) 241-6522

ual.com

Nonstop daily to Chicago–O'Hare and Washington, DC–Dulles.

US AIRWAYS

Reservations: (800) 428-4322

usairways.com

Nonstop daily to Boston, Charlotte, Philadelphia, and New York–La Guardia.

i Route 30 in Lancaster County can be a bumper-to-bumper, slow-going crawl during peak tourist times in summer or fall. You can get a preview of whether you can expect smooth sailing or should seek an alternate route by checking out the live Route 30 cam sponsored by Lancaster Newspapers on the website lancasteronline.com/pages/cams/?name=30cam. Located at some of Route 30's busiest exits—to the Fruitville, Lititz, and Oregon Pikes—this traffic-tracking technology provides both east and west perspectives of the road.

Hershey

If you're staying at one of the Hershey resorts, shuttle service to and from Harrisburg International Airport can be arranged for a reasonable fee. Baltimore–Washington Airport (BWI) is about 90 minutes away by car.

By Train

Lancaster County

Amtrak operates 2 rail lines with stops at the Lancaster Amtrak Passenger Station (code LNC) in the city's downtown area (53 McGovern Ave.; 800-USA-RAIL or 800-872-7245;

amtrak.com). Lancaster Station offers an enclosed waiting area with ATM and Quik Trak Automated Ticketing System availability.

Amtrak's Keystone Service, which provides daily service between New York City and Harrisburg by way of Philadelphia, stops at stations in Harrisburg, Elizabethtown, Mount Joy, and Lancaster. *The Pennsylvanian,* which travels daily between New York City and Pittsburgh via Philadelphia and Harrisburg, stops at Lancaster Station.

Taxis and rental cars are available from Lancaster Station.

Hershey

The Harrisburg Train Station (code HAR), serviced by Amtrak, is a 15-minute drive from Hershey (4th and Chestnut Streets, Harrisburg; 800-USA-RAIL or 800-872-7245; amtrak .com). Guests of Hershey resorts may arrange for a reasonably priced shuttle service to their particular accommodation.

By Bus

Lancaster City
GREYHOUND BUS LINES

Greyhound Bus Lines (53 McGovern Ave.; 800-231-2222 or 717-397-4861) offers daily service to Lancaster.

Hershey
GREYHOUND BUS LINES

Greyhound at the Harrisburg Train Station (4th and Chestnut Streets, Harrisburg; 800-229-9424; greyhound.com) is the closest station. Hershey Resort guests may arrange for a reasonably priced shuttle service to their particular accommodations.

GETTING AROUND

Car Rentals

Lancaster County

Both Avis (717-569-3185) and Hertz (717-569-2331) have rental facilities at Lancaster Airport.

Most major car rental companies also have locations throughout Lancaster County. To reach them, call: Avis—Lancaster (717-560-5353, 717-343-3963); Enterprise (717-391-7080, 717-290-1111); Hertz (717-396-0000).

Hershey

The following rental companies have locations on the first floor of the Multi-Modal Transportation Facility, adjacent to the terminal at Harrisburg International Airport:

Alamo (717-948-0395)
Avis (717-948-3721)
Budget (717-944-4019)
Enterprise (717-948-5910)
Hertz (717-944-4018)
National (717-948-0390)

Parking

Lancaster City

A number of downtown Lancaster hotels, motels, bed-and-breakfasts, and inns offer free off-street parking for overnight guests. For day-trippers, there are plenty of strategically located parking lots, garages, and meters.

PARKING GARAGES

The Lancaster Parking Authority (717-299-0907) operates 5 garages. The 3 largest and most convenient to city attractions, shopping, and dining cost $2 per hour, $1 per additional or any part of an hour to a maximum of $14 per day.

DUKE STREET GARAGE
150 N. Duke St.
Lancaster, PA 17602

EAST KING STREET
150 E. King St.
Lancaster, PA 17602
(Directly behind the East King Street Garage is the Mifflin Street Surface Lot, 146 E. Mifflin St. Fees are the same as for the garages.)

PENN SQUARE GARAGE
28 S. Duke St.
Lancaster, PA 17602

PRINCE STREET GARAGE
111 N. Prince St.
Lancaster, PA 17603

WATER STREET GARAGE
220 N. Water St.
Lancaster, PA 17603
Flat $5 fee all day.

i If you're driving, the major streets of downtown Lancaster are 2 lanes but in only 1 direction. If you want to head south, use either Prince or Duke Streets; to go north, use either Queen or Lime Streets. It's westward on Orange and Walnut Streets, eastbound on King and Chestnut Streets.

CITY-OWNED PARKING LOTS

The **Lancaster Parking Authority** operates 2 public metered surface lots. Cost is 25 cents per 12 minutes. The **Christian Street Lot** is located on Christian Street behind the Fulton Bank and the Courthouse. The **Library Lot** is located on Christian Street behind the Duke Street Library.

ON-STREET PARKING METERS

Downtown on-street metered parking is available for 25 cents for 12 minutes, 8 a.m. to 6 p.m. Mon through Sat. Outside of the downtown area, parking costs 25 cents for 15 minutes. Most have 2-hour limits.

Hershey

Most of the major attractions, accommodations, and dining spots have parking lots on their premises. Some charge a parking fee, depending on the site and time of year.

i If you park your car in one of the Lancaster Historic Area public garages, be sure to take your ticket when you tour. Many downtown merchants will validate parking garage tickets. Just ask wherever you shop or dine.

Limos, Passenger Vans & Private Charter Buses

Lancaster County
EXPRESSIONS LIMOUSINE OF LANCASTER
(717) 556-5466
expressionslimo.com

FRIENDLY TRANSPORTATION SERVICE
(800) 795-FAST, (717) 392-2222
friendlytransportation.com
Twenty-four-hour, 7-day-a-week taxi service or chauffeur-driven Lincoln town cars or passenger vans. Wheelchair-accessible buses are available.

LANCASTER YELLOW CAB CO. INC.
(717) 397-8100

Public Transportation

Lancaster
RED ROSE TRANSIT AUTHORITY (RRTA)
45 Erick Rd.
Lancaster, PA 17601
(717) 397-4246
redrosetransit.com

RRTA operates 17 bus routes that serve Lancaster City and County. In the city, bus stops are marked by signs. If you're traveling outside the city, make sure you have a schedule with you to note the route of the bus you want. If you want to get on and there is no sign nearby to indicate a regularly scheduled stop, just wait at a safe spot (that is, out of the path of traffic) on the side of the road and wave when you see a bus approaching. The driver will stop to allow you to board. Each RRTA bus is clearly marked on the front, sides, and back with a route number and a name. Fares are determined by zone, beginning at $1.60 to a maximum of $2.80. Transfers are an additional 5 cents plus any applicable zone fares (20 cents to $1.25). Persons with special physical needs and those under age 65 with a Medicare card can ride for half fare during off-peak hours (peak hours are 7 to 8 a.m. and 4:30 to 5:30 p.m. weekdays). To qualify, passengers must show a Half Fare ID card (available to qualified individuals from RRTA). Students (kindergarten through grade 12) are eligible for a student rate; high schoolers must show proof of student status to obtain the discount rate. Children ages 5 and under ride free when accompanied by a full-fare paying passenger. Senior citizens age 65 and older with a transit ID or Medicare card ride free anytime.

i Touring downtown Lancaster is a bargain when you leave your car at the Red Rose Transit Authority's Park 'n Ride lot at Clipper Magazine Stadium (use main entrance from North Prince Street at Clay Street) and hop on the Historic Downtown Trolley shuttle. Parking at the lot is free for trolley passengers, and an all-day ticket to ride costs only $3.25 (regular per-ride ticket price is $1.50). The trolley leaves the lot every 15 minutes Mon through Fri during peak hours. Stops for pick-up and drop-off also include the Amtrak Station and Greyhound Bus Terminal and the Downtown Lancaster Visitors Center. The trolley runs from 7:10 a.m. to 6:30 p.m.

Bicycling

Lancaster County
Lancaster County's back roads are just made for long, leisurely bike rides. If you have a basket on your handlebars, you can stock up on just-picked produce from the farms that tend to pop up all along these less-traveled trails. There's no better way to tour the county's famous covered bridges. For weekend athletes looking for an easy ride, keep to the flatter areas around Bird-in-Hand and Leola. More challenging are the hills south of Strasburg and Route 741. Lancaster County has more miles of road than any other county in Pennsylvania, most of which remain untainted by motorists and commercial establishments. The Lancaster Bike Club has graciously detailed some of its members' favorite scenic routes on its website (lancasterbikeclub.org) to help you plan a ride to remember. When you access the site, click on the heading "Scenic Tours of Lancaster County."

THE PENNSYLVANIA "DUTCH"

Despite the working windmills that still power a number of the farms that dot the rolling green hills of Lancaster and surrounding counties, the term "Pennsylvania Dutch" refers to neither Holland nor the Netherlands. Historians tend to agree that Dutch is an Anglicized version of the word *Deutsch*, meaning "German," a reference to the language spoken by many of the settlers who came here in the early 1700s.

While many people associate Pennsylvania Dutch with the Old Order Amish, a religious group that differentiates itself from others by dressing in simple, dark clothing, eschewing the use of electricity in their homes, and choosing the horse and buggy as their primary mode of transportation, there is actually a wide range of other nationalities and religions represented here. This diversity is what actually gives Pennsylvania Dutch Country its unique flavor. But it is still the Amish and the other "Plain People" who give the area its special mystique.

THE PLAIN PEOPLE

For many tourists, the sight of bearded men in broad-brimmed hats and women in aprons and bonnets, horse-drawn buggies, and windmills may be a novelty. But for about 52,000 (double the number from 2004) of the total close to 508,000 residents of the Pennsylvania Dutch heartland, this no-frills lifestyle is a matter of faith that has been passed down through generations over hundreds of years.

"Plain People" is a term commonly identified with the most conservative members (or "Old Order") of the religious group known as the Amish. In reality, the Amish make up only about one quarter of the area's total "Plain" population. There are also a number of other denominations that base their lifestyles on modesty and humility. For example, Lancaster County has one of the world's largest Mennonite communities. Both of these religious groups are Anabaptists because, unlike other Christian faiths, they don't believe in baptism at birth. Instead they believe that baptism should be a conscious and voluntary choice that can be made only by an adult.

For this and their basic principle of separation of church and state, the Anabaptists were persecuted and, if not killed, banished from their European homelands. Their belief in nonresistance or pacifism would not allow them to take up a sword to defend themselves, their families, or their homes. Even today, pacifism remains a central tenet in all Anabaptist sects.

Over the centuries, immigrants from all over Europe brought their religions and customs to Lancaster County, and it continues to be a diverse and constantly evolving area today. All live physically side by side, but the

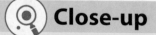

Close-up

Rumspringa

Just because the "Old Order" Amish choose to separate themselves from the rest of the world doesn't mean they have no experience with it. From the age of 16 until they choose to be (or not to be) baptized, youngsters are given the opportunity to "flirt with the world," as Donald Kraybill, author of *The Riddle of Amish Culture*, describes the tradition known as rumspringa, or the "running around years."

During rumspringa, boys and girls join social groups called "gangs," each of which has a distinctive personality and determines its own activities. Some like to enjoy sports and dances; others take their freedom further by shucking their "Plain" clothes and hairstyles. Some boys even buy cars to transport them to places they've never seen and are not likely to see again after rumspringa.

Non-Amish people may assume that tasting the temptations of the outside world will lure great numbers of Amish young people from the "Plain" life. The reality is quite the contrary. Over the past 20 years the Amish population has actually doubled, according to the Pennsylvania Dutch Convention and Visitors Bureau. Some of this growth can be attributed to average family sizes of 7 to 10 children, but, just as important, it seems that people who are born Amish usually choose to remain Amish. The general consensus among experts is that between 80 and 90 percent of the young people opt for baptism.

"Old Order" Amish and Mennonites remain separate. The conservative "Old Order" Amish and Mennonites do everything they can to keep the influences of the outside world from affecting their way of worship and their way of life. They even have a separate name for anyone who is not a member of the Amish faith—"English" (or "Englishers").

Within their own communities, the Amish live, work, and worship as a tightly knit unit. Every aspect of their lives is governed by a set of rules called the Ordnung ("order").

i Unless you're invited into someone's home, the best glimpse you'll get of "Plain" living is at the Amish Farm and House, located at 2395 Route 30 E in Lancaster (717-394-6185; amishfarmandhouse.com).

They do, however, pay the same taxes as everyone else, with the exception of Social Security and workers' compensation, from which self-employed Amish individuals are exempt.

Any perception of the Amish life as all work and no play would not be correct. It's just that these people have learned to combine fun with function. Sometimes a frolic is gender-specific, as is the case when women get together for a day of quilting, canning, or baking (these occasions are often referred to as "bees"). Men may form a "threshing ring" to help harvest one another's crops, and all will participate in the building of a new home or school. Such get-togethers offer members a chance to socialize as they work toward a common goal.

Programs such as Social Security, Medicare, Medicaid, and other public subsidy programs administered by the government are totally opposite to the self-sufficiency that characterizes the Amish community. It may seem odd that in a country where individuality is so prized the Amish live according to a code that places such emphasis on obedience to God and yielding to the general will of the community. While this way of life may seem foreign and even harsh to outsiders, to the Amish it is a means of preserving a culture that is based on humility and brotherhood, in which neighbors and generations take care of one another. For example, if a neighbor has a fire, the community gets together at a barn raising to help rebuild. When one member is ill or disabled, other community members immediately pitch in to help with chores and, if necessary, finances.

While an estimated 85 percent of the Amish adhere to Old Order traditions and beliefs, there are actually other subgroups within the Amish faith, including the "New Order" Amish, who also dress plainly, use horses and buggies as their primary mode of transportation, and hold their worship services in one another's homes. The main difference is that the New Order Amish will use electricity and telephones in their homes and modern farming equipment, including tractors, in their fields.

For more information about the history or present-day lives of the Amish and Mennonites, or to conduct your own genealogical search, visit the Lancaster Mennonite Historical Society, 2215 Millstream Rd., Lancaster (717-393-9745; fax 717-393-8751; e-mail lmhs@lmhs.org). It's open Tues to Sat 8:30 a.m. to 4:30 p.m. Also, check the website for the schedule of guided "learning tours" that focus on the history of particular places.

ONE-ROOM SCHOOLHOUSE

Like all other citizens of Lancaster County, the Plain People pay school taxes, even though they don't use the public schools. Instead their formal education is conducted in one-room schoolhouses and goes up to 8th grade.

Subjects generally include English, arithmetic, health, history, and geography. Some schools may substitute agriculture for history and geography. Formal religious teaching is saved for the home.

Amish and Mennonite sects that are not "Old Order" usually choose to send their children to public or their own schools. Many young people attend high school and go on to college.

THE AMISH & TECHNOLOGY

Even though technology doesn't play a major role in daily Amish life, it would be foolish to believe that it has had no impact. That doesn't mean they automatically reject every new innovation. But for them, every technological advance requires a great deal of examination to determine how and to what degree it might fit in with—or disrupt—the community's overall lifestyle.

Take automobiles, for example. According to Amish law, members may not have a driver's license let alone own, drive, or finance a car. However, they are permitted to ride in cars, vans, and buses owned by nonmembers and often rent drivers (often non-Amish neighbors who refer to themselves as "Amish taxis"). But horse and buggy continues to be the premier mode of transportation.

Far from being a contradiction, this example demonstrates how technology can be integrated into Amish life on a limited

Mind the Sign

Along the back roads of Pennsylvania Dutch Country, you'll often see yellow diamond-shaped signs with a black horse-and-buggy silhouette in the middle. These are more than quaint reminders of a bygone era when traffic was slower paced. Horse-drawn buggies remain the primary transportation for Amish families, and you'll often see them interspersed with car and bus traffic on area roads. It's important for visitors to remember that these horse-drawn vehicles travel at top speeds of 5 to 8 miles per hour, so, if you're traveling behind one, give it lots of leeway.

Only pass where road markings indicate (never on a curve, when you can't clearly see in front of you). Horses are usually used to traffic, but they can still be spooked by honking horns and gunning motors.

Although many of the Amish regard flashing lights, headlights, and red and yellow reflective safety triangles as gaudy, they abide by state law to display these warning signals at night. However, a report by the Ohio Department of Transportation (the largest Amish population in the world is located in Holmes, Ohio) found that more than half of all buggy/motor vehicle accidents occur in the daylight. At least 60 percent are caused by cars following too closely. So give the buggy drivers plenty of road, and if you slow down, you'll see much more of the beautiful countryside.

basis. Because the church prohibits car ownership, there is no concern about the division of the community into haves and have-nots. The difficulty of long-distance horse-and-buggy travel also serves to keep members close to home.

Telephones have also found a place in Amish life, even though they are still not allowed in the home. Members are permitted to use public or community-owned telephones (often housed in sheds or shanties) for a variety of purposes, including business, medical emergencies, and contacting family members who live in distant areas. Social chatting is not encouraged for fear that it will replace face-to-face communication.

Whenever possible and practical, the Amish continue to use waterwheels and windmills to power their homes, farms, and businesses. You won't see them plugging into public electric power lines, but, for certain purposes such as running milking machines and cooling units (required by state sanitation laws) or providing power to operate a home-based craft, produce, or other business, they may use diesel-powered generators, bottled gas for heating water, and natural gas or kerosene lanterns for lighting.

WORSHIP

Unlike most Christian sects, the Amish do not worship in churches, nor do they meet every Sunday.

Congregations are determined by "church districts," each of which comprises about 30 or 35 families living within close geographical proximity of one another. This proximity is important because the 3-hour worship services are held in the district members' homes every other Sunday. (Alternate Sundays are for visiting friends and family.) Whether or not worship services are scheduled, there is no business conducted on Sunday.

Keeping the faith is the number one concern of the Amish church, so those who stray from its precepts know that they must answer for their indiscretions. First, they are encouraged to repent before the church.

If all other attempts fail, the church will administer what is considered its harshest punishment—the bann ("ban"), the excommunication of a congregant. The person under the bann may attend worship services but must leave right after. The isolation also disallows participation in other community activities or dining at the same table as other church members, even family. This practice of avoiding an excommunicated individual is known as "Meidung," or shunning.

No Photographs

Ironically, the modes of dress, transportation, education, work, and religious practice that are supposed to separate the Amish from the rest of the world are also the things that pique the curiosity of tourists from all over the world. But while these people may be almost irresistibly photogenic, they really don't want to be part of your vacation scrapbook. Some experts say that their camera shyness is based on a biblical commandment or goes against the basic humility-based culture and customs. Whatever their reason, please refrain from invading their privacy, trespassing on their land, or taking photographs.

For people whose lives are so bound up in community, losing the sense of belonging, even temporarily, can be devastating. And, in most cases, the bann is temporary. Excommunicated individuals can—and usually eventually do—repent. When they do, the bann is lifted, shunning ceases, and they are welcomed back to community life.

MENNONITES

In 1536 Menno Simons, a former Catholic priest from Holland, joined the Anabaptist movement and became an influential teacher whose followers became known as "Mennists" or "Mennonites." Toward the end of the century, a Swiss Mennonite named Jakob Ammann took issue with what he viewed as a lack of sufficient discipline of church members who had strayed from their baptism vows. In 1693 Ammann split from the Swiss Mennonite church. His followers became known as the "Amish" (pronounced AH-mish).

Continued persecution throughout Europe resulted in the emigration of groups of Anabaptists across the Atlantic to the colony of Pennsylvania, particularly in the early 1700s. For them, William Penn's "Holy Experiment" of religious tolerance offered hope of a life of peace and freedom. So many German-speaking immigrants settled in the south-central area of the state that it became known as Pennsylvania "Deutsch," or "Dutch," Country.

Like their Amish counterparts, the Old Order Mennonites wear plain dress, reject the need for higher formal education, and believe in separating themselves from the world outside their religious communities. They use some technology on their farms, and, while many still travel by horse and buggy, some

Close-up

The Milton Hershey School and Hershey Medical Center

Having no children of their own, Milton Hershey and his wife, Catherine ("Kitty"), focused a great deal of their wealth on the establishment of a boarding school for orphan boys at Milton's birthplace, the 486-acre Homestead. In 1909 it opened with an enrollment of 10. To ensure ongoing support for the school, Hershey transferred ownership of his company to a trust, which is still responsible for the education and welfare of the more than 1,500 students—girls as well as boys—who live and attend classes on the 9,000-acre campus of the Milton Hershey School. These students are provided with a free education, room, board, and medical care from kindergarten through 12th grade.

At the Milton Hershey School & Founders Hall Visitors Center (US Route 322/ Governor Road; 717-520-2000; mhs-pa.org), you can learn more about the school by watching a brief video and chatting with a host.

In 1963 the Hershey Trust contributed $50 million and land to Pennsylvania State University to establish the Penn State Milton S. Hershey Medical Center. With more than 200 specialty physicians, the Penn State College of Medicine (opened in 1967), and a children's hospital, this state-of-the-art health care institution is now one of the nation's most renowned and respected health care facilities.

Milton Hershey also created the nonprofit M. S. Hershey Foundation to fund local educational and cultural activities. It still supports a number of important institutions including the Hershey Theatre, Hershey Gardens, and Hershey Community Archives.

During the Great Depression, Hershey kept his employees working, not just in the chocolate factory but in continuing to build up their hometown. In the 1930s, many of the town's landmark buildings were constructed, including the grand Hotel Hershey—based on a design Milton Hershey and his wife had seen during a trip to the Mediterranean. It took over 600 workers to build the accommodation that commentator and author Lowell Thomas described as "a palace that out-palaces the palaces of the maharajas of India."

Now North America's largest manufacturer of chocolate and sugar confectionery products, Hershey reports annual revenues of more than $5 billion. Over the years, the company has added numerous household-name brands to its family of products. Some of these are Reese's peanut butter products, Kit Kat, Twizzlers, Jolly Rancher, and Ice Breakers mints and gum.

do drive cars. About 10 percent of the total Mennonite population is Old Order. Another group of Mennonites, the "Conservatives," put fewer restrictions on technology for agriculture or business, allowing telephones and electricity (but still eschewing some modern marvels such as computers, the Internet, and video games). About two-thirds of total Mennonites are "Assimilated" or "Contemporary," embracing modern dress; technology, including television and computers; higher education (there are some Mennonite-run universities in the US); and interaction with the rest of the world.

ACCOMMODATIONS

Whether in the middle of the city or in the heart of the country, on the deck of a steamboat moored on its own private lake, a romantic hideaway for two or a family-size vacation accommodation, there's a place for any preference and price in Pennsylvania Dutch Country.

Most hotels, motels, and other accommodations prohibit smoking. I will specify the ones that do allow it. Same for pets. Wireless Internet is generally included in the room rate.

HOTELS & MOTELS

Although rates are subject to change, we use the following pricing code to indicate the average rate for a 1-night stay, in season, for 2 adults. Note that these rates do not include taxes, gratuities, or add-on services such as room service or premium TV channels unless otherwise indicated. Off-season rates are, of course, lower. October (especially weekends) and June through August are usually considered peak seasons.

$................ **Less than $100**
$$ .... **$100 to $150**
$$$ .... **$150 to $200**
$$$$ .... **$200 to $250**
$$$$$......... **More than $250**

In Pennsylvania Dutch Country, you'll find just about every major name in lodging, from Hilton to Holiday Inn Express; however, there are many not-so-familiar family-operated options here that can save you money and provide a more local flavor. Don't be shy about pulling in and asking for a look around.

Bird-in-Hand

AMISH COUNTRY MOTEL $$$$
3013 Old Philadelphia Pike
Bird-in-Hand, PA 17505
(800) 665-8780
bird-in-hand.com

You can soak in the surrounding ambience of Amish farmland or splash in the indoor or outdoor pools located at its nearby sister property, Bird-in-Hand Family Inn. Guests also receive a complimentary 2-hour guided Amish back roads tour on a climate-controlled bus. Standard rooms have 2 double beds so couples might want to go for a king room. Family suites and 2-night packages including meals are available.

i Check-out time may be at 10 or 11 a.m., but if you want to squeeze in a little more sightseeing or shopping or maybe a farewell buggy ride, ask your accommodation's front desk staff if they will store your luggage for a few extra hours. Many offer this service as a customer courtesy.

i Before you hit the theme parks, museums, or shopping outlets, be sure to check for discounts at the front desk. Many hotels and motels will reserve tickets to entertainment venues in advance, eliminating waits in line as well as saving you money.

AMISHVIEW INN & SUITES $$$–$$$$
3125 Old Philadelphia Pike (Route 340)
Bird-in-Hand, PA 17505
(866) 735-1600
amishviewinn.com

The location is particularly convenient because it's part of the 9-acre Plain & Fancy Farm complex that includes Amish educational attractions, a family-style restaurant, and plenty of shopping. Every room and suite comes with a kitchenette, full breakfast, Disney Channels, and access to the indoor pool and whirlpool.

i At AmishView Inn & Suites, rates are typically lower from Sunday through Thursday.

Hershey

HERSHEY LODGE
Hershey, PA 17033
(see Resorts, p. 207)

THE HOTEL HERSHEY
Hershey, PA 17033
(see Resorts, p. 208)

**HOWARD JOHNSON INN OF
  HERSHEY** $$$
845 Chocolate Ave.
Hershey, PA 17033
(717) 533-9157, (800) 800-5845
howardjohnsonhershey.com

These rates apply to peak season; you can find rooms for as low as $59.99 other times of the year. Recently renovated and renamed (for many years it was an independently owned accommodation named Spinners Inn), this new name in Hershey offers in-room microwave and fridge, free deluxe continental breakfast, and outdoor heated pool. There is a restaurant on-site.

MILTON MOTEL $$–$$$
1733 E. Chocolate Ave.
Hershey, PA 17033
(717) 533-4533, (866) MILTON4
miltonmotel.net

The rate range noted for this accommodation really applies to the peak summer season; the rest of the year you can get a room with a double or queen bed for as low as $45 or $55. Guest rooms come with refrigerator, microwave, free HBO with 60+ channels, and access to the heated indoor pool. Suites with kitchenettes are available.

Intercourse

**BEST WESTERN INTERCOURSE
  VILLAGE & INN** $$
Routes 340 and 772
Intercourse, PA 17534
(800) 717-6202
amishcountryinns.com

Park your car and forget it; you're within easy walking distance of all of the village of Intercourse's shops and attractions. Barn-style exteriors with Pennsylvania Dutch hex signs and antique-style lamps outside the doors give the hotel an out-in-the-country ambience. There's also a restaurant on the premises where you'll be served a complimentary breakfast.

THE INN AT KITCHEN KETTLE VILLAGE $$–$$$
3529 Old Philadelphia Pike
Intercourse, PA 17534
(717) 768-8261, (800) 732-3538
kitchenkettle.com

You can shop 'til you drop in Kitchen Kettle Village's over 40 stores, then rest up in one of a wide array of accommodation options tucked away in cottages and over shops (really, they're very charming; the views are great and the shops close at 6 p.m., so evenings are nice and quiet) right on the premises. Breakfast at the popular on-site restaurant is included every day except Sun (that's when it's closed).

i With so many great farmers' markets and roadside stands in the area, why not stock up on some fresh fruits, veggies, and home-baked goods to stow in your room for snacking? Beats the prepackaged stuff in any vending machine!

THE TRAVELERS REST MOTEL $$–$$$
3701 Old Philadelphia Pike
Intercourse, PA 17534
(800) 665-8780
bird-in-hand.com

Start the day with a continental breakfast, then board the climate-controlled bus for your complimentary 2-hour guided back roads tour. You can also stretch your legs with a short stroll to the village. All rooms have refrigerators and come with continental-plus breakfast.

Lancaster City

BEST WESTERN EDEN RESORT INN AND SUITES $$$–$$$$
222 Eden Rd.
Lancaster, PA 17601
(717) 569-6444, (866) 801-6430
edenresort.com

I usually think of Best Western as offering nice but pretty standard accommodations, but this one's a beauty that offers some pretty special amenities. There are 2 pools—one indoor, one outdoor—and a whirlpool, lighted tennis court, basketball court, 3 restaurants from fun to fine dining (the Sunday Champagne Brunch is a local favorite), and a lounge that serves spirits and light fare. Pets are more than welcome (fee is $15). The Eden offers doggie day care, grooming, overnight accommodations, and emergency veterinary care.

CONTINENTAL INN $$
2285 Lincoln Hwy. East
Lancaster, PA 17602
(717) 299-0421
continentalinn.com

Location is a big draw here; it's right next door to Dutch Wonderland and a few minutes from the 2 big outlet centers. There are also indoor and outdoor swimming pools, a sauna, full breakfast, and on-site restaurant for breakfast and dinner. Ask about attraction discount tickets. Some smoking rooms are available.

i Some hotels offer babysitting referrals upon request.

CORK FACTORY HOTEL $$$
480 New Holland Ave., Ste. 3000
Lancaster, PA 17602
(717) 735-2075
corkfactoryhotel.com

One of the city's upscale boutique hotels is housed in one of its oldest, most historic buildings, an 1865 cork factory that maintains its industrial, redbrick-inside-and-outside look, yet manages to have a cool upscale urban appeal. Don't expect plush here; the minimalist decor is deliberate. Cork Factory is a member of the Historic Hotels of America. There's a casual restaurant and bar on the premises. On-site parking is free. This is a good deal in the heart of the city.

FULTON STEAMBOAT INN $$$
1 Hartman Bridge Rd.
Routes 30 and 896
Lancaster, PA 17602
(717) 299-9999, (800) 922-2229
fultonsteamboatinn.com

Moored in a private lake just outside Strasburg, next to an Amish farm and across the street from Rockvale Outlets, this 3-deck, old-fashioned steamboat isn't transportation. It's an accommodation named to honor Lancaster native son Robert Fulton. The decor is an interesting combination of nautical and Victorian, but it works nicely. The property has a heated indoor atrium pool and whirlpool, playground, indoor and outdoor pools, sauna, and on-premises restaurant.

HOLIDAY INN EXPRESS AT
ROCKVALE $$
24 S. Willowdale Dr.
Rockvale Outlets
Lancaster, PA 17602 (Routes 30 and 896)
(888) 465-4329, (717) 293-9500
hiexpress.com

Situated right in the middle of Lancaster's Rockvale Outlets, this place is a shopper's paradise. It's clean, it's comfortable, and it offers a complimentary breakfast to fuel you for a full day of store-hopping.

*LANCASTER ARTS HOTEL $$$
300 Harrisburg Ave.
Lancaster, PA 17603
(866) 720-ARTS (2787), (717) 299-3000
lancasterartshotel.com

Rustic brick walls and wood beams are reminders of this historic building's background as a tobacco warehouse listed on the National Register of Historic Places. But the experience at this heart-of-Lancaster-City hotel is surprisingly luxurious. Each guest room is a showcase for area artists. Suites are available. The on-premises restaurant, John J. Jeffries, features seasonal, sustainable American cuisine, the majority of which is organic and gleaned from local farms. The lounge has Lancaster-produced microbrews on tap.

> **i** Lancaster is known as "The Red Rose City," a nickname that actually has its roots in the 15th-century War of the Roses in England. During that long-ago struggle for the English throne, the two contenders—the Houses of Lancaster and York—both had roses as their emblems. The House of Lancaster's was red; York's was white. (York, about 25 miles from Lancaster, calls itself "The White Rose City.")

Leola

LEOLA VILLAGE INN & SUITES $$$
38 Deborah Dr., Route 23
Leola, PA 17540
(717) 656-7002, (877) 669-5094
theinnatleolavillage.com

At this National Trust for Historic Preservation site, you can stay in buildings more than a century old from a converted tobacco barn with vaulted and beamed ceilings to a wine cellar with fireplace to an original farmhouse decorated with antiques and reproductions of period pieces. You get a complimentary continental breakfast and there's an outdoor pool, full-service spa, and upscale restaurant on the premises.

Ronks

THE OLDE AMISH INN $
33 Eastbrook Rd.
(Route 896, ¼ mile north of Route 30)
Ronks, PA 17572
(717) 393-3100
oldeamishinn.com
Amish farmers at work outside your window; clean rooms with queen beds inside; complimentary coffee and pastry in the morning. This economy-minded, family-operated accommodation's location between Bird-in-Hand and Strasburg puts you in easy reach of attractions, shopping, and entertainment, but the setting is pure country.

THE RED CABOOSE MOTEL &
RESTAURANT $$
312 Paradise Ln.
Ronks, PA 17572
(888) 687-5005, (717) 687-5000
redcaboosemotel.com
If you're into trains, you won't want to miss this opportunity to stay in one of these vintage, 25-ton cabooses that once traveled the tracks for the Pennsylvania Railroad. Accommodation sizes vary from cozy quarters for couples to family units. Dine in the on-premises family restaurant housed in a refurbished coach car.

Strasburg

CARRIAGE HOUSE MOTOR INN $–$$
144 E. Main St.
(Routes 896 and 741)
Strasburg, PA 17579
(717) 687-7651
amishcountryinns.com
Located within easy walking distance of the railroad museum and downtown area, this cozy accommodation has a 2-acre lawn so kids can get out and play. Free continental breakfast is included, and pets are welcome.

Strasburg Rail Road

If the whistle of a steam train is music to your ears, the village of Strasburg in southeastern Lancaster County at the intersection of Routes 896 and 741 is a locomotive lover's dream. America's oldest short-line steam train, the passenger- and freight-carrying Strasburg Rail Road had its maiden 4.5-mile chug sometime in 1851. Now it takes riders on a 45-minute trip to Paradise (the town, that is). Just across the street is the Railroad Museum of Pennsylvania, with more than 100 historic trains, and less than a mile away the National Toy Train Museum with 5 working layouts spanning more than a century.

HERSHEY FARM INN $$–$$$
240 Hartman Bridge Rd. (Route 896)
Strasburg, PA 17579
(800) 827-8635
hersheyfarm.com
Set on 23 acres, this property has fruit, vegetable, and flower gardens, a fishing pond,

a 1-mile wooded walking trail, and friendly farm animals. Accommodations are motor lodge–like, but suites, some with whirlpool tubs, are available and all are very clean and prettily appointed. There's an outdoor pool (with separate baby pool) and on-premises family restaurants. If you like the scenery you see at the Hershey Farm Inn, there are signs all around the gardens to help you re-create them at home—even the waterfall.

BED-AND-BREAKFASTS & INNS

Lodging at a bed-and-breakfast is a lot like staying at a friend's home. Unlike most hotel and motel chains, there is little standardization as far as room layout and decor. Some have live-in owners, some offer rooms in their main residence only, and others provide the option of separate carriage houses, cottages, or cabins.

i If you're not sure about tipping protocol for a bed-and-breakfast or other family-owned operation, keep in mind that your hosts probably have to hire part- or full-time staff to make sure accommodations are always guest-ready. Therefore, you'll probably want to tip as you would at a hotel or motel.

"Breakfast" can mean anything from a buffet spread of muffins, cold cereals, and coffee to a multicourse candlelight feast. If you have any particular physical, dietary, or other lifestyle restrictions or requirements, call ahead to make sure the operator can handle them.

Some bed-and-breakfasts and inns are not set up to accommodate young children at all, some only those above a particular minimum age. Most prohibit smoking indoors. I will designate any lodgings that do permit smoking.

Many bed-and-breakfasts and inns have their own resident pets but are unable to accommodate additional animals. If you are allergic to dogs or cats, be sure to check to determine if your accommodation of choice already has a pet. I will indicate whether there is room at the inn for yours.

i Ask about the availability of off-street parking and whether it is included in your daily tariff. Parking spaces can be at a premium—in terms of both availability and price—in some of the area's more populated and visited areas, so be sure to factor that in when comparing room rates.

Most properties accept credit cards, but some family-owned lodging places may prefer traveler's or personal checks, or even cash. Check before you book.

Some accommodations have 2-night stay requirements for weekends, particularly during peak seasons. Holidays may also require minimum 2- or 3-night stays.

Although rates are subject to change, we use the following pricing code to indicate the average rate for a 1-night stay, in season, for 2 adults. Note that these rates do not include taxes, gratuities, or add-on services, such as room service or premium TV channels, unless otherwise indicated. Off-season rates are lower. October (especially weekends) and June through August are usually considered peak seasons. Many accommodations offer seasonal packages that may include dining, theater, golf, tours, and other extras.

$	Less than $100
$$	$100 to $150
$$$	$150–$200
$$$$	$200–$250
$$$$$	More than $250

Adamstown

**ADAMSTOWN INNS AND
COTTAGES** $$–$$$
144 W. Main St.
Adamstown, PA 19501
(717) 484-0800, (800) 594-4808
adamstown.com

Five distinctive lodging options are available. Housed in a Victorian-era "painted lady," the Amethyst Inn bed-and-breakfast is furnished with period antiques and has 2-person whirlpool tubs and gas log fireplaces. "Well-behaved" children over 12 are invited. Two-bedroom cottages and a 5-bedroom vacation home are also available; children of any age are welcome. Cottages and vacation home only are pet-friendly.

Annville

⁕ANNVILLE INN $$–$$$$$
4515 Hill Church Rd.
Annville, PA 17003
(888) 868-4515, (717) 867-1991
annvilleinn.com

You're just a few miles away from the hustle and bustle of Hershey, but you're in a beautiful haven surrounded by peaceful countryside. The inn has 5 distinctively decorated guest rooms (ask about the "Secret Surprise" room), some with fireplaces and whirlpools; an outdoor pool; and in-house movie theater. Full breakfast is served.

Bird-in-Hand

**BIRD-IN-HAND VILLAGE INN
& SUITES** $$–$$$
2695 Old Philadelphia Pike
East Lampeter, PA 17505
(800) 914-2473
bird-in-hand.com

Four 18th- and 19th-century buildings house period-furnished rooms and suites, some with whirlpool tubs, fireplaces, and kitchenettes. A complimentary continental-plus breakfast and 2-hour Amish farm country bus tour are included.

> **i** One legend has it that the name Bird-in-Hand came about in the 1730s when two workmen were trying to decide if they should spend the night at the nearest inn or keep going. The decision was made when one observed that they should stop at the inn because "a bird in the hand is worth two in the bush." Another story attributes the name to a picture on a sign in front of an inn on the then—and still—well-traveled Old Philadelphia Pike (Route 340). Today the 18th-century brick inn, listed on the National Register of Historic Places, is a popular accommodation called the Bird-in-Hand Village Inn & Suites.

**⁕GREYSTONE MANOR BED &
BREAKFAST** $$–$$$
2658 Old Philadelphia Pike
Bird-in-Hand, PA 17505
(717) 393-4233
greystonemanor.com

Like Cinderella, this mid-1800s farmhouse blossomed into a graceful Victorian mansion when stained-glass windows, cut crystal

---

Reservation Services

Want to know what accommodations are available without calling around or find a last-minute vacancy for an impromptu getaway? Try one of the following free central reservation services.

The Innkeepers of Authentic Bed and Breakfasts of Lancaster County Association
23 Cottage Ave.
Lancaster, PA 17602
(800) 552-2632
authenticbandb.com
This organization of more than 40 bed-and-breakfasts/inns hosts a detailed website with descriptions of their individual facilities, available dates, price ranges, direct links to each accommodation, and online reservations. Click on the website's "Specials" tab for specials and discounts.

Lancaster County Bed & Breakfast Inns Association
62 W. Main St.
Adamstown, PA 19501
(717) 464-5588, (800) 848-2994
padutchinns.com
Check out locations, amenities, prices (including specials), and available dates from around a dozen local bed-and-breakfasts. Link directly with the accommodations of your choice and make your reservations online.

---

and double-leaded glass doors, gleaming woodwork, and other regal accoutrements were added later in the century. There's also a more rustic carriage house.

i If you're interested in sampling the local wine, chocolates, or other specialty foods produced in the area, a number of bed-and-breakfast owners and innkeepers will get the items of your choice or even make up entire gift baskets for you. Look on the accommodation's website or ask when you book your reservation.

Elizabethtown

✳MOONSTONE MANOR $$–$$$
2048 Zeager Rd.
Elizabethtown, PA 17022
(717) 361-0826
conewagomanorinn.com
Surrounded by lush gardens, this Conewago Creek–side abode, which was built between the mid-18th and early-19th centuries, has a surprising interior combining Victorian opulence, rugged leather and wood, and breezy tropical wicker and palm. (It works!) All 9 guest rooms feature lovely antiques, fireplaces, and whirlpool baths. Full breakfast is included.

TWIN PINE MANOR BED & BREAKFAST $$–$$$
1934 W. Main St.
Ephrata, PA 17522
(717) 733-8400, (888) 266-0099
twinpinemanor.com

The Alpine Suite is the most expensive room in this circa-1970s A-frame house, but it's a truly lovely hideaway with cathedral A-frame ceilings, big stone fireplace, and 2-person Jacuzzi. But even the other 7, more economical, guest rooms have fireplaces and are cute and comfy. Children 16 and older are welcome. Full breakfast is included on Sat and Sun.

i Was your bed-and-breakfast meal so yummy that you'd like to try to duplicate it at home? You may be surprised to find out that many owners offer photocopies of guests' favorite recipes, and some have even created their own cookbooks (usually available for sale at the front desk).

WEST RIDGE GUEST HOUSE $$–$$$$
1285 W. Ridge Rd.
Elizabethtown, PA 17022
(717) 367-7783, (877) 367-7783
westridgebandb.com

Four rooms in the main house and another 5 in the guest house are individually decorated; some come with whirlpool tub, fireplace, and deck. Full breakfast is included as well as access to the swimming pool and tennis court (bring your own racket).

Intercourse

AMISH GUEST HOUSE AND COTTAGE $
3625 E. Newport Rd. (Route 772 East)
Intercourse, PA 17534
(717) 768-8914
theamishguesthouse.com

For the Amish, senior citizenship doesn't mean a move to Florida. Instead, parents who are downsizing move into a smaller *Grossdaadi* or *Dawdi Haus* (pronounced DAH-dee HAHS) built by their children on their property, so the family can remain close and connected. The cottage here is one of these houses. It sleeps up to 6 and has a fridge, microwave, and sitting room. The 2-bedroom guest house, which can sleep up to 8, has a full kitchen and dining room.

CARRIAGE CORNER BED & BREAKFAST $–$$
3705 E. Newport Rd. (Route 772)
Gordonville, PA 17534
(717) 768-3059, (800) 209-3059
carriagecornerbandb.com

Although the busy little village of Intercourse is just a 5-minute walk away, the setting in this 5-guest-room residence with its home-spun accents of handcrafted folk art is serene and idyllic. Full breakfast is included.

i Bring your friends and family (up to 16 of them) and rent a vacation home in Intercourse (717-768-3204; amishcountryinns.com). These fully equipped homes are tucked among the rolling farmlands for maximum scenery and privacy. Two have private pools and some require 2-night minimum stays.

INN AND SPA AT INTERCOURSE VILLAGE $$$

Intercourse Village
3542 Old Philadelphia Pike
Intercourse, PA 17534
(800) 644-0949
amishcountryinns.com

The indicated rates refer to the 2 period-decorated, fireplace-equipped guest rooms in the lovingly restored 1909 Victorian home. (There are no in-room televisions or phones.) Just down the pathway are 4 country-style suites with fireplaces, wet bar, fridge, phone, and TV, and 3 Grand Suites ($$$$$) with Jacuzzi for 2. All come with 5-course breakfast, and there is an on-premises spa.

Lancaster City

AUSTRALIAN WALKABOUT BED AND BREAKFAST $$$-$$$$

837 Village Rd.
Lancaster, PA 17602
(717) 464-0707, (888) WALKABT
walkaboutinn.com

In Australia, a walkabout means to go and discover new places. This 1925 4-suite home with warm American chestnut wood interiors is the perfect place from which to begin and end your daily forays. Each suite has a fireplace; 2 have whirlpool tubs. Full breakfast is included. The property also offers a private cottage ($$$$$). Be sure to check the website for some super seasonal, last-minute, romance and baby moon specials.

E. J. BOWMAN HOUSE $$-$$$

2674 Lititz Pike (Route 501)
Lancaster, PA 17601
(717) 519-0808, (877) 519-1776
ejbowmanhouse.com

Route 501 is a busy main road, but you won't even think about it once you step into this circa-1860s Italianate home, known locally simply as "the Big Yellow House," that's as colorful on the inside as it is on the outside. Fourteen murals depict seasonal life in 19th-century Lancaster. Choose from 4 fireplace rooms or 1 whirlpool suite. Jam by the grand fireplace in the music room on the inn's instruments or your own. Full breakfast is included. Children over age 10 are welcome. No credit cards. Ask about discounts for military personnel, teachers, musicians, seniors, and people riding 2-wheeled vehicles.

KING'S COTTAGE $$$-$$$$

1049 E. King St.
Lancaster, PA 17602
(717) 397-1017, (800) 747-8717
kingscottagebb.com

You don't have to be a newlywed to love the private Carriage House or main-inn "Majestic Chambre," both of which feature double Jacuzzi, fireplace, and in-room breakfast delivery. All of the other rooms in this restored National Register of Historic Places–listed Spanish mansion have fireplaces (the Princess also has a whirlpool), and 2 have bathrooms that are private, though located steps down the hall. Full breakfast is included as well as private, off-street parking, a real plus at this downtown Lancaster City accommodation.

*O'FLAHERTY'S DINGELDEIN HOUSE $$-$$$

1105 E. King St.
Lancaster, PA 17602
(800) 779-7765, (717) 293-1723
dingeldeinhouse.com

Okay, first things first. Dingeldein was the name of former owners of this 1910 Dutch colonial residence that now serves as the main house for this bed-and-breakfast. O'Flaherty is a nod to the Irish heritage of later owners. Originally built for Armstrong family flooring tycoons, the residence now houses 2 guest rooms and 2 suites, some with fireplaces. Across the garden is a cottage with 2 additional guest rooms. Children over age 12 are welcome. Home-cooked breakfast is included. On-premises parking is available.

SECRET GARDEN $$
445 W. Chestnut St.
Philadelphia, PA 19106
(717) 399-9229

It's just a 4-block-walk from this pretty, 1-guest-room, 3-suite Victorian to all of the downtown Lancaster City attractions. The Tropical Suite has a Jacuzzi; the Garden Suite a fireplace and fully equipped kitchen. Full breakfast is included.

SILVERSTONE INN & SUITES $$–$$$$$
62 Bowman Rd.
Lancaster, PA 17602
(877) 290-6987
silverstoneinn.com

You won't believe the outlet shopping hub of Route 30 is just right around the corner when you stay at the serenely elegant, circa-1750 Silverstone Inn & Suites, situated on a 15-acre sheep farm. Most rooms have fireplaces and Jacuzzis; the private Butternut Cottage has its own porch and large outdoor hot tub. A full breakfast is included.

i If you are planning a late arrival or find yourself stuck in traffic or otherwise running behind schedule, it's courteous to call your bed-and-breakfast or inn to let them know. Many of these operations are small and/or in family residences and do not have 24-hour front desk staff like a hotel, motel, or resort would.

WALNUT LAWN BED & BREAKFAST $
1027 Village Rd.
Lancaster, PA 17602
(717) 464-1382
walnutlawn.com

Tom and Sarah Murphy have done everything possible to maintain a safe and healthy refuge for guests with environmental allergies or other conditions. Even breakfast features hormone-free milk and eggs from local farms and produce from their own orchards. But the ambience here is anything but sterile; the 4 guest rooms in their 1909 2-story brick home are warm and welcoming. Ask to see (or stay in) the Siam Room, an homage to the Murphys' experience in the Peace Corps.

i Most bed-and-breakfasts serve their morning meal between specified hours, particularly when they offer full, hot, multicourse repasts. In many cases, if you snooze, you lose.

Lititz

ALDEN HOUSE BED AND BREAKFAST $$
62 E. Main St.
Lititz, PA 17543
(717) 627-3363
aldenhouse.com

Right outside your door are all of the shops, eateries, and other fun stuff in downtown Lititz, but this is an oasis from busy Main Street. Choose from among 2 guest rooms, 4 suites (the Tea Rose Suite has a gas fireplace), and a carriage house. Children over age 10 are welcome. Full breakfast and private lot parking are included.

FORGOTTEN SEASONS BED & BREAKFAST $

304 E. Newport Rd.
Lititz, PA 17543
(717) 626-3088
forgottenseasons.com

If you're looking for authenticity, this circa-1735 former tavern is one of the oldest remaining homes in Lititz, and each of its 3 guest rooms has a story about the people who lived or stayed here. Full farmhouse-style breakfast is included. Be sure to peek into Barbara's Room, where the walls are covered with hand-painted artwork from the early to mid-1800s that are being studied and documented. There's also a linear park next door with a 1-mile hiking and biking trail.

i Founded in 1756 by members of the Moravian Church, Lititz, located about 7 miles north of Lancaster City, was named by a missionary, Count Zizendorf, after a castle in the eastern part of the current Czech Republic that provided refuge to persecuted Moravians. The Lititz Moravian Church, built in 1787, still stands on Moravian Square on Main Street. The town is also the home of Wilbur Chocolate Candy (their "buds" predated the Hershey Kiss by 14 years) and Sturgis Pretzel House, the first commercial pretzel bakery in the US, making it a popular tourist destination. Lititz also has the distinction of being named a Distinctive Destination by the National Trust for Historic Preservation. It is also my adopted home.

THE LITITZ HOUSE $$–$$$

301 N. Broad St.
Lititz, PA 17543
(717) 626-5299, (800) 464-6764
lititzhouse.com

Three blocks north of Main Street, this 1904 Colonial Revival with wraparound porch overlooking a peaceful garden features 3 guest rooms, 1 suite, and a private 3rd-floor loft (2-night minimum).

✳SPEEDWELL FORGE BED & BREAKFAST $$$$–$$$$$

465 Speedwell Forge Rd.
Lititz, PA 17543
(877) 626-1760
speedwellforge.com

This is a one-of-a-kind, don't-miss-it place—a gorgeous circa-1760, National Register of Historic Places–listed colonial mansion tucked away on 120 acres of parklands plus home to the Pennsylvania Wolf Sanctuary, refuge to more than 40 rescued residents. Bed-and-breakfast owner Dawn Darlington also operates the sanctuary. There are 3 guest rooms in the main house (Kathryn's Room has a whirlpool) and 2 cottages. Most spectacular is the "Paymaster's Office," a cottage with vaulted beamed ceilings, massive brick fireplace, and whirlpool tub. Room rates include full breakfast and evening desserts. Children 12 and over are welcome.

Marietta

✳ASCOT HOUSE BED & BREAKFAST $$$

219 W. Market St.
Marietta, PA 17547
(717) 426-2518
ascothousebandb.com

Marietta is a little bit off the beaten track, but this circa-1800 Georgian home is a find.

Yes, it's partly the antique-filled decor of the warm and welcoming common room and 5 guest rooms, most with fireplace and Jacuzzi. But just as important is the charm of owner Wendy Codd, who will cook you a bountiful breakfast in the morning and authentic British tea in the afternoon. Dogs are welcome (pet-sitting is available for $10 per hour).

i Back in the early 19th century, prosperous Marietta residents built homes and mansions in the grand colonial, Federal, and Victorian architectural styles. Fortunately, these majestic abodes were sturdy enough to withstand the passing years, even when Hurricane Agnes ravaged the town in 1972, and 45 percent of Marietta is designated as a National Historic District.

Mount Joy

THE CAMERON ESTATE INN $$$–$$$$
1855 Mansion Ln.
Mount Joy, PA 17552
(717) 492-0111, (888) 4-CAMERON
cameronestateinn.com
Two of the rooms in this 3-story, 17-room and suite 1805 mansion that was built by President McKinley's great-grandfather are more expensive, but the rest fall within the indicated parameters. Some of the antiques-filled rooms have a fireplace and whirlpool. Full breakfast is included, and an upscale dinner-only local landmark restaurant is on the premises.

i It's not situated on a mountain, so don't call this western Lancaster County town Mt. Joy. It was actually named after Englishman Lord Mountjoy, who served under Queen Elizabeth I.

THE OLDE SQUARE INN $$$–$$$$
127 E. Main St.
Mount Joy, PA 17552
(800) 742-3533
oldesquareinn.com
Located on Mount Joy's historic square within steps of one of my favorite dining, social, and entertainment spots (Bube's Brewery—see under the chapter heading, "Other Area Restaurants,"), this 5-guest-room, 1-guesthouse accommodation home is a place guests come back to again and again. Some rooms come with a fireplace and/or whirlpool; all come with full breakfast. Pets are welcome ($20 fee).

Palmyra

1825 INN $$
409 South Lingle Ave.
Palmyra, PA 17078
(717) 838-8282, (877) 738-8282
1825inn.com
Situated only a few miles' drive from the town of Hershey and all of its attractions, this 1825 country-style home has a fun, informal personality all its own. Antiques, reproductions, and locally made crafts make for comfortable surroundings in the 6 main house and 2 cottage rooms (these cost a little more). Full breakfast is served.

Strasburg

**✳LIMESTONE INN BED AND
  BREAKFAST $–$$**
33 E. Main St.
Strasburg, PA 17579
(717) 687-8392
thelimestoneinn.com
An architectural melding of Georgian and German styles makes this circa-1786 home one of the most unusual and, according

to owners Richard and Denise Waller, one of the most photographed historic buildings around. Its location at the heart of Strasburg's Main Street means you can park your car (off-street parking is provided) and forget it as you walk to shops, restaurants, museums, and all kinds of other in-town attractions. Furnishings in the 6 guest rooms include many antiques; half have fireplaces. The Tower Room has a private bathroom down the hall. Full breakfast and off-street parking are included. Children over age 12 are welcome. Some rooms have low ceilings, so you might want to let the Wallers know if you're tall.

i Limestone Inn co-owner Denise Waller can arrange for you to dine with an Amish family if you give her sufficient notice.

FARM STAYS

Nature didn't intend for us to rise and shine every morning to the clanging of an alarm clock. That's why there are roosters. A farm stay can be a great wake-up call in more ways than one.

For a big helping of country living, you may want to stay in the farmhouse with your host family or in a converted barn. Some other farms offer totally posh and private rooms and suites or family-size cabins or cottages.

Smoking in these accommodations is usually prohibited. I will point out in the listings any accommodations that do allow smoking. If you need a phone in your room, or can't live without a television or high-speed Internet connection, check with the accommodation before booking.

i While a stay at a farm can be a delightful and educational experience for children, not all farms are equipped to accommodate very young ones. Be sure to check with the farm of your choice.

Summer is prime time for farm stays, but no matter what the season, the scenery is always spectacular, and the livestock still need tender loving care. Spring is planting season and the time when many baby animals make their world debut. Fall is a time of harvests and colorful foliage. Winter can be serene or a playground for building snowmen and taking sleigh rides. In other words, there's never a dull season down on the farm.

While many farm lodgings accept major credit cards, some small, family-owned operations may prefer traveler's checks, personal checks, or even cash. Check before you book.

Although rates are subject to change, we use the following pricing code to indicate the average rate for a 1-night stay, double occupancy, in season, for 2 adults. Note that these rates do not include taxes, gratuities, or add-on services such as room service or premium TV channels, unless otherwise indicated. Off-season rates are lower. October (especially weekends) and June through August are usually considered peak seasons. Many accommodations offer seasonal packages that may include dining, theater, golf, tours, and other extras.

$	Less than $100
$$	$100 to $150
$$$	$150 to $200
$$$$	$200 to $250
$$$$$	More than $250

Hummelstown

*INN AT WESTWYND FARM
BED AND BREAKFAST $$–$$$
1620 Sand Beach Rd.
Hummelstown, PA 17036
(717) 533-6764, (877) WESTWYND
(877-937-8996)
westwyndfarminn.com

Hummelstown is located about 3 miles north of Hershey, but this wonderful 32-acre working horse farm is a destination on its own. The inn itself is gorgeous as are all of its 9 antique-decorated guest rooms, many with fireplace and/or Jacuzzi. (There's also a separate carriage house that's priced a little bit higher.) Breakfast is served anytime you want it, and there are home-baked treats available all day. Early risers can help co-owner Frank Troxell feed the horses, goats, and alpacas (Paco and Taco).

i Visit afarmstay.com for descriptions and links to a large local association of farm accommodations.

Lancaster

EQUESTRIAN ESTATES HORSE FARM
BED & BREAKFAST $$–$$$
221 Schultz Rd.
Lancaster, PA 17603
(717) 464-2164, (717) 464-1345
equestrianbnb.com

If you are equine-inclined, you'll love this farm where the Stoltzfus family breeds show and quarter horses. Stay in one of the 3 each guest rooms and suites, some with working fireplace and/or Jacuzzi, in their circa-1800 brick farmhouse. Guests are invited to help feed the steeds or accompany their hosts

to a horse auction or show. Amish country breakfast is included.

i David Stoltzfus was raised in the Old Order Amish faith and is now pastor of the House of the Lord Mennonite Fellowship Church. He and his family are happy to share the traditions of both faiths with guests. No alcohol is permitted on the premises.

PHEASANT RUN FARM $$–$$$
200 Marticville Rd.
Lancaster, PA 17603
(717) 872-0991
pheasantrunfarmbb.com

It's only about a 15- to 20-minute drive to downtown Lancaster, but all you'll see is scenic countryside when you stay at this restored 1809 stone bank barn on this 48-acre working farm. Henry and Anna's room, one of the 4 in the barn, has a fireplace and whirlpool. Full breakfast is included. Children age 12 and older are welcome.

Manheim

COUNTRY VISTAS BED &
BREAKFAST $$
448 W. Sun Hill Rd.
Manheim, PA 17545
(717) 664-2931
countryvistas.net

Your family will have an authentic hands-on farm experience, feeding the animals, collecting the eggs, even riding a pony on this 5-acre "farmette" located halfway between Hershey and Intercourse. The 2 guest rooms and 1 suite are clean, homey, and tastefully decorated. Full breakfast is included. No credit cards.

Amish Accommodations

Many accommodations are located near Old Order Amish farms; these two are actually on them. But though your hosts eschew electricity, they don't expect you to follow suit. Both even offer air-conditioning in their guest quarters (but you don't have to use it if you want a more authentic experience). Just don't expect any frills. Note that neither of these farms offers hands-on experiences, but the owners will be happy to show you around if you ask in advance. Neither accepts credit cards. And keep in mind that the owners probably don't have telephones in their homes, so leave a message when you call and they'll get back to you.

The guest cottage on Ben Riehl's dairy farm, **Beacon Hollow Farm Amish Guest House** (130 Beacon Hollow Rd., Gordonville; 717-768-8218; $$), located 1 mile north of Intercourse, has 2 bedrooms and a kitchen to accommodate up to 4. Breakfast provisions are provided for a do-it-yourself meal. At **Smucker's Guest House** (484 Peters Rd., New Holland; 717-354-6879; $$), located 3 miles from Intercourse, you'll find 3 guest rooms. Continental breakfast is provided.

Marietta

*OLDE FOGIE FARM $
106 Stackstown Rd.
Marietta, PA 17547
(717) 426-3992, (877) 653-3644
oldefogiefarm.com

That's "olde" as in quaint, not ancient, joke the good-natured owners of this organic (been that way for about 40 years), free-range farm, who, by the way, are named Tom and Biz Fogie. This is truly a feel-good place, as much because of the Fogies as for their comfy accommodations and gorgeous garden (including one that is alive with butterflies). Two types of accommodations are available here: traditional bed-and-breakfast rooms and family efficiency suites (cook your own breakfast—you're welcome to gather your own eggs). Chore participation is optional, but I say, get up and do it.

Mount Joy

COUNTRY LOG FARM HOUSE $$
1175 Flory Rd.
Mount Joy, PA 17552
(717) 653-4477
countryloghouse.com

Helping Jim and Mim Brubaker gather eggs and milk the goats is sure to work up a hearty appetite for your farm-style breakfast. The log house features 3 guest rooms and a suite, all well-equipped to accommodate families. No credit cards.

ROCKY ACRE FARM BED &
BREAKFAST $$–$$$
1020 Pinkerton Rd.
Mount Joy, PA 17552
(717) 653-4449
rockyacre.com

Get a double dose of family-and-farm fun here when you stay at Galen and Eileen Benner's 200-year-old working dairy farm and join their son Arlin and daughter-in-law Deborah for a hands-on tour of their even bigger Yippee Farms just down the road (880 Pinkerton Rd.; 717-653-2314; yippeefarms.com). Guest rooms in the Victorian-style farmhouse (said to have once been part of the Underground Railroad) are large; most accommodate between 4 and 5 people (nightly rates are based on 4 occupants rather than the usual 2). Full breakfast is included. Two-night minimums are required on all weekends, on weekdays during school breaks, and in June through August.

RESORTS

In a place most closely identified with the humble austerity of its Old Order religious communities, it may seem surprising to find resorts with world-class golf courses, spas, and other major amenities representing the epitome of luxury. But rather than being an anomaly, this coexistence of opposites is one of the main reasons why Pennsylvania Dutch Country has such a unique, multifaceted personality and appeals to such a broad spectrum of visitors.

Although rates are subject to change, we use the following pricing code to indicate the average rate for a 1-night stay, in season, for 2 adults. Note that these rates do not include taxes, gratuities, or add-on services, such as room service and premium TV channels (unless otherwise noted). Off-season rates are lower. October (especially weekends) and June through August are usually considered peak seasons.

$................ Less than $100
$$ ....$100–$150
$$$ ....$150–$200
$$$$.................$200–$250
$$$$$.........More than $250

Hershey

Hershey Resorts

What began as a project to keep construction workers gainfully employed during the Great Depression has evolved into a world-class destination resort. Guests who stay at the Hotel Hershey, Hershey Lodge, or Hershey Highmeadow Campground receive exclusive access to the 18-hole, championship East and West courses of the Hershey Golf Collection plus free admission to Hershey Gardens, shuttle service to Hersheypark, and exclusive children's activities.

If you really want to immerse yourself in chocolate, the Spa at the Hotel Hershey (717-520-5888; chocolatespa.com) offers a menu that will make you feel like a kid in a candy shop. Aside from its signature head-to-toe chocolate treatments, you'll find other irresistible "flavors" such as mojito, coffee, and milk and honey as well as gentle floral scents both familiar and exotic.

The Hershey properties have numerous restaurants ranging from the über-elegant to the kick-back casual, coffee shops to cupcake boutique. If you're hungry for it, you'll find it here—even if it isn't made of chocolate.

✳HERSHEY LODGE $$$$–$$$$$
West Chocolate Avenue and University Drive
PO Box 446
Hershey, PA 17033
(717) 533-3311, (800) HERSHEY
hersheylodge.com
Although this facility wasn't opened until 1967, 21 years after the death of Milton Hershey, its style and service definitely live up to his original standards. You can see the influence of Milton Hershey's Pennsylvania Dutch heritage and the beauty of the surrounding

countryside throughout this 665-room and suite accommodation. Amenities include heated indoor and two outdoor pools, basketball and tennis courts, s'mores roasts, and drive-in movies. Babysitting is available.

i The Hotel Hershey's Cocoa Kid's Club gives guests age 5 and over special activities such as tennis, basketball, arts and crafts, and swimming under the supervision of trained camp counselors. Babysitting services are available for kids under 5. Half-day and full-day programs are available in summer and on weekends and holidays year-round. Prices vary.

✳THE HOTEL HERSHEY   **$$$$$**
100 Hotel Rd.
PO Box 400
Hershey, PA 17033
(717) 533-2171, (800) HERSHEY
hersheypa.com

Surrounded by acres of magnificent formal gardens and manicured lawns, the 278-room, 20-suite, Mediterranean-inspired accommodation, built in the 1930s and upgraded during the $67 million "Grand Expansion" in 2009, is as posh as you can get. Another new addition during the "Grand Expansion" was the building of 10 private, 4- to 6-bedroom Woodside Cottages on the grounds of the Hotel Hershey that are perfect for vacationing with family and friends. The Hotel/Cottages complex shares a host of recreational facilities including an indoor pool, two outdoor pools (one just for adults, the family one has slides), and cabanas; year-round outdoor skating rink; basketball and tennis courts; and hiking trails.

CAMPGROUNDS & CABINS

For some people, camping is a chance to air out the old tent and pitch it in a beautiful spot under the stars or to rough it in a primitive log cabin. To others, it's a comfortable road trip in a fully appointed RV. Some apply the term camping to accommodations that range from quaint cottages to amenity-loaded resorts. The only key factor that seems to define the camping experience for all is an abundance of opportunities to enjoy the great outdoors. Many facilities are pet-friendly when it comes to their tent and RV sites but not in cabins or cottages.

Campers can find facilities open year-round. Rates range by type of site and time of year, so please call for specifics.

ELIZABETHTOWN

ELIZABETHTOWN/HERSHEY KOA
1980 Turnpike Rd.
Elizabethtown, PA 17022
(717) 367-7718, (800) 562-4774
campwithrusty.com, koa.com
Open from Apr through early Nov, this wooded 50-acre property offers accommodations: individual camp sites (primitive or with utilites), RV pull-throughs and back-ins, heated and air-conditioned cottages that sleep up to 6, and RV park models with bathrooms and kitchenettes. Facilities include a swimming pool and stocked catch-and-release fishing pond.

HERSHEY CONEWAGO CAMPGROUND
1590 Hershey Rd.
Elizabethtown, PA 17022
(717) 367-1179
hersheyconewago.com
Only 6 miles south of Hershey is this 26-acre campground (formerly Hershey KOA), with sites for tents (both primitive and with utilities) and RVs along with rustic log cabins overlooking a 1-acre pond. Amenities include free hot showers, swimming pool, minigolf, and basketball/tennis court.

HERSHEY/HUMMELSTOWN

*HERSHEY HIGHMEADOW CAMPGROUND
1200 Matlack Rd.
Hummelstown, PA 17036
(800) HERSHEY, (717) 534-8999
hersheypa.com/accommodations/
hershey_highmeadow_campground
Part of the Hershey Resorts family and conveniently located only a brief, free shuttle ride from Hersheypark, this 55-acre, year-round facility offers the entire gamut of camping accommodations, from open and shaded tent sites (primitive and with utilities) and RV pull-throughs to rustic log and

deluxe cabins that sleep up to 8. Amenities include 2 swimming pools, basketball and volleyball courts.

INTERCOURSE

BEACON HILL CAMPING
West Newport Road (Route 772)
(0.5 mile north of Route 340
intersection)
Hummelstown, PA 17036
(717) 768-8775
beaconhillcamping.com

No frills, no recreational facilities or activities, and guests must be over 16. Peace and quiet are main selling points here—that plus the convenience of being in walking distance to everything the village of Intercourse has to offer. RV pull-throughs have full hookups; camping cabins and cottages, all with air-conditioning and heating, sleep 2. Only cottages have indoor plumbing.

LANCASTER

OLD MILL STREAM CAMPING MANOR
2249 Lincoln Hwy. East
Lancaster, PA 17602
(866) 386-2839, (717) 299-2314
oldmillstreamcampground.com

Although you're within steps of Dutch Wonderland and a short drive to the outlets, you'd never know it, situated as it is in a country setting beside a quiet stream. Open year-round, this property offers full RV hookups and tent sites (primitive and with utilities). Pets are permitted.

Positively Primitive

There's a portable toilet nearby and water spigots at 4 locations, but that's it as far as the modern camping amenities go at the Mill Creek Camping Area at the southern end of Lancaster County Central Park (1050 Rockford Rd., Lancaster; 717-299-8215; co.lancaster.pa.us/parks). Four primitive campsites each accommodate up to 4 people ($18 for the group); there's also one site for larger groups. Everyone needs a camping permit. Park activities include a swimming pool (admission is charged), skate park (free), basketball and tennis courts, softball and soccer fields, playgrounds, environmental center, and naturalist-led programs. To get there from Lancaster City, take Duke Street south through the city to Chesapeake Street. Take a right onto Chesapeake Street; go 0.2 mile and turn left into the park.

RONKS

✳FLORY'S COTTAGES AND CAMPING
99 N. Ronks Rd.
Ronks, PA 17572
(717) 687-6670
floryscamping.com

Surrounded by Amish farmland, this family-owned and operated campground offers 3 overnighter options: RV sites with utilities; 1- to 3-bedroom housekeeping facilities with fully equipped kitchen, TV, heat, and air-conditioning, and guest rooms on the 2nd floor of the owner's residence. Open year-round. There's a public pool at nearby Leola Community Park.

MILL BRIDGE VILLAGE CAMP RESORT
101 S. Ronks Rd.
Ronks, PA 17572
(800) 645-2744, (717) 687-8181
millbridge.com

This lively spot attracts tourists to see its 2 historic landmarks, an 18th-century mill and mid-19th-century covered bridge. So if you're looking for something out of the way, this isn't it. But you'll find canoe rentals, buggy rides, a swimming pool, and other fun stuff. Paved RV sites with hookups; resort cabins with heat, air, and kitchenette; 2-story loft suite with full kitchen; and Native American–style tepees with water and electric on-site. Ask about off-season specials.

STRASBURG

BEAVER CREEK FARM CABINS
2 Little Beaver Rd. (1.5 miles
southeast of Strasburg on Route 896)
Strasburg, PA 17579
(717) 687-7745
beavercreekfarmcabins.com

Just 8 two-bedroom single cabins (and one double for larger families) with heat and air-conditioning, kitchen, and bathroom set amid 29 acres of quiet, beautiful farmland. Eighteen holes of mini disc golf on-site. Open year-round.

DINING DEUTSCH STYLE

Many restaurants offering authentic Pennsylvania Dutch food either serve smorgasbord or family style (pass the potatoes, please). The majority of the smorgasbords and family-style dining spots serve pretty much the same fare—fried and roasted chicken, ham, roast turkey, pork and sauerkraut, chicken potpie (made with wide noodles, not a pastry crust), homemade soups, salad bar, and Dutch Country sides such as chowchow (a pickled vegetable mixture served cold) and red beet pickled eggs. Dessert spreads are bountiful—don't miss the shoofly pie, fruit cobblers and crisps, and chocolate cake with peanut butter icing. I will indicate the restaurants that also offer a la carte menus.

Prices indicate dinner for 1 adult without beverages, tax, and gratuity. Most of these restaurants also serve breakfast and/or lunch at bargain prices. Most of these dining spots are closed Sun unless otherwise indicated.

$................. Less than $20
$$ .... $20 to $30
$$$ .... $30 to $40
$$$$................. $40 to $50
$$$$$.......... More than $50

i Many fresh vegetables, potatoes, and noodles are served simply, accented only with a gloss of browned butter to add a richer, almost nutty taste. A favorite flavoring for everything from chicken and corn soup to potpies and cakes is saffron. Pennsylvania Dutch homemakers prize the rich golden color and distinctive flavor that this spice lends to their recipes.

Look for discount coupons for Pennsylvania Dutch family-style and smorgasbord meals at official area visitor centers (visit paputchcountry.com for addresses) or online at the individual restaurant websites.

BIRD-IN-HAND

BIRD-IN-HAND FAMILY RESTAURANT & SMORGASBORD $$
2760 Old Philadelphia Pike
Bird-in-Hand, PA 17505
(717) 768-1500
bird-in-hand.com
A cute feature at this family-owned eatery is the Noah's Ark–themed buffet that's just the right height so kids can serve themselves.

PLAIN & FANCY FARM RESTAURANT $–$$
3121 Old Philadelphia Pike (Route 340, 1 mile east of Bird-in-Hand)
Bird-in-Hand, PA 17505
(717) 768-4400
plainandfancyfarm.com

Pennsylvania Dutch Cuisine

Pennsylvania Dutch Country native and cookbook author Betty Groff fondly recalls her mother serving "French Goose" to her family after a day working on the farm. Actually, the dish was really pig stomach stuffed with a savory mixture of pork sausage, potatoes, and vegetables. This is a good example of the waste-not, want-not creativity of Pennsylvania Dutch farm cooking. Another is scrapple, which was pork trimmings mixed with cornmeal and spices (today, pork butt instead of trimmings is generally used). Don't knock them if you haven't tried them. They can be really delicious and they're key to the culture. If you get a chance, sample schnitz and knepp, a dried apple-and-dumpling dish that's usually served with home-cured ham.

One of the best known of the area's family-style restaurants, Plain & Fancy has been serving Pennsylvania Dutch specialties in a converted farm setting for more than 40 years. Open 7 days. A la carte menu is available.

i Shrove Tuesday, the day before the beginning of Lent, is known as Fastnacht, the night before the fast begins. To use up all of their fat and eggs, the Pennsylvania Dutch follow the German tradition of making dough-nuts, or fastnachts, coated in regular or confectioner's sugar, in square or round shapes. Churches often sell them at fund-raisers.

EAST EARL

✳**SHADY MAPLE SMORGASBORD $–$$**
129 Toddy Dr.
East Earl, PA 17519
(717) 354-8222, (800) 238-7363
shady-maple.com
Expect to wait in line to get into this super-popular—with both tourists and natives—family-owned and operated spot. At 200

feet long, it may well live up to its billing as the longest buffet in Lancaster County (in all honesty, I've never measured any of them, but this one is certainly big).

INTERCOURSE

✳**STOLTZFUS FARM RESTAURANT $**
Route 772, East Newport Road
Intercourse, PA 17534
(717) 768-8156
stoltzfusfarmrestaurant.com
Located 1 block east of Intercourse, this authentic Amish homestead farm (owner Amos Stoltzfus grew up here) serves family-style fare in all-you-can-eat portions. You can't get fresher meats because they come from the family's butcher shop, Stoltzfus Meats & Deli, located only 0.25 mile away. Make sure you try some of the sausage (it's made fresh daily) and the special-recipe ham loaf. Closed Dec through Mar.

i To cleanse the palate during and between rich courses, many Penn-sylvania Dutch eat various sweet-and-sour (sugar-vinegar brined) relishes such as chowchow or pickled vegetables or rinds.

Dining in an Amish Home

To supplement their farm income, some Amish families will invite area visitors into their homes for a home-cooked dinner featuring local specialties. Most of these families prefer to take reservations through selected hotel, inn, and bed-and-breakfast owners, but one that you can contact directly is the Fisher Family Farm (4010 Old Philadelphia Pike [Route 340], Gordonville; 717-768-0733). Donations are welcome (the average is usually about $15 per diner). Elam and Barbara Fisher's farm has no electricity.

LITITZ

**✳LITITZ FAMILY CUPBOARD
   RESTAURANT & BUFFET** $
12 W. Newport Rd. (just off Route 501
North)
Lititz, PA 17543
(717) 626-9102
lititzfamilycupboard.com
This is a local favorite and a home-cooking
go-to place for my husband and me. Thursday is French Goose night. A la carte is available, too.

ℹ In Pennsylvania Dutch homes, pork and sauerkraut is the traditional New Year's Day good luck meal. Some say that the reason for the pork is that pigs root "forward," while chickens and turkeys scratch "backward." If you happen to be in the area, a number of firehouses feature this fortuitous fare at their New Year's Day fund-raiser dinners.

MOUNT JOY

**COUNTRY TABLE RESTAURANT BAKE
   SHOPPE & DELI** $
740 E. Main St., 2 miles off Route 283 just
east of Mount Joy
Mount Joy, PA 17552
(717) 653-4745
countrytablerestaurant.com
A la carte breakfast, lunch, and dinner. All of the Pennsylvania Dutch favorites plus steaks and seafood.

RONKS

**HERSHEY FARM RESTAURANT &
   INN** $–$$
240 Hartman Bridge Rd. (off Route 30,
south of Rockvale Outlets on Route 896)
Ronks, PA 17572
(800) 827-8635
hersheyfarm.com
The higher price applies to Saturday dinner. Two carving stations serve ham and turkey, on Saturday it's prime rib instead of turkey. A la carte menu, too. Hershey Farm is known for its whoopee pies—it holds a festival every fall. There are minis on the buffet and usually a basket of regular size in the cashier area.

MILLER'S SMORGASBORD　　　**$–$$**
2811 Lincoln Hwy. East (Route 30, 1 mile
east of Route 896)
Ronks, PA 17572
(800) 669-3568
millerssmorgasbord.com

It began as a truck stop in 1929; now it's a
smorgasbord landmark. Choose from 3 buffet options: soup, salad, and bread; entrees,
carving station, and grilled veggies; or the
Traditional, which has all of the above and
more. Open 7 days.

i For breakfast, be sure to order a
bowl of "Amish oatmeal." Every
family has its own recipe of this dried
fruit and nut, vanilla- and cinnamon-
scented treat that tastes like a fresh-
from-the-oven oatmeal cookie. Top it
with milk or cream, whipped cream, or
nothing at all.

SMOKETOWN

GOOD N' PLENTY RESTAURANT　　　**$**
150 Eastbrook Rd.
(between Routes 340 and 30)
Smoketown, PA 17576
(717) 394-7111
goodnplenty.com

Seating is truly family style (i.e., long communal tables) and so is the service at this
1871 farmhouse. But don't be afraid to pass
the platters, because the refills will continue
until every appetite is satisfied. Open 7 days.
Closed for the month of Jan.

OTHER AREA RESTAURANTS

In Pennsylvania Dutch Country, the Amish and Mennonites aren't the only ones who know how to make the most out of local ingredients. This diverse area has attracted stellar chefs, white-tablecloth restaurants, pubs, microbreweries, and tea and coffeehouses.

The pricing code designates the basic price of a dinner entree (unless otherwise stated) for 1 adult. Tax, gratuities, and alcoholic beverages are not included in this price. Many establishments have been designated nonsmoking, and those that do allow smoking are identified whenever possible. Most restaurants accept major credit cards. Those that do not are identified.

$. . . . . Less than $20
$$ . . . . $20–$30
$$$ . . . . $30–$50
$$$$ . . . . More than $50

ADAMSTOWN

**STOUDT'S BREWING CO. AND
  BLACK ANGUS RESTAURANT
  & BREW PUB $$–$$$**
2800 N. Reading Rd.
Route 272 North (1.5 miles north of
Pennsylvania Turnpike exit 286)
Adamstown, PA 19501
(717) 484-4386
stoudtsbeer.com

Steaks have been the specialty here for more than 40 years, but, in reality, it's the brews that get the bravos. The pub's good bet—try the crab calzone or one of the wursts. (Brewery tours are available on Sat and Sun.)

EAST PETERSBURG

✴HAYDN ZUG'S RESTAURANT $$–$$$
1987 State St. (4 miles north
of Lancaster on Route 72)
East Petersburg, PA 17520
(717) 569-8450
haydnzugs.com

The menu is huge and a bit of a challenge to follow until you get used to it, but persevere; it's worth it. This is my favorite "going out nice" place—it's cozy, colonial, and candlelit. I love the lamb Dijonnaise and the grilled shrimp with lobster sauce. Order your entree in a half-portion; it's plenty for all but the biggest appetites.

HERSHEY RESORT
RESTAURANTS

At the Hotel Hershey (100 Hotel Rd., Hershey, PA 17033; 717-534-8800; hersheypa.com/dining):

✳THE CIRCULAR DINING ROOM $$$

Milton Hershey wanted his grand hotel's dining room to be built in a circular configuration because, he explained, "in some places, if you don't tip well, they put you in a corner. I don't want any corners." Although it's a bit too large to be called "intimate," this is a truly romantic restaurant with a menu to match. Look for the innovative ways chocolate is used throughout the menu, and don't miss the cocoa-dusted scallops. The Circular Dining Room has long been renowned for its Sunday Brunch ($39.95), but you can have the same first-class experience sans the seafood, carving stations, and other dinner selections at the breakfast-focused Grand Breakfast Buffet ($18.95) any other day.

HARVEST $-$$$$

Dark chocolate–braised pork shank, smoked baby back ribs with chocolate barbecue sauce? Of course, you're in Hershey! But not everything on the menu of this casual eatery is chocolate-centric. There's also an extensive selection of locally sourced USDA Prime steaks—for a Pennsylvania Dutch twist, try yours with a birch beer reduction sauce. Open for lunch, too.

TREVI 5 $-$$

House-made pasta is the specialty here. The wine list is extensive and international.

At the Hershey Lodge (325 University Dr.; Hershey, PA 17033; 717-533-3311; hershey lodge.com):

FOREBAY $-$$$

Whatever you're craving, you'll find it here, from a big, beefy (or lamb) burger to house-smoked barbecue ribs to stuffed lobster.

Don't miss the Peanut Butter Cup Martini or Small Batch Bourbons!

HERSHEY GRILL $-$$

The dinner entrees are excellent, but if you're looking for some Hershey dining experience on the less pricey side, order a lamb bacon BLT brick or chicken margherita sandwich or share some of the special small plates.

LEBBIE LEBKICHER'S $

Bring the family for breakfast. The kids will love the chocolate chip pancakes and banana bread french toast; for a more sophisticated wake-up call there's eggs Benedict or the salmon and wild mushroom omelet.

OTHER HERSHEY RESTAURANTS

DEVON SEAFOOD GRILL $-$$

Hershey Press Building
27 W. Chocolate Ave.
Hershey, PA 17033
(717) 508-5460
devonseafood.com

The almond-crusted talapia with orange buerre blanc is nothing short of crave-worthy. Ditto for the lobster mac and cheese.

> **i** Dinner can cost upward of $30 at Devon Seafood Grill, but on weekdays, you can get a bargain "power lunch" for $11.50.

HERSHEY PANTRY $

801 E. Chocolate Ave.
Hershey, PA 17033
(717) 533-7505
hersheypantry.com

Even the locals don't mind standing in line to get into this cute eatery with its

Close-up

Dinner Theaters

Want some entertainment or education with your entree? Some comic or musical diversion with your dessert? Check out the area's year-round dinner theaters. Quoted price is for adult theater ticket and dinner with tax and gratuity.

CHRISTIANA

Freedom Chapel Dinner Theatre
15 N. Bridge St.
Christiana, PA 17509
(610) 593-7013
The building is historic (a former church built in 1858), and the productions and pre-show meal are pure Pennsylvania Dutch—two favorites are the charmingly romantic *Amish Vows in Paradise* and the holiday-themed *Amish Family Christmas*. Cost is $49 (show without dinner $30).

LANCASTER

*Dutch Apple Dinner Theatre
510 Centerville Rd.
Lancaster, PA 17601
(717) 898-1900
dutchapple.com
I'm not a dinner theater aficionado, but I've enjoyed every performance I've seen here—and the food, American favorites served buffet-style plus carving station, is really good, too. The shows are classic and contemporary musicals, and there are children's offerings as well. Prices range from $51 to $54.

*Living the Experience
Bethel AME Church
450–512 E. Strawberry St.
Lancaster, PA 17603
(ChurchTowne)
(717) 393-8379
bethelamelancaster.org
Through personal accounts and spiritual song, this thoughtful interpretation of the lives of free and enslaved Africans in the Lancaster County area performed in this 1821 church that was a "station" on the Underground Railroad is anything but your usual, from-the-book history lesson. Afterwards, the audience is invited to discuss the presentation and issues it raises with the cast over a buffet dinner featuring African-American specialties. $38.

Rainbow Dinner Theatre
Route 30 (3 miles east of Rockvale
Outlets), Paradise
(800) 292-4301, (717) 687-4300
rainbowdinnertheatre.com
All Broadway-caliber comedy all the time plus an extensive buffet of American favorites. $48 to $52.

everything-homemade menu. The lines move fast, so don't be deterred, or you'll miss out on one of the best and most reasonably priced options—everything's under $10, including the yummy french toast. This is also a great place for lunch or dinner, too. Closed Sun.

WHAT IF . . . OF HERSHEY $–$$
845 E. Chocolate Ave.
Hershey, PA 17033
(717) 533-5858
whatifdining.com

You'll find a good number of dinner entrees under $20 on this varied, upscale, Italian-inspired menu. Think lobster ravioli and crab alfredo.

INTERCOURSE

KLING HOUSE $
Kitchen Kettle Village
Route 340 (10 minutes east of Lancaster)
Intercourse, PA 17534
(800) 732-3538, (717) 768-2746
kitchenkettle.com

If peach melba pancakes sound good to you, then head here for breakfast where everything's under $10, even the create-your-own omelets. Open for lunch, too. Closed Sun.

LANCASTER CITY

*CHECKERS BISTRO $–$$
300 W. James St.
Lancaster, PA 17603
(717) 509-1069
checkersbistro.com

This Euro casual-cool spot is where I meet friends for some good food, wine, and a chat. We often share a bunch of small plates (tamale with lobster and shrimp, Moroccan

lollipop lamb chops), but I've never been disappointed when I ordered any of the luxury pizzas and regular entrees.

i Intercourse? Get your mind out of the gutter! The origins of this eyebrow-raising moniker are not known for sure, but there are three different theories. One is that it comes from the village's location at the intersection—or intercourse—of two famous roads. Another is that it was named for a long stretch of road (aka an Entercourse) that led to a nearby racetrack. And third is the thought that in the early 19th century the word "intercourse" was used to describe everyday social interaction, and that this area was the center of local life.

*FENZ $–$$
398 Harrisburg Ave.
Suite 100
Lancaster, PA 17603
(717) 735-6999
fenzrestaurant.com

Pure comfort food, including a super-delicious meat loaf with mac and cheese and ricotta-stuffed ravioli with stewed wild mushrooms.

THE GREENFIELD RESTAURANT
AND BAR $$–$$$
595 Greenfield Rd.
Lancaster, Pennsylvania 17601
(717) 393-0668
theoldegreenfieldinn.com

Romance is a table for two in the wine cellar of this 1780 stone farmhouse. Prime rib and steaks are cut to order, and the seafood pasta is a longtime signature.

JOHN J. JEFFRIES $-$$$
Lancaster Arts Hotel
300 Harrisburg Ave.
Lancaster, PA 17603
(717) 431-3307
johnjjeffries.com

Okay, so triple-filtered water may be a little pretentious and it tastes like—water. But this restaurant and its executive chef/owners have their hearts in the right place. Housed in a late-19th-century tobacco warehouse, this dining spot focuses on local, seasonal, and sustainable ingredients prepared simply and elegantly.

i In the 1840s, so many German immigrants opened "lager bier" breweries in the area that one local newspaper dubbed Lancaster City "Munich of the United States."

LANCASTER BREWING CO. $-$$
302 N. Plum St.
(corner of Walnut and Plum Streets)
Lancaster, PA 17602
(717) 391-6258
lancasterbrewing.com

This former late-19th-century warehouse-turned-brewery makes liberal use of its blockbuster beers in the preparation of dinner entrees such as milk stout meat loaf and ale-battered fish-and-chips.

Sushi in Amish Country?

Yup, and it's really good, too, at **Mojo Asian Cuisine & Sushi Bar** (245 Bloomfield Dr., Lititz; 717-509-3888; $) and **Wasabi** (2600 Willow Street Pike, Willow Street; 717-464-8878; $).

Need a coffee break?

Here are three local favorites:

Merenda Zug Espresso Bar (11 E. Main St., Strasburg; 717-687-8027)
Spill the Beans Cafe (43 E. Main St., Lititz; 717-627-7827)
Square One Coffee (145 N. Duke St., Lancaster; 717-392-3354; squareonecoffee.com)

✳LEMON GRASS THAI RESTAURANT $-$$
Cocalico Outlet Center
2481 Lincoln Hwy. East
(across from Rockvale Outlets)
Lancaster, PA 17602
(717) 295-1621
thethailemongrass.com

Hot or not, the choice is up to you. If it's tongue-tingling you're after, order the Evil Jungle Princess; if not, go for the Angel Breast. Extensive vegetarian menu, too. Open daily for lunch and dinner.

THE PRESSROOM $$-$$$
26–28 W. King St.
Lancaster, PA 17603
(717) 399-5400
pressroomrestaurant.com

The building might be a 250-year-old Queen Anne, but inside the ambience is comfy and clubby with its mahogany decor, booths and banquettes, and open hearth kitchen. Dinners range on the high side—a number are over $30—but the lunch sandwiches, named after newspaper comics characters, are all under $10.

✳RACHEL'S CAFE & CREPERIE $
309 N. Queen St.
Lancaster, PA 17603
(717) 399-3515
rachelscreperie.com

There's nothing better on a nice day than to grab a sweet or savory crepe to go at Rachel's, so you can fuel up while you window shop your way through downtown Lancaster.

STRAWBERRY HILL
RESTAURANT $$–$$$
128 W. Strawberry St.
Lancaster, PA 17603
(717) 393-5544
strawberryhillrestaurant.com

If you're passionate about wine, this late-19th-century vintage Victorian is a don't-miss destination. The award-winning list features more than 1,000 selections. The food is top-notch, too, with its fresh takes on seasonal (and local whenever possible) ingredients.

LITITZ

CAFE CHOCOLATE OF LITITZ $
40 East Main St.
Lititz, PA 17543
(717) 626-0123
chocolatelititz.com

Located in Pennsylvania Dutch Country's other chocolate capital, this tiny eatery is known for its fondue fountain, but the savory menu has some interesting global specialties such as South African Baboti meat loaf and vegetable curry Siam.

GENERAL SUTTER INN $–$$
14 E. Main St.
Lititz, PA 17543
(717) 626-2115
generalsutterinn.com

General John Sutter claimed a stake in history when his California mill became the epicenter of 1800s Gold Rush hysteria; his connection to Lititz? He moved here, died here, and is buried here. The inn that bears his name serves upscale fare with some interesting accents (grilled salmon brûlée with jalapeño glaze, for example). Small plates are almost all under $10.

i Wilbur's isn't the only chocolate in Lititz. Right down the street is Cafe Chocolate (40 E. Main St.; 717-626-0123; chocolatelititz.com), featuring sweet stuff from around the world. Look for the chocolate fountain in the window.

MARIETTA

✳JOSEPHINE'S RESTAURANT $$–$$$
324 W. Market St.
Marietta, PA 17547
(717) 426-2003
josephinesrestaurant.net

Exposed beams and walls made of stucco-stacked log walls provide 18th-century ambience, but chef/owner Daniel LaBoon's French-inspired menu is anything but old-fashioned. I can never resist the short ribs, but I'm told there are other good things on the menu as well. Save room for the homemade ice cream.

(Q) Close-up

*Bube's Brewery: A Complex Experience

When you drive by, you'd probably dismiss this building at 102 N. Market St., Mount Joy (717-653-2056; bubesbrewery.com) as an old factory. And it was, dating back to 1876 when Bavarian immigrant Alois Bube (boo-bee) began brewing German-style lager here—and opened a Victorian-style hotel. After shutting down right before Prohibition, the brewery was abandoned until some local entrepreneurs turned it into a complex of exciting, high-concept restaurants—and, once again, a working brewery.

The original hotel bar now serves up a menu of killer martinis. Speaking of killer, it is also the scene of a regular schedule of history-based Murder Mysteries. When no one's being murdered, there's often live music. $$$.

Forty-three feet below, the brewery's original stone-lined vaults are now the Catacombs Restaurant, an interestingly upscale concept where the menu is a la carte ($$–$$$) most evenings, except on Medieval or Pirate Feast nights.

More casual and less expensive are the outdoor Biergarten and outdoor Bottling Works restaurants (both $), where you can enjoy everything from burgers to steaks with your favorite Bube's brew.

PARADISE

HISTORIC REVERE TAVERN $–$$
3069 Lincoln Hwy. East
(US Route 30)
Paradise, PA 17562
(717) 687-8601
reveretavern.com

Built in 1740, this stone building has a name-dropper-worthy history. Stephen Foster wrote some of his best-known music here; 15th US president James Buchanan once owned it. Today, steaks and seafood are the specialties here.

STRASBURG

IRON HORSE INN RESTAURANT $–$$
135 E. Main St.
Strasburg, PA 17579
(717) 687-6362
ironhorsepa.com

After a day of railroad recreation in Strasburg, your best choice for dining is this more-than-century-old transport waiting room. Entrees range from local faves such as chicken and waffles to "Triple Steak" featuring marinated portobello mushroom, Atlantic salmon, and filet mignon.

VARIOUS LOCATIONS

*ISAAC'S RESTAURANT & DELI $
Eight locations
Lancaster
25 N. Queen St. (in the heart of historic downtown in the Fulton Bank Building);
(717) 394-4455
The Shoppes at Greenfield (565 Greenfield Rd., right off Route 30); (717) 393-6067
Granite Run Square (1559 Manheim Pike); (717) 560-7774

⊙ Close-up

Dining on the Rails

For a taste of old-fashioned locomotive luxury, plan to have lunch ($) or dinner ($$$–$$$$) on the restored vintage, mahogany-and-polished-brass-appointed Lee E. Brenner Dining Car at the Strasburg Rail Road (Route 741 East, Strasburg; 717-687-7522; strasburgrailroad.com), America's oldest steam railroad, as you watch the scenic countryside glide by.

The Strasburg Rail Road also hosts Murder Mystery Trains on selected dates from Apr to mid-Nov. Tickets (including dinner, entertainment, train fare, and taxes) cost $54.95 for adults, $36.95 for children ages 2 to 11. For adults only is the Wine and Cheese Train available on selected evenings in July and Aug ($27).

Sycamore Court (245 Centerville Rd., Centreville exit off Route 30 between Lancaster and York); (717) 393-1199

Ephrata
Cloister Shopping Center (120 N. Reading Rd.); (717) 733-7777

Lititz
4 Trolley Run Rd. (just off Lititz Pike/ Route 501); (717) 625-1181

Strasburg
Route 741 East (The Shops at Traintown); (717) 687-7699

Hershey
1201 W. Chocolate Ave.; (717) 533-9665
isaacsdeli.com
The pink flamingo logo will lead you to a tropical-themed spot where the sandwiches are named for birds and flowers. The one in Lititz is one of my favorite places to grab a quick lunch or dinner. Isaac's is known for its grilled soft pretzel roll sandwiches and house-made soups of the day.

THEATER, MUSIC & NIGHTLIFE

It's not unusual to hear visitors to Pennsylvania Dutch Country complain that "nothing's open" after dark. While it's true that many of the museums and other popular attractions close at around 5 or 6 p.m., Lancaster County is still a pretty lively place after dark. There are plenty of theaters offering everything from big Broadway-style musicals to avant-garde community and historic productions. Lancaster City and Hershey both have their own symphony orchestras. Lancaster also has its own opera company. Just keep in mind that Lancaster County is not New York and it's not Podunk, so expect ticket prices to be somewhere in between—and often higher than you might think.

EPHRATA

EPHRATA PLAYHOUSE IN THE PARK
Ephrata Community Park
320 Cocalico St.
Ephrata, PA 17522
(717) 733-7966
ephrataplayhouseinthepark.org

Well-known for its lavish Broadway musical productions, the theater also showcases original works and presents the Family Series of original and classic tales for children. Tickets are $25 to $27. If there are any seats remaining on Saturday right before the show, you may pay as you wish.

> ℹ️ Check out the photos on the Playhouse in the Park lobby wall and you'll find a resume from Robert De Niro—he wasn't hired. There's also a well-circulated rumor that a young Philadelphia actor named Sylvester Stallone auditioned here (he didn't get a final callback).

HERSHEY

HERSHEYPARK SPORTS AND ENTERTAINMENT COMPLEX
100 W. Hershey Park Dr.
Hershey, PA 17033
(717) 534-3911, (800) HERSHEY
hersheypa.com

Three distinctly different venues—**Giant Center** hosts the biggest headliners in music, Disney ice shows, WWE wrestling, and other major events; seating is 16,000 for sporting events, 30,000 for concerts. The outdoor **Hersheypark Stadium** can accommodate between 10,500 to 12,500 spectators for sporting events and musical acts such as U2 and James Taylor. The Stadium's more intimate **Star Pavilion** offers reserved and lawn seating for 8,000 music fans.

✳HERSHEY THEATRE
15 E. Caracas Ave.
Hershey, PA 17033
(717) 534-3405
hersheytheatre.com

Touring Broadway shows, classical music and dance programs, and headline performers from around the world provide entertainment from Sept through Apr at this absolutely gorgeous historic theater, which was built between 1929 and 1933 as part of town founder Milton S. Hershey's Depression-era "Great Building Campaign." Tickets for even the most popular shows rarely go over $70. The theater is also home to the Hershey Symphony Orchestra (adult ticket is $18). Come early so you can admire the lobby with its walls and arches fashioned from four different types of imported and domestic marble. The ceiling with bas-relief scenes and figures and "canopy of gold" in the inner foyer was modeled after St. Mark's Cathedral in Venice, Italy.

i Families with young children can get a free introduction to classical music at the Hershey Symphony Orchestra's annual "Young Person's Concert" held at the Milton Hershey School. A highlight is the chance for children to interact with a "petting zoo" of orchestra instruments.

LANCASTER

AMERICAN MUSIC THEATRE
2425 Lincoln Hwy. East
Lancaster, PA 17602
(800) 648-4102, (717) 397-7700
amtshows.com
This popular venue hosts headliner musicians representing all genres, comedians, national Broadway tours, and original holiday productions. Tickets can range from $20 to close to $70.

i On 13 summer Sunday evenings from June through August, Lancaster's Long's Park (located just off Route 30 on the Harrisburg Pike, across from Park City Center; 717-295-7054; longspark.org) hosts a free musical series represents a range of genres including jazz, blues, Celtic, Southern rock, and zydeco.

CHAMELEON CLUB
223 N. Water St.
Lancaster, PA 17603
(717) 299-9684
chameleonclub.net
Since the late 1980s, the Chameleon Club has been presenting live original music from national touring artists (including Creed and Limp Bizkit) and hot local bands in an intimate venue. Ticket prices are usually under $20, with a few exceptions, some as low as $10. In the Lizard Lounge downstairs, you'll find DJs and karaoke.

✳THE FULTON OPERA HOUSE
12 N. Prince St.
Lancaster, PA 17603
(717) 397-7425
fultontheatre.org
After more than a century and a half, the affectionately nicknamed "Grand Old Lady of Prince Street" and one of only 8 theaters to be named a National Historic Landmark is more than alive and well; she's singing, dancing, and emoting with the energy of an ingénue. Home of Lancaster's professional regional theater group and symphony orchestra, the Fulton presents a year-round schedule of major musicals, comedies, and dramas. Opened in 1852, this venue is considered to be the nation's oldest continuously operating theater and has hosted, through its

history, such legends as Sarah Bernhardt, W. C. Fields, Al Jolson, and George M. Cohan. Tickets generally range from $20 for bargain seats to up to $55 for platinum (Lancaster Symphony Orchestra performances begin at $17 and can cost up to $62).

i **If you're interested in learning what goes on behind the scenes at a theater, a number of the local venues offer guided backstage tours for a separate ticket price.**

STITCHES COMEDY CLUB
Lancaster Host Resort
2300 Lincoln Hwy. East
Lancaster, PA 17602
(717) 826-3472
stitchescomedy.com
See headline touring comedy acts at reasonable prices. $13 to $15. Must be 21 years old.

RONKS

SIGHT & SOUND MILLENNIUM THEATRE
300 Hartman Bridge Rd. (Route 896)
Ronks, PA 17572
(800) 377-1277
sight-sound.com
Described as "the largest faith-based live theater in America" and "the Christian Broadway," this venue, which draws audiences from all over the country, stages big, big, big-scale original biblical-inspired productions. When I say big, I mean more than 50 professional performers, hundreds of costumes, live trained animals ranging from camels and horses to flight-trained birds, and elaborate special effects. A perennial holiday favorite is the *Miracle of Christmas*. Productions are definitely family-friendly but generally run about 2 to 2.5 hours, so they may be a little long for very young children. Adult tickets are $57.

HOMEGROWN & HOMEMADE

Everywhere you look you'll find evidence of the abundance of Pennsylvania Dutch Country. It's in the displays of homegrown fruits and vegetables at farm stands tucked away on narrow back roads. Look for hand-lettered signs offering just-gathered brown eggs, goat's milk, homemade root beer or birch beer, and oven-fresh baked goods.

Some of the stands work on the honor box system.

You also can find the wares of lots of local growers and crafters in one convenient place at one of the area's extensive, historic, and fun-to-shop farmers' markets.

The abundance is as much artistic as it is agricultural. You can see it in the multi-colored quilts, with their intricate patterns. It is in the masterfully crafted furnishings, toys, and decorative pieces that come from the barns and basements that have been converted into workshops.

Many of these home-based businesses are owned and operated by members of the Amish community (upward of 80 percent at last count) who, due to soaring land prices, have had to turn to public commerce for their livelihoods. Some operate their own cottage industries, ranging from small shops staffed by family members to factories that offer employment opportunities to other members of the community. Others hire non-Amish distributors to market their products to customers across the nation and around the world.

Statistics cited by local authorities on Amish life note that while the rate of failure for other American small businesses exceeds 50 percent, it is only 5 percent for those that are Amish-owned. Even more surprising is that 20 percent of Amish businesses are owned by women.

Due to religious considerations, most Amish- and Mennonite-owned businesses (both small and large) are closed Sun. Operations that are open on that day will be specified in the text.

ART

PENNSYLVANIA ARTS EXPERIENCE
Arts Orientation Center
114 N. Prince St.
Lancaster, PA 17603
(717) 299-9496
paartsexperience.com

The small towns in and around Lancaster County are home to a wealth of talented painters, weavers, quilters, printmakers, potters, glassblowers, woodworkers, and other artists, many of whom are nationally and even internationally known and exhibited.

This nonprofit organization will help you to find and set up visits with many of these artists at their private studios along the area's extensive "art trail." (The service is free.) You can also download maps from the website.

BAKERY PRODUCTS

ACHENBACH'S PASTRIES, INC.
375 E. Main St.
Leola, PA 17540
(717) 656-6671
achenbachs.com

This family business, which traces its roots back to the Great Depression, is famous for its long johns (rectangular doughnuts topped with a chocolate, vanilla, or peanut butter icing) and "sticky" rings (just call them "stickies" like everybody else does).

THE SPRINGERLE HOUSE
15 E. Main St.
Strasburg, PA 17579
(717) 687-8022
springerlehouse.com

Springerle, cookies imprinted with pictures in hand-carved molds, have been around for over a thousand years in Europe, and Heather Botchlet's family has been making them in Lancaster County for more than 100. They're as artistic as they are delicious. Botchlet also has a stand at the Lancaster Central Market.

CANDY

GROFF'S LANCASTER CANDY STORE
3587 Blue Rock Rd. (Route 999)
Lancaster, PA 17603
(717) 872-2845
groffscandies.com

Founded in 1969, this family-owned and operated, made-from-scratch-at-home candy

company is renowned for its fudge, chocolates, brittles, and "sugar-free" treats. The Groffs also have a stand at the Bird-in-Hand Farmers' Market.

Whoopee!

Everywhere you look in Pennsylvania Dutch Country, you'll see whoopee pies. Actually, they're not pies at all, but, rather, a "sandwich" of two big cake-like cookies with a thick layer of fluffy (or sometimes not so fluffy) icing in between. Traditionally, the cookies are chocolate—usually devil's food—and the filling is vanilla, but some adventurous types have come up with other flavor variations, including pumpkin and peanut butter. They're yummy, but almost tooth-achingly sweet. You might want to share one.

✳WILBUR CHOCOLATE CANDY AMERICANA MUSEUM AND FACTORY STORE   FREE
48 N. Broad St.
Lititz, PA 17543
(888) 294-5287
wilburbuds.com

OK, there are more than 1,000 antique and vintage chocolate-making and consuming artifacts on display here, and you can peek through the window of the "Candy Kitchen" to watch all kinds of sweets get dunked and drizzled. But, really, you have to walk past all kinds of displays of chocolate-covered everything to get to the museum part, and there's no way to do that without at least tasting

Close-up

Humble Pies

Do you prefer your bottom to be wet or dry? If you're a shoofly pie connoisseur, you know that "wet bottom" means that there's a generous layer of sweet molasses filling under the crumb cake–like topping of this regional favorite. "Dry bottom" has a much thinner (sometimes almost barely there) layer of molasses filling, so it is more cake-like and less sweet throughout. Most locals will tell you the name was derived from the fact that flies attracted to the sweet filling constantly had to be shooed away from pies cooling on windowsills and kitchen tables or that it was often made with the once-popular Shoo Fly brand of molasses. Here are my favorites:

Bird-in-Hand Bake Shop
542 Gibbons Rd.
Bird-in-Hand, PA 17505
(717) 656-7947
bihbakeshop.com
This is really, really off the beaten path, so make sure you get directions from the bakery's website.

Dutch Haven Shoo-fly Pie Bakery
2857A Lincoln Hwy. East
(US Route 30)
Ronks, PA 17572
(717) 687-0111
dutchhaven.com
You can't miss the white windmill on its roof. They also ship.

Lititz Family Cupboard Bakery
12 W. Newport Rd.
Lititz, PA 17543
(717) 626-9102
lititzfamilycupboard.com
This bakery has a drive-through window for speedy service, but then you'd miss all the wonderful aromas and other temptations inside.

---

one of the company's world-famous Wilbur Buds, which have been a staple here since 1893. If you haven't tasted Wilbur chocolate, you're in for a treat. It's very different from anything you'll find at Hershey. Closed Sun.

DAIRY PRODUCTS

Lancaster County produces more than 1.9 billion pounds of milk each year, and where there's that much milk, there's bound to be some great ice cream. Here are some of the best. All merit ✴.

Adamstown

BOEHRINGER'S DRIVE-IN
3160 N. Reading Rd. (Route 272)
Adamstown, PA 19501
(717) 484-4227
Super-premium stuff (17 percent butterfat) made with real crushed vanilla bean, big

chunks of strawberry, and treasured family recipes since 1936. Open Mar through Sept.

Lancaster

PINE VIEW ACRES DAIRY
2225 New Danville Pike
Lancaster, PA 17603
(717) 872-5486

You can choose from 25 varieties made from cream from the dairy's own herd. Nothing envelope-pushing flavor-wise here, just good ice cream. Open year-round.

Lititz

*GRECO'S ITALIAN ICES & HOMEMADE ICE CREAM
49 N. Broad St.
Lititz, PA 17543
(717) 625-1166

Don't miss this little hidden gem tucked away beside a parking lot directly across from Wilbur Chocolate behind the Freez 'n Frizz. Greco's homemade ice cream repertoire includes around 40 flavors (if coconut is on the menu, get it), and the banana splits are hefty 32-ouncers.

New Holland

LAPP VALLEY FARM
244 Mentzner Rd. (between Routes 23 and 340)
New Holland, PA 17557
(717) 354-7988

You can watch the cows being milked on John Lapp's dairy farm, then cool off with a cone of any of 16 flavors of homemade ice cream—and just-made waffle cones. You can also find Lapp's ice cream at Kitchen Kettle Village.

Strasburg

THE STRASBURG COUNTRY STORE AND CREAMERY
1 W. Main St.
Strasburg, PA 17579
(717) 687-0766
strasburg.com

You can smell the waffle cones from blocks away. The ice cream is pure, super-creamy (14.5 percent butterfat), and made daily. Pick your pleasure at the marble soda fountain— a 600-pound souvenir of the 1890s.

FARMERS' MARKETS

*Each one is distinctive and an integral part of its community. Visit them all if you can. If you can only get to one, Lancaster Central Market has the most history; Green Dragon the widest variety.

BIRD-IN-HAND FARMERS' MARKET
2710 Old Philadelphia Pike
Bird-in-Hand, PA 17505
(717) 393-9674
birdinhandfarmersmarket.com

More than 30 local vendors gather here to offer a wide selection of edible, wearable, and decorative items from candy to candles, Amish bonnets to leather jackets, hand-carved wooden toys, homemade candy and fudge, smoked meats and cheeses, fresh produce, hand-dipped candles, and all kinds of traditional sweet-and-sour side dishes. Open year-round; check the website for seasonal days and hours.

GREEN DRAGON FARMERS' MARKET & AUCTION
955 N. State St.
Ephrata, PA 17522
(717) 738-1117
greendragonmarket.com

The dragon comes alive every Friday year-round with indoor and outdoor shopping featuring 400 local growers, merchants, and craftspeople. Open since 1932, it's one of the largest farmers' markets on the East Coast.

LANCASTER CENTRAL MARKET
23 N. Market St. (northwest corner of Penn Square)
Lancaster, PA 17603
(717) 291-4723
centralmarketlancaster.com

There has been a farmers' market on this site since the 1730s, making it America's oldest. The current Romanesque Revival building with its 72-foot-high, Spanish tile–covered towers dates back to 1889. Every Tues, Fri, and Sat close to 60 vendors (some whose family businesses have been "on market" since the early 1900s) sell food, crafts, and other products that reflect both local and international cultures.

ROOT'S COUNTRY MARKET & AUCTION
705 Graystone Rd.
Manheim, PA 17545
(717) 898-7811
rootsmarket.com

Begun in 1925, Root's (pronounced like "foots"), which is open only on Tues, is the oldest single-family-run country market in Lancaster County. More than 200 stand holders (some of whom are second and third generations of family businesses) offer farm-fresh produce, meats, bakery items, flowers and plants, handmade crafts, and all manner of household items.

FURNITURE & OTHER WOODWORKING

Bird-in-Hand

GLICK'S FOOD & CRAFTS
248A Monterey Rd.
Bird-in-Hand, PA 17505
(717) 656-1343

This working Amish farm, home to Eli Glick and family, is a great place to see all kinds of Pennsylvania Dutch crafts in the making, from cedar chests, hickory rockers, and tables to fruit, shoofly, and whoopee pies. Woodworking equipment is air powered (no electricity on this Amish farm), baking is done in a huge old-time iron oven, and ice cream cranked in a machine attached to a gas engine.

Intercourse

LAPP'S COACH SHOP
3572 W. Newport Rd.
(Route 772)
Intercourse, PA 17534
(717) 768-8712 (call between 9:30 and 10 a.m. or leave message)
lappscoachshop.com

Established in 1944, this shop sells Amish-made furniture, decorative items, and toys. Check out the toy wagons and scooters.

Lititz

CHERRY ACRES FURNITURE
23 E. Main St.
Lititz, PA 17543
(717) 626-7557
cherryacres.com

Reclaimed lumber from sources that range from barn siding to house floors gets a new lease on life in the hands of local artisans, who craft it into original rustic-style furnishings made for today's lifestyles.

THE SHAKER SHOPPE
616 Owl Hill Rd.
Lititz, PA 17543
(717) 626-9461
shakershoppe.com

Prized for its elegant simplicity, expertly crafted Shaker furniture has a timeless appeal that makes it true heirloom quality. This showroom has hundreds of handmade-in-Lititz, historically accurate pieces in Pennsylvania cherry, sugar pine, and tiger maple on display. You can also commission a custom piece in any wood or color.

Marietta

GEORGE'S WOODCRAFTS, INC.
9 Reichs Church Rd.
Marietta, PA 17547
(717) 426-1004, (800) 799-1685
georgeswood.com

Even the drawer bottoms and cabinet backs of these artisan home and office furnishings are made from solid, air-and-kiln-dried hardwood: no skimping, no shortcuts. And each piece of furniture is signed by the craftsman who made it. The rocking chairs are divine.

New Holland

CARSON'S IN THE CORNFIELDS
245 Grist Mill Rd.
New Holland, PA 17557
(717) 354-7343
carsonsinthecornfields.com

Mother and daughter Nancy Carson and Melissa Nordhoff create one-of-a-kind

furniture, wall decor, and other accessories by combining recycled antique parts and other rescued materials such as barn boards and shutters. Call for hours.

Ronks

CITY DUMP AT DUTCH HAVEN SHOO-FLY PIE BAKERY
2857A Lincoln Hwy. East
(US Route 30)
Ronks, PA 17572
(717) 687-0111
dutchhaven.com

There's no fancy showroom, but look around and you'll find some excellent handcrafted cedar chests and wood porch furniture, including my favorite gliders.

FISHER'S QUALITY FURNITURE
3061 W. Newport Rd.
(Route 772)
Ronks, PA 17572
(717) 656-4423
fishersqualityfurniture.com

Levi Fisher and his two craftsmen (his son, Mervin, is learning the trade) make cherry and oak furniture sets for every room in the house.

LAPP'S WOODEN TOYS
3006 Irishtown Rd.
Ronks, PA 17572
(717) 768-7234
lappstoysandfurniture.com

About as far from today's techno-toys as you can get, these simple, well-crafted playthings allow children to exercise their imaginations. Everything's produced in the adjoining woodshop.

JAMS, JELLIES & RELISHES

INTERCOURSE CANNING COMPANY
3612 E. Newport Rd.
Intercourse, PA 17534
(717) 768-0156
intercoursecanning.com
Proprietor Susan Adams and her staff refer to the preserved and jarred locally grown products such as pickled and dilled veggies, red beet eggs, and chowchow as "Amish hors d'oeuvres." You'll also find fruit butters and all kinds of other products usually found in Pennsylvania Dutch pantries. Feel free to taste before you buy.

Seven Sweets & Sours Festival

According to Pennsylvania Dutch tradition, every dinner should be accompanied by seven "sweets and sours," referring to any of the wide assortment of pickled vegetables, relishes, jellies, jams, fruit butters, spiced fruits, and other preserved produce that make use of the bounty of the area's farms. Every third weekend of September, Kitchen Kettle Village hosts a festival celebrating this tradition.

KITCHEN KETTLE VILLAGE
3529 Old Philadelphia Pike
Intercourse, PA 17534
(717) 768-8261, (800) 732-3538
kitchenkettle.com
This place is really touristy, but it's also really fun. It has more than 40 boutique shops selling everything from punched tin lighting to clothespin dolls, music boxes to pet paraphernalia. They've been "putting up" jams, jellies, and relishes like farm families do for more than 50 years. You'll find more than 70 original recipes for old-time regional specialties, including chowchow, apple butter, poppy seed dressing, and peanut butter schmier (like nut fudge with a hint of brown sugar), as well as an array of new-fangled nibbles, including Vidalia onion relish, zesty salsa, and jalapeño jam.

POTTERY

THE CLAY DISTELFINK
2246 Old Philadelphia Pike
Lancaster, PA 17602
(717) 399-1994
claydistelfink.com
The distelfink, the Pennsylvania Dutch name for the goldfinch, is considered to be a symbol of good luck. Artist Marilyn Stoltzfus incorporates the distelfink as well as many other images that the Pennsylvania Dutch relate to good fortune into designs for her handcrafted redware plates, made in the style of German pottery of the 1600s to 1800s. Open by appointment.

ELDRETH POTTERY
Production: 902 Hart Rd.
Oxford, PA 19363
(717) 529-6241
Showroom: 246 N. Decatur St. (Route 896)
Strasburg, PA 17579
(717) 687-8445
eldrethpottery.com
Each piece of salt-glazed stoneware and redware pottery is signed and dated by the craftsman who made it. Look for bargains in the "seconds" section at Eldreth Pottery;

Pennsylvania Pottery

Two forms of pottery that are particularly identified with Pennsylvania Dutch Country are salt-glazed stoneware and redware. Salt glazing, used in Germany for over 500 years, got its name from the process of introducing salt into the kiln at above 2000° Fahrenheit so it forms a sodium vapor. The vapor is carried throughout the oven by the flames and sticks to the clay, forming a random design coating.

Redware, which also traces its origins to Germany, is made by applying a glaze to the pottery before it is placed in the kiln. A lower oven temperature of just under 2000° Fahrenheit allows the glaze to melt evenly, making it possible for the artisan to have better control over color and decoration.

these items may not be perfect, but you can usually find some good bargains.

POTS BY DE PERROT
201 S. Locust St.
Lititz, PA 17543
(717) 627-6789
potsbydeperrot.com
Steve and Shirley de Perrot create decorative and functional stoneware pottery and tile art in a variety of styles and glazes. You'll find everything from trivets and platters to tables and mirrors. Open Wed through Sat.

i Steve de Perrot's tile art can also be seen in a special alcove at the Lititz Public Library (651 Kissel Hill Rd., Lititz; 717-626-2255; lititz library.org) honoring beloved community members.

VILLAGE POTTERY
3510 Old Philadelphia Pike
Intercourse, PA 17529
(800) 390-8436, (717) 768-7171
thevillagepottery.com
Handmade mostly by local artisans, the functional and decorative pottery here

demonstrates a wide range of redware and stoneware decorating techniques.

PRETZELS

In Philadelphia, they like them soft and chewy; in Pennsylvania Dutch Country, the most prized pretzels are hard, crisp, and crunchy. Bakers make the twisting look easy, but if you've ever tried it yourself, you know that turning out batch after batch of perfect pretzels with speed and precision takes a lot of practice.

Local legend has it that bread baker Julius Sturgis was given a pretzel recipe in 1850 as a thank-you gift from a hobo to whom he had given a meal. Eleven years later, he switched his entire operation to pretzel baking, making his the first commercial pretzel bakery in America. The Sturgis family continues to bake pretzels in the original Lititz bakery (the building dates back to 1784). Take a tour, take a twisting lesson, sample, and stock up at Julius Sturgis Pretzel Bakery, 219 E. Main St. (Route 772); (717) 626-4354; juliussturgis.com. All the pretzel bakeries listed are ✳.

Akron

MARTIN'S PRETZELS
1229 Diamond St.
Akron, PA 17501
(717) 859-1272
martinspretzels.com
Conservative Mennonite owned and staffed, the production room rings with hymns sung by the women who roll, twist, and pinch an average of 12 sourdough pretzels apiece every minute, just as they have been doing for more than 60 years. You can see (and hear) most of the process through the large lunchroom window most days (not Sunday) from around 8 a.m. to 3 p.m. Call if you want to be sure of the schedule.

i Forming 12 pretzels each minute may be fast for a human, but a machine can extrude 245 pretzels in the same time. Just one more reason to support the locals.

Intercourse

IMMERGUT HAND-ROLLED SOFT PRETZELS
3537 Old Philadelphia Pike
Intercourse, PA 17534
(717) 768-0657
Watch the bakers as they work, then enjoy a twisted treat (regular or whole wheat) with a cold glass of hand-squeezed lemonade. (I know I said Dutch Country pretzels are generally hard, but everybody likes a little variety now and then and these are too good to miss.)

INTERCOURSE PRETZEL FACTORY
3614 Old Philadelphia Pike
Intercourse, PA 17534
(717) 768-3432
intercoursepretzelfactory.com
The twisters here turn out about 100 pounds of pretzels per day. You can take a free tour, then test your twisting wrist action.

Lancaster

HAMMOND PRETZEL BAKERY
716 S. West End Ave.
Lancaster, PA 17603
(717) 392-7532
hammondpretzels.com
In operation since 1931, Hammond is the nation's oldest continuously family-operated, handmade pretzel bakery. (The recipe dates back to the 1800s).

QUILTS

Gordonville

ESH'S QUILTS AND CRAFTS
3829 Old Philadelphia Pike
Gordonville, PA 17529
(717) 768-8435

Leola

COUNTRY LANE QUILTS
221 S. Groffdale Rd.
(1 mile south of Route 23)
Leola, PA 17540
(717) 656-8476

RIEHL'S QUILTS & CRAFTS
247 E. Eby Rd.
Leola, PA 17540
(717) 656-0697

(Q) Close-up

Quilts

It is believed that Pennsylvania Dutch women learned the art of quilt making from Quakers and others already living in the commonwealth at the time of their arrival. But when you see the variety and artistry demonstrated by today's seamstresses (many of them working out of their homes), you'll understand why their talent and skill have made Lancaster County the "Quilt Capital of the World." Traditional Amish pattern designs are generally made up of various combinations of squares and rectangles, with such visually evocative names as Diamond in the Square, Sunshine and Shadow, Log Cabin, Bars, Double Wedding Ring, Irish Chain, and Bear's Paw.

As you travel through Pennsylvania Dutch Country, you will see quilts that reflect the plain colors of Amish clothing and others that incorporate a myriad of brights, pastels, and print fabrics. In Amish households, only traditional colors are permissible. But just because a quilt isn't "Plain" doesn't mean it is not authentic. Amish women do use other colors and prints to make quilts to sell to tourists and others outside of their community.

Many places will custom-make quilts based on an original or your design. Keep in mind that they are handmade and may take months to complete.

Because so many visitors are looking for authentic, locally handmade quilts, I'm listing some of my favorite Amish and Mennonite farm businesses. Most employ many of their neighbors to sew the quilts in their homes. Check the websites, if I list one, for directions to these out-of-the-way businesses. Otherwise, you might never find them.

New Holland

SMUCKER'S QUILTS
117 N. Groffdale Rd.
(right off Route 23)
New Holland, PA 17557
(717) 656-8730

WITMER QUILT SHOP
1070 W. Main St. (on Route 23)
(717) 656-9526

Ronks

FAMILY FARM QUILTS
3511 W. Newport Rd.
Route 772
Ronks, PA 17572
(717) 768-8375
familyfarmquilts.com

Here you'll find Amish- and Mennonite-made quilts, wall hangings, and other fabric crafts including dolls (the "washcloth" dolls are especially cute), Log Cabin quilt pattern placemats and coasters, quillows, hot pads, spice pads, and potholders.

LAPP'S QUILTS & CRAFTS
206 N. Star Rd.
Ronks, PA 17572
quiltart.com
Homemade quilts and other decorative items are for sale in the basement of this Amish farmhouse. Take Route 30 from Lancaster to Route 896 South to N. Star Road East; it's the first farm on your right after the schoolhouse.

i If you like to quilt, you'll find more than 6,000 bolts of 100 percent cotton fabric at The Old Country Store in Intercourse (3510 Old Philadelphia Pike, Intercourse; 800-828-8218; theoldcountrystore.com) and 10,000 at Burkholder's Fabrics in Denver (2255 W. Rte. 897; 717-336-6692; burkfabrics .com).

MISCELLANEOUS HANDMADE ITEMS

THE OLD CANDLE BARN
3551 Old Philadelphia Pike
Intercourse, PA 17534
(717) 768-8926
oldcandlebarn.com

Visit the candle factory Mon through Fri from 8 a.m. to 4 p.m. and watch local artisans dip and pour the old-fashioned way. This company has been making its candles this way for more than 35 years.

WINE

*MOUNT HOPE ESTATE AND WINERY
83 Mansion House Rd.
Manheim, PA 17545
(717) 665-7021, ext. 129
parenfaire.com

At the home of the annual Pennsylvania Renaissance Faire, you might not be surprised to find a honey mead—but how about one with blueberry? Yum. The Fantasy Series blends such as Maiden's Blush and Knight's Reward are fun, too.

NISSLEY VINEYARDS & WINERY ESTATE
140 Vintage Dr.
Bainbridge, PA 17502
(717) 426-3514, (800) 522-2387
nissleywine.com

Set on 300 acres, this family-owned winery has been producing estate-bottled Seyval Blanc and Vidal Blanc as well as some very interesting red, white, and rosé blends that range from dry to sweet.

SHOPPING

Nowhere is Pennsylvania Dutch Country's juxtaposition of old and new, plain and fancy, frugal and lavish more apparent than in its range of retail options, from out-in-the-woods rustic markets to hole-in-the-wall, one-of-a-kind mom-and-pop boutiques; from tiny workshops, studios, and galleries of artists whose names you've yet to learn to as-far-as-the-eye-can-see stretches of name brands in huge outlet malls. And if you're into antiquing, wear your comfiest sneakers and eat a big breakfast to fuel you up for a busy day.

ANTIQUES

Adamstown

Any town that promotes itself as "Antiques Capital USA" had better have the collectibles to back up its claim. Adamstown definitely does (antiquescapital.com). More than 5,000 dealers in all manner of items ranging from the reminiscent to the rare, from the 18th through 20th centuries, line the "Adamstown Antique Mile," which runs north and south along Route 272, a short way from the Route 286 exit of the Pennsylvania Turnpike. Some of the shops have addresses in Reinholds and Denver. Otherwise, their addresses are in Adamstown.

In the Adamstown area, you'll find everything from individual dealers who specialize in particular items or eras to co-op enterprises where a number of dealers operate their own booths in a single location. Some co-ops call themselves "showcase shops" because the dealers in them display their offerings in glass cases. An example is the Antique Showcase at the Black Horse, 2180 Reading Rd. (Pennsylvania Turnpike exit 286 and Route 272), Denver (717-335-3300), with 300 showcases, open 7 days a week year-round.

Some of the area's antiques shops and markets are still weekend-only operations, while others are also open for several days—and some even every day—during the week. During Antique Extravaganza weekends (the last full weekends in April, June, and September), many antiques dealers extend their days and hours.

ADAMS ANTIQUES
2400 N. Reading Rd.
Denver, PA 17517
(717) 335-3116
adamsantiques.com
Over 200 antiques and collectibles dealers display vintage and antique furniture, fabrics, pottery, china, books, advertising signs, and toys in more than 85 large booths and 125 showcases. Open 7 days year-round.

THE COUNTRY FRENCH COLLECTION
2887 N. Reading Rd.
Adamstown, PA 19501
(717) 484-0200
countryfrenchantiques.com
Eighteenth- and 19th-century French furniture and suites set in a barn that's an antique itself (built in 1790).

✳**OLEY VALLEY ARCHITECTURAL ANTIQUES**
2453 N. Reading Rd.
Denver, PA 17517
(717) 335-3585
oleyvalley.com
The selections of reclaimed stained, beveled, and leaded glass windows; fireplace mantels (Victorian, formal, period, country) in a variety of sizes from small to extra large; and antique bars (front and back wall units) are particularly impressive. Open Thurs through Mon.

RENNINGERS ANTIQUES MARKET
740 Noble St.
Kutztown, PA 19530
(717) 336-2177
renningers.com
Come early (as in 5 a.m.) to join the seasoned shoppers who will be searching for finds by flashlight in the 300-dealer outdoor part of this huge market. Then you'll be warmed up when the indoor part opens at 7:30 a.m., giving you access to an additional 375 dealers.

SHUPP'S GROVE
607 Willow St.
Reinholds, PA 17569
(717) 484-4115
shuppsgrove.com
Open since 1962, Shupp's was the first outdoor antiques market in the Adamstown area. Each week highlights—but is never limited to—a particular theme, such as vintage kitchen and cast iron, garden and architecture, retro '60s and '70s, and science fiction. Nice to know for specialty item collectors who may want to plan a trip to coincide with a certain theme. Open Sat and Sun Apr through Oct.

Hershey

CROSSROADS ANTIQUE MALL
825 Cocoa Ave.
(intersection of Routes 743 and 322)
Hershey, PA 17033
(717) 520-1600
crossroadsantiques.com
Dozens of dealers with a variety of antiques and collectibles, including rustic furniture, primitives, pottery, china, porcelain, glass, dolls, and toys set up shop in this 2-story stone barn. Call for seasonal hours.

i If you're in town the second week of October during the AACA Eastern National Antique & Classic Car Show, visit the Crossroads Antique Mall for car-related collectibles.

Hummelstown

✳**OLDE FACTORY ANTIQUES & CRAFTS**
139 S. Hanover St.
Hummelstown, PA 17036
(717) 566-5685
Consider it an aerobic workout to take in all 3 floors and 200 booths of antiques, collectibles, and crafts. If you're a rare book collector or just a voracious reader, don't miss Tarmans Books on the 2nd floor. Open 7 days.

i Looking for those rare DC and Marvel classics? You'll find them at Comic Store (Station Square Shopping Center, 28 McGovern Ave.; 717-397-8737; comicstorepa.com).

CLOTHING

Lititz

SPOILED SILLY BOUTIQUE
56 E. Main St.
Lititz, PA 17543
(717) 823-6453

This is a great place to find a gift for any age from infant to preteen. Many of the clothing and accessory items are handmade.

> **i** While you're walking on Main Street in Lititz, be sure to peek into the little alleyways between the stores. In many of them you'll find—more stores!

THE TIGER'S EYE
49 E. Main St.
Lititz, PA 17543
(717) 627-2244
tigerseyelititz.com

Nadine Buch Poling represents over 400 vendors of fashion-forward, wearable art garments and accessories. If you travel a lot, you'll like the Pleats separates by Babette, which always look crisp no matter how you pack them. For style, you can't beat the appliquéd jackets and coats from Beppa.

> **i** Clothing and shoe purchases are not taxable in Pennsylvania.

HOME ACCESSORIES & GIFTS

Bird-In-Hand

BIRD-IN-HAND IRON WORKS
3109 Old Philadelphia Pike (Route 340)
Bird-in-Hand, PA 17505
(717) 768-8101
birdinhandiron.com

Displayed here are home decor items made of cast iron, wrought iron, tin, pewter, and cast aluminum ranging from the smallest hooks and brackets to chandeliers and weathervanes representing 200 vendors, the majority of whom are American and 25 percent of whom are local. Many items are one of a kind.

Lititz

✳THE NORTH STAR OF LITITZ STUDIO AND GALLERY
521 E. Main St.
Lititz, PA 17543
(717) 625-1945

Hand-blown glass in a rainbow of colors and a dazzling array of intricate designs are fashioned into jewelry, Christmas ornaments, lamps, bottles, and other home decor items. Whimsical and fashion pieces are priced from inexpensive to serious collector level.

Mount Joy

WILTON ARMETALE FACTORY STORE
903 Square St.
Plumb and Square Streets
(1 block south of Route 230)
Mount Joy, PA 17552
(800) 553-2048
armetale.com

Armetale metal is a food-safe alloy made using a technique perfected long before the American Revolution. The resulting gift items, cookware, and dinnerware are virtually indestructible as well as striking, with the class of silver and the warmth of pewter. At the factory store, set in an old end-of-the-19th-century tobacco barn, you can save up to 60 percent off the prices that you would find in upscale department stores and specialty shops. Some are seconds, closeouts,

Mud Sales

You could get dizzy trying to keep up with the buying and selling that goes on all day when mud sale season comes around. (The events take place in the late winter/early spring when the ground begins to thaw and get muddy— get it?) These sale/auction extravaganzas are where Amish and Mennonite residents come to get everything from home furnishings to horses and buggies. This is also where the local ladies who don't make quilts buy them. The mud sales are held in different towns each weekend; proceeds benefit the local volunteer fire departments. Don't miss this opportunity to take part in at least one of these always highly anticipated community events. Mud sales start early (often at 8 or 8:30 a.m.), and they start on time. Parking can be a little tricky in some of the smaller towns, too, so stake out your place as early as you can. It will be worth it.

and discontinued items, and the inventory changes weekly.

Columbia

SUSQUEHANNA GLASS COMPANY FACTORY STORE
731 Ave. H
Columbia, PA 17512
(717) 684-2155, (800) 592-3646
theglassfactory.com
Come for a free factory tour on any Tues or Thurs and watch as the artisans hand cut, silkscreen, engrave, and etch glass as the processes have been done for more than a century. The on-site shop carries a wide range of the sparkling accessories.

Ephrata

✳TEN THOUSAND VILLAGES
240 N. Reading Rd. (Route 272)
Ephrata, PA 17522
(717) 721-8400
tenthousandvillages.com
You have probably seen Ten Thousand Villages shops in various parts of the US and Canada, but Ephrata is where it all began and where this nonprofit program of the Mennonite Central Committee (MCC), which has been working to fight poverty around the world since 1946, has its headquarters. In this shop, the MCC sells exquisite crafts handmade by third-world adult artisans from more than 30 countries. The wide selection of truly unique crafts includes pottery, jewelry, baskets, toys, crèches, hand-loomed textiles, and musical instruments.

JEWELRY

Lancaster

✳J A SHARP CUSTOM JEWELER
322 N. Queen St.
Lancaster, PA 17603
(215) 295-9661
jasharp.com
Jude Sharp designs extraordinary custom gold, silver, and platinum jewelry. She offers a wide collection of original designs, or she'll sit down with you to sketch out something completely different. If you want stones in your piece, Sharp can get them, or she can

use stones from jewelry that you already own.

TOYS

Ronks

AIMEE & DARIA'S DOLL OUTLET
2682 Lincoln Hwy. East
Ronks, PA 17572
(717) 687-8118
dolloutlet.com

It began when mother and daughter Aimee and Brenda Sheaffer decided to sell their personal doll collections to raise money for children in need. Now their shop has more than 5,000 dolls in stock, as well as clothes, furniture, and other accessories. Just about every size and price range are here, representing just about every major company. Aimee & Daria's periodically offers doll-making classes, no experience necessary. Participants must be 4 years old and accompanied by an adult. Fee includes all necessary materials and tools.

Hey, Farm Toy Fans . . .

You will have a field day at **A.B.C. Groff** in New Holland (110 S. Railroad Ave.; 800-346-8319; groffsfarmtoys.com) and **Outback Toys—Binkley & Hurst** in Lititz (101 W. Lincoln Ave.; 888-414-4705; outbacktoystore.com). Both stores have thousands of tiny tractors and other die-cast collectibles by Farmall, IH, John Deere, and other major manufacturers.

FACTORY OUTLETS

Shoppers come by the busloads to take advantage of the bargains at the many brand-name factory outlet stores and malls throughout Pennsylvania Dutch Country. Unless otherwise specified, the outlet complexes listed here include a range of merchandise, from fashion to home furnishings, jewelry to gourmet food, luggage to electronics.

Hershey

THE OUTLETS AT HERSHEY
46 Outlet Sq.
Hershey, PA 17033
(717) 520-1236
tangeroutlet.com/hershey

You'll find savings of between 30 and 70 percent off regular retail at 60 stores located right next to Hersheypark. (For additional savings, stop by the management office and pick up a free Preferred Shopper Card and a listing of monthly discounts from participating merchants.

Lancaster

✳**ROCKVALE OUTLETS**
35 S. Willowdale Dr.
(intersection of Routes 30 and 896)
(717) 293-9595
rockvaleoutletslancaster.com

With more than 100 stores covering 76 acres, it's no wonder that this center operates a courtesy shuttle to get shoppers from one end to the other. (It runs from Apr through Dec.) Be sure to visit the information center to pick up your Rockvale Rewards Club membership card, which can entitle you to even deeper discounts. Money-saving Senior Citizens Priority Club Cards are also available.

TANGER OUTLETS

311 Stanley K. Tanger Blvd.
Lancaster, PA 17602
(717) 392-7260
tangeroutlet.com

Tanger rhymes with hanger, and you'll find plenty of them in the many designer outlets that are among the 60 name-brand outlet stores here. You can expect to save between 20 and 40 percent below retail. AAA members can get an exclusive savings book with an additional 15 to 20 percent discount from participating merchants by coming to the Tanger Outlet Center Management Office. The outlets are open year-round (holiday hours may vary) Mon to Sat from 9 a.m. to 9 p.m., Sun from 10 a.m. to 6 p.m.

MULTIPLE-SHOP CENTER

Lancaster

PARK CITY CENTER
142 Park City Center (Route 30)
Lancaster, PA 17601
(717) 393-3851
parkcitycenter.com

Over 170 stores and restaurants are here. The mall is anchored by retail giants Sears, JCPenney, Bon Ton, Boscov's, and Kohl's.

MISCELLANEOUS

Lititz

THE PILOT SHOP AT AIRWAYS
Lancaster Airport, 520 Airport Rd.
Lititz, PA 17543
(717) 569-4496, ext. 102, (800) 247-8294
flyairways.com

This "aviation superstore" sells all kinds of pilot supplies, from aircraft parts to headsets and GPS, charts and maps, simulators, and software, at discounted prices. For aficionados there are extensive collections of collectibles, radio-controlled models, aircraft replicas, toys, and kites.

ATTRACTIONS

If you have the time and energy, Pennsylvania Dutch Country has enough attractions to keep you busy from when the roosters crow until the cows come home.

Although rates are subject to change, we use the following pricing code to indicate the adult admission charge for each attraction. Keep in mind that many attractions have special discounted rates for youngsters and for seniors. Some also offer money-saving combination or package prices with other nearby attractions.

$ .... Under $10
$$ .... $10 to $15
$$$ .... $15 to $20
$$$$ .... $20 to $25
$$$$$ .... More than $25

AMUSEMENT PARKS

Hershey

HERSHEYPARK $$$$$
300 Park Blvd.
Hershey, PA 17033
(800) HERSHEY
hersheypa.com

This is big coaster country. There are 11 to be exact, and they include some real screamers. One recent addition, The Boardwalk, with its centerpiece 54,000-gallon East Coast Waterworks, is a combination of slides, interactive water toys, ropes, and bridges; surf-simulating Waverider and Coastline Plunge, which sends you plummeting down one of four watery chutes from 50 feet above the ground; and an Aquatheatre where Atlantic bottle-nosed dolphins and California sea lions put on a splashy spectacular. The 36-inch-tall and under crowd has more than 25 rides to call their own.

Check the website for seasonal hours and discounts.

ℹ Make a beeline for the coasters and water rides as soon as you arrive at Hersheypark in the morning; otherwise, you could find yourself standing in long, long lines. Also try to plan your visit for Sunday through Thursday and you'll avoid some of the biggest crowds.

Lancaster City

DUTCH WONDERLAND $$$$$
2249 Lincoln Hwy. East
Lancaster, PA 17602
(866) FUN-AT-DW
dutchwonderland.com

At some amusement parks, little kids can feel somewhat left out when they're too big for the "baby rides" and too small for everything else. But Dutch Wonderland actually caters to children ages 10 and under with more than 30 just-the-right-size rides, including two roller coasters and two water adventures plus live shows. Steps away from the amusement park is the 18-hole Wonderland Mini-Golf Course.

That Fish Place/That Pet Place

A fun rainy day (or Sunday) activity is a visit to That Fish Place/That Pet Place in Lancaster (237 Centerville Rd.; 888-842-8738; thatpetplace.com), a huge pet store where more than 500 species of fresh- and saltwater fish swim in more than 800 aquariums; another room is filled with snakes, reptiles, chameleons, hamsters, rats, ferrets, frogs, gerbils, guinea pigs, iguanas, rabbits, and hedgehogs; and a colorful aviary features parakeets, finches, lovebirds, cockatiels, and other winged wonders. Stroke a starfish, handle a horseshoe crab, and interact with a ray in the 2,000-gallon Marineland Touch Tank. Admission is free.

ANIMALS

Hershey

FALCONRY EXPERIENCE AT THE
HOTEL HERSHEY $$$$$
Hershey, PA 17033
(800) HERSHEY
hersheypa.com

It's a thrilling experience to watch these magnificent birds of prey in free flight. See for yourself why falconry has been the sport of royalty for more than 4,000 years. It's really a breathtaking experience. Available Memorial Day through Labor Day.

ZOOAMERICA: HERSHEY $$
North American Wildlife Park
100 W. Hersheypark Dr.
Hershey, PA 17033
(717) 534-3900
zooamerica.com

Located just across a walking bridge from Hersheypark is this 11-acre walk-through zoo, where over 200 animals, representing 75 species native to the 5 regions of North America, live in naturalistic habitats. Open year-round. Visit the website for seasonal hours. Same-day admission to ZooAmerica is included in the Hersheypark one-price admission plan during the regular summer season when entered from within Hersheypark.

i Find out where to go and what's going on at the Pennsylvania Dutch Country Visitors Center (501 Greenfield Rd., just off Route 30, Lancaster; 800-PA-DUTCH; padutchcountry.com).

Lititz

✳WOLF SANCTUARY OF
PENNSYLVANIA $$
465 Speedwell Forge Rd.
Lititz, PA 17543
(717) 626-4617
wolfsancpa.com

Visit and learn about the 40 rescued wolves that live in safety on this 22-acre natural woodland sanctuary. Without government or corporate assistance, these magnificent animals are given food, shelter, and veterinary care for life, while, whenever possible, being able to form their own packs, choose their own mates, and raise their offspring.

i Many attractions offer admission price discount coupons available from their individual websites.

HERSHEY TOURS

HERSHEY'S CHOCOLATE WORLD   FREE
251 Park Blvd.
Hershey, PA 17033
(717) 534-4900
hersheys.com/chocolateworld

You can't actually tour the Hershey factory, but you can learn about the chocolate-making process on a free, fun-filled ride narrated by a comely trio of crooning cows and their bull buddy, Hef. The Hershey Company's Official Visitor Center and a store that's stocked to overflowing with confectionery creations are conveniently located in the same building. Open 7 days a week year-round. Chocolate World also offers a number of other activities and attractions including a "create-your-own-candy-bar" experience ($$), 30-minute, 3D animated musical extravaganza starring the Hershey product characters ($), and a guided chocolate-tasting adventure ($).

*HERSHEY TROLLEY WORKS $$
Hershey's Chocolate World
251 Park Blvd.
Hershey, PA 17033
(717) 533-3000
hersheytrolleyworks.com

Take a tour through town as singing conductors provide a musical and historical background. It's great fun and you get to eat chocolate.

FILMS & HISTORIC PRODUCTIONS

Intercourse

*THE AMISH EXPERIENCE F/X THEATER $
3121 Old Philadelphia Pike (Route 340)
Bird-in-Hand, PA 17505
(717) 768-3600, ext. 210
amishexperience.com

Located at the Plain & Fancy Farm restaurant and shopping complex, The Amish Experience F/X Theater presents a multimedia production, *Jacob's Choice*, that tells the story of the Old Order Amish culture and lifestyle throughout history from the perspective of one young man and his family. Open Sun.

i If you plan to also visit the Amish Experience F/X Theater, visit the property's Amish Country Homestead (see "Films and Historic Productions") and/or take an Amish Farmlands Tour (see "Tours"); you can save on combination tickets.

FUN & GAMES

Hershey

ADVENTURE SPORTS IN HERSHEY $
FOR INDIVIDUAL ACTIVITIES
3010 Elizabethtown Rd.
Hershey, PA 17033
(717) 533-7479
adventurehershey.com

The whole family will love the wide variety of sports activities that are offered here, including 18-hole miniature golf, bumper boats, batting cages (lighted for night fun), go-karts, and 20-acre lighted driving range. New outdoor laser tag, a hybrid of indoor laser tag and paintball. Season begins early

Meeting Mennonites

The **Mennonite Information Center** in Lancaster (2209 Millstream Rd.; 717-299-0954, 800-858-8320; mennoniteinfoctr.com) offers a variety of opportunities to learn about the faith. You can chat with members of the community who staff this information center and watch a free 17-minute movie. For a more in-depth exploration of the Pennsylvania German culture, watch the 30-minute film called *Who Are the Amish?* ($). You can also hire a guide of Mennonite or Amish heritage to give you an insider's perspective of the culture and daily life during a 2-hour, self-driven tour of farm country with stops of your choice along the way ($$$$$).

Apr and continues to the end of Oct. Open daily in summer; check the website for the rest of the seasonal schedule.

Strasburg

✴**THE VILLAGE GREENS MINIATURE GOLF** $
1444 Village Rd.
Strasburg, PA 17579
(717) 687-6933
villagegreens.com
Two courses over 13 landscaped acres make minigolfing a challenge for a range of ages and skill levels. For an easygoing round, stick to the Orange course. Only go for the Gold if you're prepared to contend with all kinds of natural obstacles including waterways and trees.

HISTORIC HOMES & GARDENS

Ephrata

✴**EPHRATA CLOISTER** $
632 W. Main St. (Route 322
West near intersection with Route 272)
Ephrata, PA 17522
(717) 733-6600
ephratacloister.com

The name, derived from the Bible, means "fruitful," and the 18th-century Cloister at Ephrata, founded in 1732, did produce an impressive amount of original art and music, particularly in the 1740s and 1750s, when about 300 members of one of America's first religious communities worked and worshiped here. The devotion of these Brothers and Sisters to a faith based on Anabaptism, asceticism, and celibacy (that's why nobody lives here anymore) is dramatically apparent everywhere on this 24-acre campus of 9 medieval-looking structures with their sparse furnishings—they slept on bare benches with "pillows" of wood. Guided tours of 2 of the houses and self-guided tours of the others are available daily, including Sun, year-round.

Hershey

✴**HERSHEY GARDENS** $
170 Hotel Rd.
Hershey, PA 17033
(717) 534-3492
hersheygardens.org
Begun in 1937 by Milton Hershey as "a nice garden of roses" for the public to enjoy, this bountiful botanical 23-acre oasis now features seasonal displays of more than 7,000

plants in 275 varieties. If you think the kids are going to get bored tiptoeing through the tulips, wait until they see the colorful "Children's Garden" with its alphabet, colors, and counting themes and step into the Butterfly House, where 300 native species flutter freely among flowers and plants. The Gardens are open daily; hours vary by season. The Butterfly House is open late May through mid-Sept. June through August is prime time for the roses of Hershey Gardens. April to May is tulip time (30,000 of them). In September and October, leaf peepers can take in the autumn array of colors and from December through March, you can stroll among the evergreen, holly berry, and crabapple trees, watching the birds forage for their winter food.

Lancaster

THE AMISH FARM AND HOUSE $
2395 Route 30 East
Lancaster, PA 17602
(717) 394-6185
amishfarmandhouse.com
This 25-acre property has been a true working farm since it was deeded from William Penn in 1715. Many buildings from the early 19th century have been preserved, including an 1803 stone bank tobacco barn and an 1805 farmhouse, home to generations of Old Amish families and furnished in their traditional style. Tours of the house are guided, then continue on your own to visit the 1803 stone bank barn, blacksmith shop, other farm outbuildings, resident animals, and a one-room schoolhouse.

CHARLES DEMUTH HOUSE AND GARDEN FREE
120 E. King St. (rear)
Lancaster, PA 17602
(717) 299-9940
demuth.org
Master watercolorist Charles Demuth (1883–1935), whose paintings hang in major museums throughout the world, created almost all of his works in the second-floor studio of his 18th-century home. His living quarters and studio have been re-created, and an on-site gallery features rotating exhibitions as well as Demuth's art. No admission (donations encouraged). Closed Mon and for the entire month of Jan.

JAMES BUCHANAN'S WHEATLAND $
1120 Marietta Ave.
Lancaster, PA 17603
(717) 392-8721
wheatland.org
Take a guided tour of this 1828 Federal-style mansion that was the home of America's 15th president for 20 years (1848–1868), including the tempestuous time of his term (1857–1861) as the nation teetered on the edge of civil war. It was in this house that Buchanan organized his presidential campaign quarters and, later, family members held his funeral. Regular guided tours are available year-round except for Jan through Mar. Closed Sun and Mon.

Willow Street

HANS HERR HOUSE AND MUSEUM $
1849 Hans Herr Dr.
Willow Street, PA 17584
(717) 464-4438
hansherr.org
Built in 1719, this medieval Germanic-style home is the oldest surviving residence in

(Q) Close-up

Fun For Free

By interspersing visits to free attractions with ones that require admission fees, you can make your travel budget—and your fun—go further, particularly if you have a youngster or two in tow. To make it easier for you to find the freebies, we've singled them out in this listing. For more free fun, check out the Parks, Recreation & Golf chapter.

Hershey's Chocolate World (Hershey, 717-534-4900)

Lancaster Museum of Art (Lancaster, 717-394-3497)

Milton Hershey School & Founders Hall Visitors Center (Hershey, 717-520-2000)

The Quilt Museum at the Old Country Store (Intercourse, 800-828-8218)

That Fish Place/That Pet Place (Lancaster, 717-299-5691)

Wilbur Chocolate Candy Americana Museum and Factory Store (Lititz, 717-626-3249)

Lancaster County and the oldest Mennonite meetinghouse left in the Western Hemisphere. Guided tours of the period-furnished building are available Mon through Sat, Apr 1 through Nov 30. During September's Heritage Day and Snitz Fest at the Hans Herr House, costumed interpreters and artisans will reenact daily life for Pennsylvania Germans of the 18th and 19th centuries. Demonstrated activities include open-fire cooking, baking, corn husk doll-making, weaving, and sausage-making. By the way, snitz is dried apples, a staple for sweet and savory dishes for farm families.

MUSEUMS

Columbia

✳NATIONAL WATCH AND CLOCK MUSEUM $
514 Poplar St.
Columbia, PA 17512
(717) 684-8261
nawcc.org

Time may fly, but it does leave some astonishing tracking devices behind to remind us of the ingenuity and creativity of artisans who used timepieces as their media. This is a surprisingly interesting museum, featuring more than 12,000 clocks, watches, and other related items including ancient sundials, early European and Asian devices, and whimsical novelty clocks. Open year-round, closed Sun in winter.

Hershey

AACA (ANTIQUE AUTOMOBILE CLUB OF AMERICA) MUSEUM $$
161 Museum Dr.
Hershey, PA 17033
(717) 566-7100
aacamuseum.org

Auto aficionados can travel through time and space, experiencing the evolution of design and the fickleness of fashion. On display are more than 90 historic cars, from

Henry Ford's Model T to the epitome of road royalty as exemplified by Packard, Pierce, Lincoln, and Cord.

THE HERSHEY STORY $$
63 W. Chocolate Ave.
Hershey, PA 17033
(717) 534-3439
hersheymuseum.org

Interactive multimedia exhibits and artifacts guide you through the history of Milton Hershey, his company, and his town. Check the website for seasonal hours. At Cafe Zooka in The Hershey Story Museum, you can sample a flight of warm drinking chocolates from around the world to surprise and educate your palate. $—1 flight can be easily shared by at least 2 people.

Bird-in-Hand

AMISH COUNTRY HOMESTEAD $$
THE AMISH EXPERIENCE
3121 Old Philadelphia Pike
Bird-in-Hand, PA 17505
(717) 768-8400, ext. 210
amishexperience.com

Inside the 9 rooms in this fully furnished and stocked (down to the home-canned veggies in the pantry) replica of an Old Order Amish home and 1-room schoolhouse, a guide will interpret the lives, beliefs, and traditions of today's Amish community. This is the only Amish house tour to be designated a Lancaster County "Heritage Site." Open Sun. Closed for the months of Jan and Feb.

Intercourse

**THE QUILT MUSEUM AT THE OLD
COUNTRY STORE** FREE
3510 Old Philadelphia Pike (Route 340)
Intercourse, PA 17534
(800) 828-8218
ocsquiltmuseum.com

A good portion of the quilts on permanent display in this museum are pre-1940 creations made by Amish and Mennonite women. However, each year also brings new exhibits of antique and contemporary works from around the world.

Lancaster

**HANDS-ON HOUSE CHILDREN'S
MUSEUM OF LANCASTER** $
721 Landis Valley Rd.
Lancaster, PA 17601
(717) 569-KIDS
handsonhouse.org

Interactive, imagination-fueling, themed exhibits and programs allow children from ages 2 to 10 to experiment with colors and multidimensional design, get hands-on with gears and pulleys in a kid-friendly "machine shop," and learn about life on the farm. Open daily, including Sun.

i Each spring and fall, downtown Lancaster becomes one big urban art gallery when many of the local businesses, including restaurants, museums, schools, and non-art-related shops, display the works of new and established artists representing a wide range of media and styles. For maps and information, call (717) 509-ARTS or visit lancasterarts.com.

LANCASTER MUSEUM OF ART   **FREE**
135 N. Lime St.
Lancaster, PA 17602
(717) 394-3497
lmapa.org

Contemporary regional artists are well represented in the permanent collection of this 4,000-square-foot facility that is a focal point for Lancaster County visual art exhibition and education. Throughout the year, 16 additional traveling or temporary shows feature the works of regional, national, and international artists in a variety of media, including children's art and juried and contemporary crafts.

Sundays Are Fun Days in Pennsylvania Dutch Country

Often people hesitate to extend their Pennsylvania Dutch Country visits to include a Sunday stay because they've heard that "everything's closed" and there's nothing to do. While it is true that Amish farm stands and workshops are closed on their worship day, there are still all kinds of things, from amusement parks to zoos, that remain open. Many Amish-oriented (not Amish-operated) attractions are open on Sunday, and you can even get yourself some authentic chowchow and shoofly pie. Sunday is also a great time to immerse yourself in the sweet experiences of Hershey, Chocolatetown USA.

✳**LANDIS VALLEY FARM AND MUSEUM**   **$$**
2451 Kissel Hill Rd. (just off Route 272/Oregon Pike)
Lancaster, PA 17601
(717) 569-0401
landisvalleymuseum.org

Don't let the word "museum" throw you; this largest living history village of Pennsylvania Dutch life draws you into the day-to-day of the mid-18th and 19th centuries as you visit 2 dozen original and re-created buildings filled with exhibits and artifacts and interact with costumed guides and artisans. Check out the online schedule for special events throughout the year. Open daily, year-round.

✳**NORTH MUSEUM OF NATURAL HISTORY AND SCIENCE**   **$$**
400 College Ave.
Lancaster, PA 17603
(717) 291-3941
northmuseum.org

Wonders of the past, visions of the future are here for the exploring with exhibits of eons-old fossils and artifacts extracted from the earth to the quest for knowledge about the unknown reaches of the universe. One particularly popular attraction is the high-definition planetarium ($$) that makes you feel as if you are actually visiting galaxies yet to be explored. The museum is open Tues to Sat.

Ronks

THE AMISH VILLAGE   **$**
199 Hartman Bridge Rd.
Ronks, PA 17572
(717) 687-8511
theamishvillage.net

🔍 Close-up

Covered Bridges of Lancaster County

From the 1820s to 1900, there were about 1,500 covered bridges built in Pennsylvania. Today, 219 of these bridges remain in 40 of the state's 67 counties. Lancaster County has 28 of them. Although romantics have dubbed these sheltered structures "kissing bridges," the actual reason covers were built over them was to protect the construction from weather damage.

The Pennsylvania Dutch Convention and Visitors Bureau publishes a map pinpointing all of the remaining covered bridges throughout the county. For a free copy, call (800) PA-DUTCH, or log on to padutchcountry.com. You can also print out 6 different covered bridge driving tours from the same site.

Your guide will explain the workings of an Old Amish farm as you tour the authentically furnished 1840 home, operating waterwheel and windmill, and outbuildings, including blacksmith shop, one-room schoolhouse, and operating smokehouse, and pay a visit to the barnyard residents. Call or check the website for seasonal hours.

NATURAL WONDERS

Ronks

CHERRY-CREST FARM $$
150 Cherry Hill Rd.
Ronks, PA 17572
(717) 687-6843
cherrycrestfarm.com
Best known for its "Amazing Maize Maze," a 5-acre labyrinth carved from the cornfields to deliberately discombobulate erstwhile explorers (each year is a new maze designed by former Disney producer and co-owner Don Frantz). Your admission also includes more than 50 other farm-focused family activities such as a wagon ride through the cornfield, animal petting and education, straw bale racing, and a singing chicken show. Call for seasonal hours and activities.

ℹ️ **If you think the maze is daunting by day, pack up your flashlight and see how well you do after dark!**

RAILROAD ATTRACTIONS

Ronks

✳NATIONAL TOY TRAIN MUSEUM $
300 Paradise Ln.
Ronks, PA 17572
(717) 687-8976
nttmuseum.org
At this national headquarters of the Train Collectors Association, you'll find 5 operating layouts from the 1920s to the present. Open Sun; call for seasonal hours.

Strasburg

CHOO CHOO BARN—TRAINTOWN, USA $
226 Gap Rd.
Strasburg, PA 17579
(800) 450-2920, (717) 687-7911
choochoobarn.com

It began with a $12.50 Lionel train set in 1961 and is now 1,700 square feet of hand-built scenes and buildings featuring over 150 hand-built animated figures and vehicles depicting familiar Lancaster County sites, including an Amish barn raising and the rides at Dutch Wonderland, as well as 22 operating trains. Open 7 days; closed Jan and Feb.

i Monday and Friday tend to be the least crowded days of the week at the Choo Choo Barn, so, if you can, it's a good idea to schedule your visit then.

RAILROAD MUSEUM OF
PENNSYLVANIA $$
300 Gap Rd.
Route 741, east of Strasburg
Strasburg, PA 17579
(717) 687-8628
rrmuseumpa.org

This museum features an indoor and outdoor world-class collection of more than 100 historical locomotives, from steam to electric, and railroad cars. There are also exhibits of railroad art and artifacts spanning 1825 to the present. Call or visit the website for seasonal hours; open Sun.

STRASBURG RAIL ROAD
Route 741, east of Strasburg
Strasburg, PA 17579
(717) 687-7522
strasburgrailroad.com

Although the Strasburg Rail Road was incorporated in 1832, the only indication of when it started running was a schedule from December 1851. The 4.5-mile straight track was used for passenger and freight transportation until around the turn of the 20th century. Now from late May through most of Nov, America's oldest short-line railroad's coal-burning steam engine once again invites passengers to come aboard for a 45-minute scenic narrated ride through the countryside. Depending on your preference—and pocketbook—you can ride in a regular coach heated with potbellied stoves in winter ($14) or upgrade to a deluxe, Victorian-ornate parlor car ($20). Pack a picnic or take a lunch, dinner, wine and cheese, or themed meal ride.

TOURS

By buggy or bus, bicycle seat or balloon basket, horse or four-wheeled horse-power—or your own 2 feet—there are unlimited opportunities to discover the best that Pennsylvania Dutch Country has to offer. If you want to go it alone, you can get suggestions and pick up maps at the Pennsylvania Dutch Convention and Visitors Bureau, 501 Greenfield Rd. at Route 30, Lancaster; (717) 299-8901, 800-PA-DUTCH; padutchcountry.com, or you can pop a 90-minute, narrated Auto Tape Tour into your CD player (order by contacting 201-236-1666; autotapetours.com; $16.95, $3 for shipping).

BUS/MOTOR COACH TOUR

AMISH NEIGHBORS TOURS/ALL ABOUT TOURS
324 Susan Ave.
Strasburg, PA 17579
(800) 63-AMISH
allabouttours.net/amish-neighbors.asp
Take a guided 3-hour guided tour through Amish farmlands with lots of interesting stops and opportunities to meet the locals and visit their barn- and home-based businesses along the way.

GHOST TOUR

LANCASTER OR STRASBURG GHOST TOUR
11 E. Main St.
Strasburg, PA 17579
(717) 687-6687
ghosttour.net
Follow the light of your guide's lantern as you visit at least 10 local haunts, including historic cemeteries in either Lancaster City or Strasburg. These 90-minute, family-friendly tours (each is less than a mile walk) include researched and documented stories, folk-lore, and ghost stories. Advance tickets are required for the Lancaster tour; reservations are strongly recommended for the one in Strasburg.

HOT AIR BALLOONS

ADVENTURES ALOFT
Meet at Ephrata Walmart
890 E. Main St.
Ephrata, PA 17522
(717) 733-3777, (877) 508-1380
Allot 3 to 5 hours for the total experience, including 1 hour in flight.

i Hot air balloon companies generally schedule flights for just after dawn or at dusk because these are the times when winds are generally lighter. If you go in the morning, you can help with the balloon inflation. Flights are available year-round (weather permitting), but peak season is April through November.

US HOT AIR BALLOON TEAM
Departure from:
2737 Old Philadelphia Pike
Bird-in-Hand, PA 17505
(800) 763-5987
ushotairballoon.com
Figure 2.5 to 3 hours for the total experience, with about 1 hour in the air.

i In keeping with a centuries-old tradition, balloonists usually drink a postflight champagne toast. According to Adventures Aloft, this tradition began in the late 1700s, when early French balloonists would frighten farmers by landing in their fields. To avoid finding themselves on the sharp end of a pitchfork, the balloonists began offering farmers champagne upon their descent as a demonstration of goodwill.

PRIVATE TOUR

OLD ORDER AMISH TOURS
63 E. Brook Rd.
Ronks, PA 17572
(Route 896 North)
(717) 299-6535
oldorderamishtours.com
Because this is a private tour, the places you visit can be customized to suit your interests. A particularly popular stop is the Old Order Amish working farm and home (the owners are friends of the guide). During your 2-hour (or longer) farmland foray, you can also visit some of the community's home-based quilt and woodworking businesses. No Sun.

BIKE, SCOOTER & SEGWAY TOURS

COUNTRYSIDE SCOOTER & BIKE RENTALS
2705 Old Philadelphia Pike (Rt. 340)
Bird-in-Hand, PA 17505
(717) 278-2142
countrysidescooters.com
Bike rentals are $12 half day/$20 full day; scooters (with free tank of gas good for about 100 "country" miles) are $35 2 hours/$45 4 hours/$65 full day. Open 7 days. You can download bike tour maps at padutchcountry.com and at lancasterbike club.org/scenictours.php.

SEGWAY TOUR

✳**RED ROSE SEGWAY**
305 N. Queen St.
Lancaster, PA 17603
(717) 393-4526, (877) 393-8345
redrosesegtours.com
Full disclosure—I love Segways. That said, you can choose from 3 different escorted and narrated 90-minute tours: City, Ghosts and Graveyards, or Arts Tour. Participants must be at least 16 years old.

i Weekdays after 5 p.m. and on weekends, you can park free across the street from Red Rose Segway in a business's parking lot. According to the Segway folks, the owners of the business "don't mind."

Buggy Rides

You know you want to . . . at least once. And there are plenty of companies that are more than willing to take you clip-clopping through the countryside. Some operators offer the closed-sided buggies often used by Amish families. Others offer the option of riding in an Amish "market wagon," which has sides that roll up. For larger families and groups, you can also find operators that provide rides in larger open wagons. According to the owners of Aaron & Jessica's Buggy Rides in Bird-in-Hand, buggy horses are usually either American standardbred or American saddlebred. Wagons are usually pulled by draft horses.

All three of these styles are good. I prefer the closed buggy because, to me, it offers the most authentic experience. An open wagon offers a better view.

Most of the buggy ride companies are not owned by practicing Old Order Amish, but by individuals and families who were brought up with and are quite knowledgeable about its tenets and traditions. Others may be members of the Mennonite or Brethren churches. Ditto for the drivers. Feel free to ask respectful questions. Tips are welcome, unless otherwise specified.

Look for discount coupons on buggy rides on the companies' websites; at visitor centers, hotels, motels, and inns; and in local publications such as the *Amish News* (a publication for tourists, not by and for the Amish community). Some operators offer rides on Sunday.

WALKING TOURS

Lancaster

HISTORIC LANCASTER WALKING TOUR

5 W. King St.
Lancaster, PA 17603
(717) 392-1776
historiclancasterwalkingtour.com

A brief film presentation lays the groundwork for your 90-minute tour that spans 250 years. Every day Apr through Oct, you can join a colonial-garbed guide who leads tours down cobbled streets to visit more than 50 locations, including historic homes, courtyards, churchyards, and gardens. Call for prices.

Bird-in-Hand

ABE'S BUGGY RIDES

2596 Old Philadelphia Pike (Route 340)
Bird-in-Hand, PA 17505
(717) 392-1794
abesbuggyrides.com

Operated by Abner Beiler, who was raised Old Amish until he was 14 years old, and his wife, Alison, this company uses original closed-sided Amish family-style buggies for its 5 different rides that range from 20 minutes to 1.5 hours. Prices start at $10 for 20 minutes. Cash or check only. No Sun.

AARON AND JESSICA'S BUGGY RIDES
3121 Old Philadelphia Pike, #3
Bird-in-Hand, PA 17505
(717) 768-2829
amishbuggyrides.com

Owned by a family with Mennonite and Brethren roots, this company offers a 50-minute, 5-mile or 35-minute, 4-mile ride on private roads that run through noncommercial working Amish farms. This company prefers to use Amish open-sided market wagons because they offer riders a broader view of the countryside. This is an all-weather operation (if there's enough snow, you can take a sleigh ride). No Sun.

Ronks

ED'S BUGGY RIDES
Route 896, 1.5 miles south of Rte. 30
Ronks, PA 17572
(717) 687-0360
edsbuggyrides.com

You can take a 1-hour tour through the farmlands or arrange for a stop-off and chat with an Amish family (note: they have a craft shop, but it's still an interesting experience). Open and closed family carriages are available. Tour guide drivers are Amish and Mennonite.

PARKS, RECREATION & GOLF

Lancaster County is well known for its bounty of bucolic beauty, but outdoor enthusiasts will be happy to know that this beauty is more than skin deep. Hikers and bikers will find multiple miles of wooded trails to explore, golfers world-class courses to conquer, and canoers and kayakers sparkling waters to ply.

PARKS

Lancaster County Parks and Recreation operates 6 regional parks and 2 recreational trails, a total of a little more than 2,000 acres, all of which are open to nonresidents.

Lancaster City

Details about and directions to each park can be found at co.lancaster.pa.us/parks or call (717) 299-8215.

Lancaster County Central Park

Named for its central location on the southern edge of Lancaster City, this 544-acre park is the largest of the county's parks. You could spend an entire day—or even more—here, visiting the tranquil Garden of the Five Senses, the public skate park, and the 15,255-square-foot, 6 feet at the deep end swimming pool with tubular slide and fountains. ($)

i Park in the lot right off Eshelman Mill Road, south of the Lancaster County Central Park skate park. Wheelchair access is available from this lot. Another small lot on Davis Drive also offers parking for those in wheelchairs.

Other Lancaster County Parks

BETWEEN COLUMBIA AND MARIETTA

CHICKIES ROCK COUNTY PARK
Lancaster County's second largest regional park, Chickies Rock spans more than 422 acres and offers a multitude of recreational amenities, including hiking, biking, and cross-country skiing trails; sledding slopes; stream fly-fishing-only area for trout. Hike up Chickies Rock 200 feet above the Susquehanna River for a fantastic view.

i To fish in Pennsylvania, all individuals age 16 and over need a current state fishing license signed in ink and displayed on a hat or outer garment. Licenses are not needed on Fish for Free days. Visit the Pennsylvania Fish and Boat Commission website (fish .state.pa.us) or call (717) 705-7800 for more information.

EASTERN LANCASTER COUNTY

MONEY ROCKS PARK
Located in eastern Lancaster County, this more-than-300-acre woodland park offers excellent hiking, cross-country skiing,

sledding, rock climbing, mountain biking, and horse trails.

SOUTHEASTERN LANCASTER COUNTY

THEODORE A. PARKER III NATURAL AREA

Named after a renowned local ornithologist, this virtually undisturbed 90 acres in a quiet valley feature a hiking trail that runs parallel to a burbling stream that teems with brown and brook trout. Fishing is permitted during authorized seasons.

WEST LAMPETER TOWNSHIP

D. F. BUCHMILLER PARK

Known for its expansive open lawn areas and arboretum-type plantings, this 79-acre park in West Lampeter Township has 6 tennis courts, a playground, a ballfield, and a disc golf course.

Other Public Parks

LANCASTER

LONG'S PARK
Intersection of Harrisburg Pike and the Route 30 Bypass
Lancaster, PA 17601
(717) 295-7054
longspark.org

Situated just northwest of Lancaster City, this 71-acre park has a 3-acre spring-fed lake, petting zoo, children's playgrounds, tennis courts, a fitness trail, and a snack bar. In addition to providing a recreational environment for locals and visitors, Long's Park also hosts a number of special events, including a free summer-long entertainment series and a major Labor Day arts and crafts festival.

STATE PARKS & PRESERVES

MIDDLE CREEK WILDLIFE MANAGEMENT AREA
100 Museum Rd.
Stevens, PA 17578
(717) 733-1512
portal.state.pa.us

Considered by many naturalists to be one of the best places for bird watchers, photographers, and hikers, this 5,000-acre area, owned by the Pennsylvania Game Commission, has a 400-acre shallow-water lake that provides prime nesting space for Canada geese (a large flock remains in the area year-round) and, in fall, tundra swans. .

Fishing is permitted in specified areas, as are hunting and trapping during legally prescribed seasons. Boats propelled by paddles and oars are allowed from mid-May through mid-Sept.

i To catch the creatures of the Middle Creek Wildlife Management Area at their most active, come just after dawn or around dusk. To avoid disturbing the wildlife, remember to stay on the roads and developed trails or in your car.

SUSQUEHANNOCK STATE PARK
1880 Park Dr.
Drumore, PA 17518
(717) 432-5011
dcnr.state.pa.us

Situated on a wooded plateau above the Susquehanna River, this 224-acre park features 380-foot-high cliffs that offer panoramic views. Most dramatic is the view from Hawk Point Overlook, from where you can see numerous islands, including Mt. Johnson Island (to the left of the overlook), the world's first bald eagle sanctuary. There's an optical viewer for eagle-, hawk-, osprey-, and vulture-spotting.

SPECTATOR SPORTS

BUCK MOTORSPORTS PARK
900 Lancaster Pike
Quarryville, PA 17566
(717) 859-4244, (800) 344-7855; track (day of event only) (717) 284-2139
buckmotorsports.com

For more than 30 years, "the Buck" has been offering weekend motorsports excitement in Lancaster County. From the May season-opener to the early October finale, there's something for every fan, from stock cars to hot rods to big rigs, truck and tractor pulls, and demolition derbies.

i Parking is free at the Clipper Magazine Stadium Lot (access via Clay Street, off Prince Street). But even if this lot is full, you can also park free at Armstrong/Liberty (both are best accessed via Clay or Liberty Streets off Prince Street; a pedestrian walkway connects these lots to the stadium lot).

HERSHEY BEARS HOCKEY CLUB
Giant Center
550 W. Hersheypark Dr.
Hershey, PA 17033
Hershey box office: (717) 534-3911
team office: (717) 534-3380
hersheypa.com

Originally named the "Hershey B'ars," this team joined the American Hockey League (AHL) in 1938 and has won the coveted Calder Cup multiple times.

LANCASTER BARNSTORMERS
Clipper Magazine Stadium
650 N. Prince St.
Lancaster, PA 17603
(717) 509-HITS
lancasterbarnstormers.com

This professional minor league (Atlantic League) baseball team played its first game in May 2005 in its specially built $23 million Clipper Magazine Stadium (it holds 6,500 fans). Regular season (70 home games, 70 away) goes Apr through Sept. Individual adult tickets are $5 in advance, $6 game day for lawn seat; $8 in advance, $9 game day for field box seat; and $10 in advance, $11 game day for dugout box seat. Kids 12 and under who come to the game wearing a youth athletic league uniform, jersey, or T-shirt get in free for field box seating (a complimentary ticket must still be obtained, beginning at 4 p.m., at the Barnstormers box office). Generally, stadium gates open 1 hour before the scheduled game time, Mon through Thurs, and 1.5 hours prior to the first pitch on weekends. Want a special announcement over the public address system or on the scoreboard to celebrate a special occasion or even offer a proposal of marriage? Just submit your request in writing or via e-mail at least 24 hours prior to the game (game-day requests will be accommodated if scheduling allows) and make a $5 donation to a designated charity. Players are happy to sign autographs before the umpires take to the field. Wheelchair-accessible parking is available—call for details.

i In winter, Clipper Stadium is transformed into an ice skating park ($). Skate rentals are available on a first-come, first-served basis.

WATER SPORTS & RECREATION

SHANK'S MARE OUTFITTERS
2092 Long Level Rd.
Wrightsville, PA 17368
(717) 252-1616
shanksmare.com
Rent a kayak (single models are $25 for up to 2 hours, tandem $33) for a leisurely paddle down the scenic Susquehanna River.

GOLF

Public Golf Courses

Hershey
THE HERSHEY GOLF COLLECTION
1000 E. Derry Rd.
(717) 533-2360, (800) HERSHEY (437-7439)
Hershey, PA 17033
hersheygolfcollection.com
Although the collection's East and West courses are reserved exclusively for resort guest use, Hershey also has 2 other excellent courses that are open to the public.

HERSHEY LINKS
101 Hanshue Rd.
Hummelstown, PA 17036
Ponds, creeks, and multilevel greens and pot bunkers up the challenge ante on this 175-acre, par 72 course. Daily Fee Play rate ranges from $59 to $120, depending on time of day.

SPRING CREEK GOLF COURSE
405 E. Chocolate Ave.
Hershey, PA 17033
A spring winds through this 9-hole, 2,200-yard course, which was designed in 1932 by Maurice McCarthy with golfers under age 18 in mind. Newly renovated, this par 33 course has a broader age appeal, but still welcomes juniors with patience and special rates. Nine holes weekday $12/weekend $14 for adults, $10/$12 for juniors.

i Taxes are additional on greens fees, unless otherwise specified.

Millersville
CROSSGATES GOLF CLUB
1 Crossland Pass
Millersville, PA 17551
(717) 872-4500
crossgatesgolf.com
None of your clubs will feel neglected on this challenging 18-hole, par-72 public course located a few minutes from downtown Lancaster. The Conestoga River and gentle hills add to the serenity of the surroundings. Greens fees are $16 to $22 weekdays/$18 to $40 (must ride before noon on weekends so includes cart) weekends.

Mount Joy
GROFF'S FARM GOLF CLUB
650 Pinkerton Rd.
Mount Joy, PA 17552
(717) 653-2048
groffsfarmgolfclub.com
Designed in the traditional Scottish links style, this scenic 18-hole, par-71 championship course follows the unique contours of this former farm terrain, with rolling hills, quick greens, open fairways, and distinctive holes. Because it's tucked away in the rural area of Mount Joy, Groff's can be a little tricky to find, so check the website or call for directions. Greens fees for weekdays $13 to $15 walk/weekends $13 to $23.

ANNUAL EVENTS

Pennsylvania Dutch Country is all about tradition, so it's no surprise that numerous annual events held here have their roots in decades, generations, and even centuries past. This is just a sampling of don't-miss celebrations and commemorations that keep the history and spirit of this area so fresh and alive. Many more are highlighted in other chapters of this book. (In October, there are so many Halloween events, from family-friendly to blood-curdling, that I can't even begin to list them. Check on the Pennsylvania Dutch Country and Hershey websites for details.)

JANUARY

BY THE LIGHT OF THE MOON TOURS
Wolf Sanctuary of Pennsylvania
465 Speedwell Forge Rd.
Lititz, PA 17543
(717) 626-4617
wolfsancpa.com
The best time to visit the wolves at the sanctuary is in the winter and, when the moon is full, you'll forget that the rest of the world exists. Campfire included. Kids 16 and older are welcome.

FEBRUARY

CHOCOLATE-COVERED FEBRUARY
Hershey Resorts
Hershey, PA
hersheypa.com
A month's worth of chocolate-centric events, special pairings with spirits, grand buffets, gala dinners, chocolate cooking schools and kids' activities, and themed spa specials.

MARCH

CHARTER DAY
Pennsylvania Dutch Country
Visitors Center
501 Greenfield Rd. at Route 30
Lancaster, PA 17601
(800) PA-DUTCH, (717) 299-8901
padutchcountry.com
Various state museums, including several in Lancaster County, offer free admission to the public on different days throughout the month of March. Check out the website or call to find specific museums and day.

APRIL/MAY

ANNUAL SHEEP SHEARING DAYS
Amish Farm and House
2395 Lincoln Hwy. East
Lancaster, PA 17602
(717) 394-6185
amishfarmandhouse.com
The name says it all!

i Like many US cities, Lancaster showcases its downtown cultural, shopping, dining, and nightlife destinations on the "First Friday" of each month. Be sure to talk a walk on "Gallery Row" (aka the 300 block of N. Queen Street) for special events. For more detailed information and a free map, visit lancasterarts.com or call (717) 509-ARTS.

MAY

ANNUAL RHUBARB FESTIVAL
Kitchen Kettle Village
Route 340
Intercourse, PA 17534
(800) 732-3538, (717) 768-8261
kitchenkettle.com

Who knew this vitamin C–packed veggie could be so versatile? There's a Rhubarb Race Car Derby, a pie-baking contest, Rhubarb Stroll parade with musicians and costumed characters, and the crowning of the Rhubarb King and Queen.

SERTOMA CHICKEN BARBECUE
Long's Park, Harrisburg Pike (Route 30, across from Park City Mall)
Lancaster, PA
(717) 295-7054
lancastersertomabbq.com

Listed in the *Guinness Book of World Records* as the largest 1-day chicken barbecue, this event is always held on the third Saturday of May. Every year since 1953, the Sertoma Club of Lancaster has cooked and sold an average of more than 30,000 complete chicken dinners on barbecue pits set up in the park. Enjoy the live entertainment or get dinner to go.

JUNE

ANNUAL CELTIC FLING & HIGHLAND GAMES
Mount Hope Estate and Winery
83 Mansion House Rd.
Route 72 and Pennsylvania Turnpike exit 20
Manheim, PA 17545
(717) 665-7021
parenfaire.com

Hundreds of traditional musicians, dancers, crafters, Scottish clans, Irish societies, and athletes from all over North America and Europe celebrate Celtic traditional athletic and strength competitions for men and women (sanctioned by the Mid-Atlantic Scottish Athletics Association). More than 800 children and young adults compete in Highland Dancing competitions, and there will be bagpipers, crafters, authentic foods, and free Scotch and whiskey samples.

INTERCOURSE HERITAGE DAYS
Intercourse Community Park
Route 340
Intercourse, PA
(717) 768-8585
intercourseheritagedays.com

Activities during the course of the 3-day event include an old-time spelling bee, shoofly pie baking contest, kids' volleyball tournament, helicopter rides, pancake breakfast, covered dish and ice cream social, fireworks, classic car show, and grand fireworks display. No admission; pay as you go.

i According to the Celtic Fling & Highland Games website, strenuous competitive games like these were held in ancient times so that kings and tribal chieftains could determine who was most fit to lead troops into battle.

JULY

FOURTH OF JULY CELEBRATION
In Lititz Springs Park
Center of Lititz, 7 miles north of
Lancaster on Route 501
24 N. Broad St.
Lititz, PA 17543
(717) 626-8981

For close to 190 years, the village of Lititz has commemorated Independence Day in grand style. The celebration actually begins the Saturday prior to the 4th with parades, live entertainment, and free fun and games. On July 4, the festivities include illumination of 7,000 candles along Lititz Springs Creek, a Queen of Candles pageant, all kinds of live entertainment, and a high-tech fireworks display.

AUGUST

NEW HOLLAND SUMMER FEST
PO Box 463, New Holland
(717) 355-0779, (717) 669-1400
nhsummerfest.org

New Holland Community Park is "Where Bikes Meet the Brisket" every summer at this dual event that pairs a motorcycle ride and show with the Pennsylvania State Championship BBQ Cook-Off. Come to compete or just to eat! Admission is $1 (all proceeds benefit the New Holland Community Park and Fire Company), children under 8 years old get in for free.

AUGUST TO OCTOBER

PENNSYLVANIA RENAISSANCE FAIRE
Mount Hope Estate and Winery
83 Mansion House Rd.
Route 72 and Pennsylvania Turnpike,
exit 20
Manheim, PA 17545
(717) 665-7021, ext. 231
parenfaire.com

From the time you enter the castle gates, you are immersed in the life and pageantry of 16th-century life as hundreds of costumed characters from peasants to pirates take to the Shire streets for morning-to-night jesting and jousting, tournaments and troubadours, 13 stages of entertainment ranging from bawdy to the Bard (there's mud wrestling, too), a gigantic human chess board, and too much more to describe.

i For one evening a week from early August to early September, Mount Hope Mansion, home of the Pennsylvania Renaissance Faire, transforms into a comedy club for "Friday Knights at the Improv." This inside evening venue allows the Ren actors to step out of their 16th-century costumes and roles, trading épées and swords for razor-sharp wit. Shows are at 7 p.m. Tickets for adults (18 and over) are $20.

SEPTEMBER

EPHRATA FAIR
Ephrata Farmers Day Association
19 S. State St.
Ephrata, PA 17522
(717) 733-4451
ephratafair.org

Pennsylvania's largest street fair traces its roots all the way back to 1919, when local businessmen sponsored a celebration to honor World War I veterans. Bigger and better than ever, this 5-day extravaganza attracts tens of thousands of locals and visitors to this tucked-away town. On the annual agenda are multiple parades, an antique tractor pull, scarecrow making, and baking. A giant midway is pay-as-you-go except on a one-price "All You Can Ride" night.

LONG'S PARK ART AND CRAFT FESTIVAL
Harrisburg Pike, across from Park City Mall
(717) 735-8883
Lancaster, PA
longspark.org
Four days and more than 200 exhibitors make this juried show one of the top events of its kind in the country.

OCTOBER

ANTIQUE CAR SHOW
Hersheypark and Giant Center Parking Lots
100 W. Hersheypark Dr.
Hershey, PA 17033
(717) 534-1910
The Eastern Division of the Antique Automobile Club of America (AACA) National Fall Meet is held every year here for 3 days during the first full week in October. One of the largest antique automobile shows and flea markets in the US, it features 1,500 show cars. Junior auto aficionados (age 15 and under) display their model cars, trucks, planes, and boats.

CHOCOLATE WALK
Various locations throughout Lititz
(717) 627-2463
Buy an official button and punch card at the Lititz Welcome Center/Train Station or another participating location and feel free to partake of the sweet sensations dreamed up by candy makers and pastry chefs at more than 20 tasting sites throughout the downtown area. Funds raised from this event are donated to local community organizations.

WHOOPIE PIE FESTIVAL
Hershey Farm Restaurant and Inn
240 Hartman Bridge Rd.
Ronks, PA 17572
(717) 687-8635
whoopiepiefestival.com
Take two moist rounds of cake and squoosh them together with lots of fluffy white icing—that's the handheld treat called a whoopee pie, an integral part of the Pennsylvania Dutch Country food tradition. Bring the kids for an active agenda of races, treasure hunts, eating contests, pony and hayrides, face painting, and a taste of the world's biggest whoopees. Free admission.

NOVEMBER

POE FOREVERMORE
Mount Hope Estate and Winery
83 Mansion House Rd.
Route 72 and Pennsylvania Turnpike exit 20
Manheim, PA 17545
(717) 665-7021
parenfaire.com
Poe returns to Pennsylvania Dutch Country for his annual November haunting of the

Victorian Mount Hope Mansion. Each year, he meets up with a new set of equally historic (and equally dead) cohorts, such as P. T. Barnum, Lord Byron, and Mary Shelley, to find adventure and a convenient forum for the telling of his most famous frightening fables.

DECEMBER

EPHRATA CLOISTER LANTERN TOURS
632 W. Main St.
Ephrata, PA 17522
(717) 733-6600
ephratacloister.org

Junior high and high school students portray the residents of this unique religious community to give a glimpse of how they may have lived in the 1700s. Reservations are required for these special post-Christmas evening (6 to 9 p.m.) tours.

HERSHEY SWEET LIGHTS
Hershey, PA 17033
(717) 534-3900
hersheypa.com

Pile the family into the car and drive through this 2-mile winding wooded trail of nearly 600 illuminated, animated displays as coordinated holiday music plays through your radio.

INDEX

INSIDERS' GUIDE®

The acclaimed travel series that has sold more than 2 million copies!

Discover: Your Travel Destination.
Your Home. Your Home-to-Be.

Albuquerque

Anchorage &
  Southcentral
  Alaska

Atlanta

Austin

Baltimore

Baton Rouge

Boulder & Rocky Mountain
  National Park

Branson & the Ozark
  Mountains

California's Wine Country

Cape Cod & the Islands

Charleston

Charlotte

Chicago

Cincinnati

Civil War Sites in
  the Eastern Theater

Civil War Sites in the South

Colorado's Mountains

Dallas & Fort Worth

Denver

El Paso

Florida Keys & Key West

Gettysburg

Glacier National Park

Great Smoky Mountains

Greater Fort Lauderdale

Greater Tampa Bay Area

Hampton Roads

Houston

Hudson River Valley

Indianapolis

Jacksonville

Kansas City

Long Island

Louisville

Madison

Maine Coast

Memphis

Myrtle Beach &
  the Grand Strand

Nashville

New Orleans

New York City

North Carolina's
  Mountains

North Carolina's
  Outer Banks

North Carolina's
  Piedmont Triad

Oklahoma City

Orange County, CA

Oregon Coast

Palm Beach County

Palm Springs

Philadelphia &
  Pennsylvania Dutch
  Country

Phoenix

Portland, Maine

Portland, Oregon

Raleigh, Durham &
  Chapel Hill

Richmond, VA

Reno and Lake Tahoe

St. Louis

San Antonio

Santa Fe

Savannah & Hilton Head

Seattle

Shreveport

South Dakota's
  Black Hills Badlands

Southwest Florida

Tucson

Tulsa

Twin Cities

Washington, D.C.

Williamsburg & Virginia's
  Historic Triangle

Yellowstone
  & Grand Teton

Yosemite

To order call 800-243-0495
or visit www.Insiders.com